MURDER BY THE BOOK?

Murder by the Book? is a critical overview of the wave of feminist crime novels which appeared during the 1980s. Both British and American novels by women authors are studied in order to examine emerging generic conventions which have enabled the expression of new sexual and gender politics. Sally Munt asks why the form has proved so attractive as a vehicle for oppositional politics; whether the pleasures of a notionally conservative genre can be truly transgressive, and why the dyke detective is striding forth as a new superhero for today.

This is an enticing book, both for teachers and their students, and for any crime fiction addict.

Sally R. Munt is a Senior Lecturer in English and Cultural Studies at Nottingham Trent University. She is the editor of *New Lesbian Criticism* (Columbia/Harvester 1992) and the author of a number of articles in the areas of feminist theory, contemporary culture, and lesbian and gay studies.

NARRATIVE FORMS AND SOCIAL FORMATIONS

(Formerly published as *Reading Popular Fiction*)

General Editor: Derek Longhurst

The enjoyment of thrillers, romances or Westerns is no longer the secret vice that it used to be. *Narrative Forms and Social Formations* offers a polemical, challenging and provocative contribution to our understanding of popular fiction and the pleasure it gives to its readers. Each volume draws on contemporary critical theory, historical contexts and the nature of readership and production to address key questions concerning the relationship between popular narrative and issues of class, gender, race, nation and regionalism.

In the same series:

EMPIRE BOYS
Adventures in a Man's World
Joseph Bristow

GENDER, GENRE AND NARRATIVE PLEASURE
Edited by Derek Longhurst

MURDER BY THE BOOK?

Feminism and the crime novel

Sally R. Munt

London and New York

First published 1994
by Routledge
11 New Fetter Lane, London EC4P 4EE

Simultaneously published in the USA and Canada
by Routledge
29 West 35th Street, New York, NY 10001

Typeset in Garamond by
Ponting–Green Publishing Services,
Chesham, Buckinghamshire
Printed and bound in Great Britain by
Clays Ltd, St Ives plc

Printed on acid free paper

British Library Cataloguing in Publication Data
A catalogue record for this book is available from
the British Library

Library of Congress Cataloging in Publication Data
Munt, Sally.
Murder by the book?: feminism and the crime novel
Sally R. Munt.
p. cm.
Includes bibliographical references and index.
1. Detective and mystery stories, English–History and criticism.
2. Detective and mystery stories, American–History and criticism.
3. English fiction–Women authors–History and criticism.
4. American fiction–Women authors–History and criticism.
5. English fiction–20th century–History and criticism.
6. American fiction–20th century–History and criticism.
7. Feminism and literature–Great Britain–History–20th century.
8. Feminism and literature–United States–History–20th century.
9. Women and literature. 10. Crime in literature. I. Title.
PR888.D4M87 1994
823'.0872099287–dc20 93–49588

ISBN 0–415–10918–3 0–415–10919–1 (pbk)

To my Mother
Rosa Dorothy Firth
(1920–87)

Contents

Acknowledgements

I wish to thank Stuart Laing and Jenny Bourne Taylor for their insightful and supportive suggestions in the process of completing this work. A number of people kindly read through and commented upon individual chapters, and hence I am grateful to the following for their contributions: Razia Aziz, helen (c)harles, Graham Dawson, Janet Harbord, Reina Lewis, Eva Mackey, Graham McPhee, Lois McNay, Marcus Roberts, Linda Rozmovits, and finally Sandra Freeman and Elaine Hobby who examined the text as a doctoral thesis at the University of Sussex, 1993.

1

Masculinity and masquerade *or* 'Is that a gun in your pocket?'

Mainstream women crime writers

> When we see a tall, dark man walking down a damp, shadowy street wearing a snap-brim hat, trench coat, and gun and hear the melancholy note of a blues trumpet wail up and over the sound of his footsteps on the wet pavement, we know everything we need to know about him. He is the man who goes unafraid down mean streets, the man who is the best in his world and yet is good enough for any world: the detective hero.[1]

Robert Skinner's cameo encapsulates the essence of the hard-boiled dick. The low-lit, monochromatic, American *film noir* of the 1940s springs to mind, with its city of mystery and shadows, violence and vengeance. Through the mist steps the messianic 'man in the mac', dispenser of commonsense justice, alone in his mission. The image is archetypal – the warrior knight, the tough cowboy, the intrepid explorer – he is the representative of Man, and yet more than a man, he is the focus of morality, the mythic hero. He is the controlled centre surrounded by chaos, and an effective reading must involve identification with this mediator of action, truth, and finally pleasure and relief through closure. Both the form and the content of this scenario are iconically masculine, in a literary and cultural sense. The popular cliché survives now through parody, in such figures as Sellers' Clouseau, but the image endures as one of the folk heroes of modern popular culture. The fact that the detective hero transferred so easily on to film resulted from his position in fiction as reified spectacle, his knowing, evaluative gaze centred the text for consumption by a subservient reader/viewer.

The origin of the detective story stressed the romantic, transcendent qualities of the criminal: Eugène François Vidocq (1775–1857), the first chief of the Sûreté and instigator of the first detective agency, Le Bureau des Renseignements, commented in his own autobiography *Mémoirs*:

> In every million men there are ten who put themselves above everything, even the law, and I am one of them.[2]

According to Julian Symons in *Bloody Murder*[3] the 'undisputed father' of the detective story, Edgar Allan Poe (1809–49), was inspired by Vidocq to write the five short stories which when combined supplied most of the elements of the subsequent genre. He invented the first fictional detective, C. Auguste Dupin, first appearing in the 'Murders in the Rue Morgue' (1841) as a man of supreme intellect and arrogance. Poe also supplied the conventional foil whose relationship to the detective forms the narrative centre of the story in that its progression, and our response to it, is judged and mediated by a figure who reveres the hero and therefore concretizes his eminence.

With the appearance of Arthur Conan Doyle's Sherlock Holmes in 1891 the figure matured into archetype. *A Study in Scarlet* was published in Beeton's Christmas Annual in 1887, and *The Sign of Four*, which owed a great debt to Collins' *The Moonstone*, in 1890. Holmes too is a man of the city and of darkness, 'wrapped in tobacco smoke and London fog',[4] accompanied by the awe-ful and faithful Watson, the reflective side-kick. Holmes was based on Dr Joseph Bell, a consultant surgeon at Edinburgh, but the mythical Holmes transcended his human prototype, becoming a representation of the 'Nietzschean superior man'. Doyle felt his readers needed 'a man immune from ordinary human weaknesses and passions'.[5] Culturally Holmes exudes and exalts a specifically upper-middle-class Victorian masculinity based on cool rationality and intellect. The formal detective story, the *whodunit*, replicated itself a thousand times before World War II, hardly deviating from the prescribed structure distilled by Ronald A. Knox in *A Detective Story Decalogue* (1929).[6]

In North America authors such as S. S. Van Dine, Rex Stout, and Ellery Queen were becoming established. In the diverse and entrepreneurial USA, the spirit of individual achievement rendered the class-bound British country-house murder inappropriate. The tradition radically diverged into a more indigenous product, the *hard-boiled* detective story, which has become the more dominant form. Characterized by action, violence, colloquialism and an ethically Manichaean 'quest', its initial medium was the pulp magazine, the most famous of which, *Black Mask*, spawned the formative novelist Samuel Dashiell Hammett (1894–1961). The private eye works outside the social order with his own moral purpose. He is tough, stoic, honest, loyal to his own values, fighting a lone battle against urban chaos, a contemporary crusader/knight. The perceived social order is inherently corrupt, 'fallen', and the outsider represents the harbinger of truth and justice amongst hostility: in fact the hero is no radical but represents the paranoia of the dominant hegemonic Christian/patriarchal order, the assertion of values very traditional, and our identification with the hero places him firmly back in the centre, 'our' values elevated and restored to common-sense status. In the classic whodunit this re-establishment of the social order is usually even more overt, with the bad apple prised from an otherwise peaceful Eden.

Fans and critics have concurred on a direct line of influence from Dashiell Hammett, Raymond Chandler (1888–1959), Ross Macdonald (1915–83), through to Micky Spillane (1918–). Chandler, in creating Philip Marlowe, refined the hero's image, 'a complete man and a common man and yet an unusual man . . . a man of honour'.[7] If the Continental Op and Sam Spade had one foot in the streets, Marlowe and Lew Archer revived the detective's code, stepping six inches above the pavement:

> The problem was to love people, to serve them, without wanting anything from them.[8]

The line turns the image in on itself with Spillane's Mike Hammer – 'the hammer of God'.[9] This Old Testament hero's personal code of violence and vengeance is absolute. Hammer is the 'totalitarian moral policeman', 'the new superman, a plainclothes Nazi',[10] and perhaps the logical twist at the end of this progression, a step into the gutter. World War II had hardened and reified a brutal masculinity, which, blended with the paranoid patriotism of the McCarthyite 1950s, created a figure of monological misogynist megalomania.

This potted schema is undoubtably subjective, but I have tried to sketch out a fairly commonly conceived belief concerning the homogeneous development of the Anglo-American form. From this point the line is seen to fragment into many types – from the spy novels of Fleming, Le Carré, Deighton, the adventures of Dick Francis, the multifarious police novels (critical and uncritical), to the psychological thrillers *et al.* This critical tradition invokes a progressive model of fathers and sons, similar to Harold Bloom's framework of influence,[11] where each writer is fully aware of writing within the shadow of his predecessor, but revises his text to push out the form and relate it to his particular milieu. The overriding principle of the hero is that he is modelled on either an idealized self-projection or a respected friend of the author, who then becomes an icon of humanity: Man. The detective/confidant relationship then forms the centre of the narrative. It is through this often homo-erotic friendship that the reader's involvement and information is disseminated. The reader's pleasure and admiration is directed uncritically at the hero who is always a unitary figure through whom all meaning in the text is distributed. Women, if appearing at all, do not act, they *react* to primary characters – men.

Fay M. Blake in her excellent study on the earliest liaisons between literary females and detection quotes the opening sentence of Old Sleuth's *Gypsy Rose, the Female Detective* (1898): Lawyer Henry Selpho opines 'I did not ask for a woman to be sent to me, I want a detective'.[12] Since Michelle Slung in her seminal collection *Crime on her Mind* (1975) points out that 'there were no women actually attached to the Metropolitan Police in London until 1882'[13] (and then only two were tolerated), and in the USA Blake identifies one operating in Chicago in 1893, one in Portland, Oregon in 1905, and one in Los Angeles in 1910, one may concur with Gwen Williams that the female detective of the late nineteenth and early twentieth centuries was 'purely an imaginative creation . . . part of the general response to the changing position of women',[14] and a strained one at that.

Despite this discursive disjunction – or perhaps because of it – male writers' models of female detectives proliferated in the mass publishing pulp markets of nineteenth century 'penny dreadfuls' (GB) and 'dime novels' (USA). One such Albert Aiken proffered the heroine 'Mignon Warner', an expert boxer who 'takes pleasure in all manly sports', of whom Fay Blake comments:

> A female engaged in a masculine occupation, especially when the Amazon uses fisticuffs and excels at sports, must have been regarded as a titillation to the predominantly male readers.[15]

It is the self-consciousness of transgression and incursion which marks out these early formulations, which resulted first in a defensive type of paradigmatically feminine sleuth, prefixed by the epithet 'lady', and located socially as upper class. This feminization is seen by Gwen Williams as undermining the development of suspense and the detective story's 'basic structure'[16] of rationality, a criticism which tends towards normalizing the masculine form as ideal. Rather, I prefer to read into these early sleuths, in their fizzling irreverence, a strategy of disruption adjunctive to *and* moderating of the genre's conventional masculinity. The parallel, or alternative history of the genre offered in this chapter is not discretely bound as a separate trajectory, but definitely implicated within the 'male-stream' version. Conversely, it would be inadequate of me to ignore the structural initiatives originated by women writers, cogniscent of a shared literary tradition of stealthy parody. I intend to introduce the early generic predisposition to an ironic mode which was consolidated by female-authored texts, which made successive feminist manoeuvres in the genre tenable.

Linda Semple, speaking at the ICA in 1988, identified the first female crime novel as being *The Dead Letter* by Seeley Register (1866), and reported that she has discovered a further 400 writers between then and 1950.[17] Although many (if not most) of the early detective fictions by women are now irretrievably lost, critics concur on the way those surviving texts 'feminized' the form by a process of intrepid infiltration. The master narratives did not accommodate them easily, and women writers had to develop inventive incursive strategies. The common device of parody was an inevitable response to their position as literary intruders. To take 'The Adventure of the Tomato on the Wall' and 'The Identity of Miss Angelica Vespers' by Ka appearing in *The Student: a Journal for University Extension Students* (1894), the widowed Mrs Julia Herlock Shomes decides to emulate her husband's penchant for mystery solving:

> He told Mrs Shomes very plainly a week after the wedding that he would expect her to be interesting, and to provide some little variety in the menage. It thus came about that Mrs Herlock Shomes used to alter her character two or three times a week. She thought of doing this herself, and Shomes was quite delighted. Sometimes she would come attired in a bonnet and shawl and shake her fist in Shomes' face and insist on being paid for a month's ironing in advance; at another time she would be the new cook, and nothing would do but he must give her a quarter's wages. Her favourite dress, however, was a doublet and hose, and in this costume she had been seen by most of her husband's clients, who had not the slightest suspicion that the quiet somewhat retiring page-boy who answered the door was other than he seemed.[18]

Added to which, Mr Shomes employs his own disguises:

> I've several times rushed to welcome a man and kissed him, thinking it was Herlock, only to discover afterwards that the creature had committed some terrible crime.[19]

This short story, with its transgressive hint towards an illicit sexuality, is a metaphorical incursion into the male detective story. At this stage, however, female authors were primarily augmenting, rather than rewriting, the form, already incipiently predisposed to caricature and self-mockery.[20]

Bibliographers disagree on who was the first female detective although Michelle Slung's proposed candidate – Mrs Paschal – seems to predominate, first appearing in 1861. Tantalisingly, the author is a *nom de plume* – 'Anonyma', leading Slung to speculate upon a writing syndicate, rather than a single author. Although Mrs Paschal does detect in order to deflect 'genteel poverty' she has the educational and family privileges of a lady, unlike Andrew Forrester Jnr's protean and denominative Female Detective of 1864.[21] Fay Blake's contender for the position is even lower down the social scale, the seamstress Anne Rodway in Wilkie Collins' *Queen of Hearts* (1856). She has categorized a second type of heroine as an antithesis to the lady sleuth, the working detective, usually a woman from a lower social class who sees detection as a form of employment, one preferable and significantly more profitable than the other primary occupations of the period such as acting, cleaning, or teaching. In contrast to the lady sleuths, 'conventional ladies who solve their puzzles as quickly as possible in order to return to the obscurity of their own homes', Fay Blake describes these working women as both 'truly subversive' and 'freakish', saying:

> The excitement of their work, the huge payments they receive, their frequent class elevation and the zest and competence with which the women attack their investigations contrast dramatically with their sisters, the lady sleuths, and with the roles Victorian working women were expected to assume.[22]

Thus even in the genre's origins certain fundamental structures emerge that are to be characteristic of the meeting between women and crime fiction: utopian models of female agency; an exploitation of the transgression of social mores by the employment of disruptive humour and parody; an irreverent 'feminizing' of male authority myths; the coded deployment of stereotypes (e.g. the refined white-haired spinster, the enthusiastic and naive young virgin) which signal to the reader the seeds of subversion.[23]

The canonization of women crime writers began with the so-called Golden Age, a period commonly conceived as being from the first novel of Agatha Christie (1920) to the last novel by Dorothy L. Sayers (1937), its two aphoristic pillars. Whilst critics generally concur on the pivotal position of these, plus Margery Allingham, Ngaio Marsh (the 'Queens of Crime' or the 'Quartet of Muses'[24]), Josephine Tey, Patricia Wentworth, and Gladys Mitchell are often also variously selected for sanctification. Marion Shaw and Sabine Vanacker are not alone in their suspicion that the term Golden Age 'misleadingly suggests a homogeneous and "classic" body of writing'.[25] One may conject that the critical elevation of some authors at the expense of others, then and now, expresses particular cultural, as well as literary concerns. Linda Semple[26] has drawn attention to the way many other women writing more explicitly feminist novels during this period have been allowed to go out of print, and working as one of the series editors, with Rosalind Coward, of 'Pandora Women Crime Writers', they reissued some of these novels in Britain in the late 1980s, attempting to re-create a more radical canon and respond to the readerly desires of a different decade. It has been part of the Anglo-American feminist process to 'recover' a tradition of women writers whose feminist content reverberates with the contemporary moment. The British press Virago exists for this very purpose. I will discuss here a number of these republished novels and by implication appear to endorse the construction of a revised canon, packaged and delivered to satisfy a newly created audience. I have selected a few syntagmatically structured texts not in order to inaugurate retrospectively a revised canon, or a new tradition, in the manner favoured by North American feminist literary critics of the 1970s, but because using texts accessible to today's reader gives a flavour of their formal innovation,[27] illustrating the way in which the social situation of women became a prime schemata within the novels of the periods in which they were written, situations still germane in the 1980s. The masculine critical tradition has *falsely* referred to the primacy of the formal rules of detective fiction precisely in order to play down the longevity of such political readings. The ritually revered formula, obsessed with timetables, maps, locked rooms, puzzles – the prescribed form – has been steadily adjusted to include realism and social commentary, for which the crime and its solution became increasingly a convenient framework. In this generic transition seemingly lies the roots of the more overt feminist crime novel of the 1980s; this self-selection by new editors incites questions of the canon.

Despite the common conception of the classic crime story taken to be typical of this 'Golden Age' (a term replete with romantic associations[28]) – symptomatically one obsessed by form, a cosy comedy of manners – there are clearly identifiable facets of 'feminization' visible in even the most cursory overview I will offer here, which would indicate a constrained resistance to prevailing mores. Agatha Christie (1890–1976) published *The Murder of Roger Ackroyd* in 1926, about which much has already been written.[29] Superficially it is superbly conventional: a country-house murder in which the patriarch is murdered in the study, leaving a small circle of suspects. By paying close attention to characterization, and by usurping the authority of the narrator (by making him the murderer), Christie employs two narrative strategies which transgress the genre. However, the detective Hercule Poirot embodies most clearly the 'feminine'. He is a parody of the male myth; his name implies his satirical status: he is a shortened Hercules, and a *poirot* – a clown. He is narcissistic, emotive, feline, apparently irrational, eccentric, quixotic, obsessed with the domestic, and socially 'other' in that he is a Belgian. In Christie's first book, *The Mysterious Affair at Styles* (1920), he is often referred to as a 'little man' – not a man, but inferior. He is a feminine hero. Christie continued to reject the masculine hero model in Tommy and Tuppence Beresford (*The Secret Adversary* 1922–), and Miss Marple (*Murder at the Vicarage* 1930–), her other main protagonists. As Marty Knepper has noted,[30] in many of her sixty-six novels she depicted a wide variety of capable women, and broadly feminist concerns, noticeably during the 1920s and 1940s when gender roles were less prescriptive. Marion Shaw and Sabine Vanacker have catalogued Christie's deployment of women sleuths and assistant sleuths, and argued that her feminized heroes appeal to women writers and readers, because in their social roles those women are 'actually the ones who put the pattern together, who restore order to a shaken world'.[31]

This reference to the changing function of femininity between the wars is taken up specifically by Alison Light whose study of the whodunit as a form of popular modernism[32] focuses on what she calls the 'literature of convalescence':[33] the bloodless, detached, dispassionate, *domestic* murder which, like the woman's role within the family, soothed and reassured a nation ravaged by war. It read to forget, and to remove the threat of violence. Christie's novels rejected the heroic, preferring instead to exploit the permeating parodic mode first implicated by her female forebears. Light's study is important in the sense that it refutes the critical institution's tendency to patronize Christie's fiction as lightweight, domestic and not worthy of sustained attention.[34] She goes on to criticize recent feminist work in crime fiction for hearing 'the voice of the English middle class as an unchanging monotone',[35] and argues that Christie's novels are fraught with social disturbance. On this Light's comments are worth representing in full, as her model also pertains to the way feminist crime fiction of the 1980s expressed the contradictions and unease percolating through that particular subculture:

> Far from suggesting a world in which every person knows their place, and in which values are firm and fixed, the fiction explores the difficulty of social belonging in a modern world in which the very idea of social status has something theatrical and impermanent about it. If they are ultimately defensive fictions, looking for an insider on whom to blame the apparent uncertainty of social life, then that same refusal to look beyond the Home Counties and their inhabitants for her psychic swindlers could surely open up for Christie's readers the unsettling implication that 'it is the middle classes who are the murdering classes', and their victims are their own selves. The fiction may work in the end to offer 'reassurance' but since her communities always thrive on suspicion their insecurities can never be resolved. Perhaps it is this contradiction which makes these fictions for many such compulsive reading and turns readers into addicts, hooked on 'crime'.
>
> Should we not read the flood of whodunits between the wars not so much as a sign of the fixity of class assumptions but as symptomatic of their instability?[36]

Now, I am not suggesting here a simple substitution of 'gender' for 'class', but in the self-reflecting process of investigating threat from inside and outside, these fictions can be read as offering a panacea to the sense of social displacement women – whether feminist or not – experience within a society which (still) fixes them within a matrix of enmity, competition, and fragmentation.

Dorothy L. Sayers (1893–1957) wrote novels which have been accused of being racist and markedly anti working class, although they are largely in line with the dominant social prejudices of her time. Aspects of Peter Wimsey, though, like Poirot, were definitely effeminate.[37] Sayers was also interested in the specific cultural limitations which femininity imposed upon women. In *Strong Poison* (1930), using her serial detective heroine Harriet Vane, she is keen to separate the enduring ideological confluence between women's active sexuality and criminality.[38] In *Gaudy Night* (1935)[39] Sayers explores women's independence in academia, and its concomitant difficulties. Setting a murder mystery in a similarly enclosed setting, a women's college, was rapidly becoming a sub-genre, and famous examples include Nicholas Blake's[40] *A Question of Proof* (1935), Gladys M. Mitchell's *Laurels are Poison* (1942), Josephine Tey's *Miss Pym Disposes* (1946), and Nancy Spain's rather camp *Poison for Teacher* (1949), set in the suggestively named Radcliffe Hall. The idea was revived in the 1980s by feminist writers such as Amanda Cross, Val McDermid and Ellen Hart (in *Hallowed Murder* (1989)).

Sue Ellen Campbell has written about the character Harriet Vane as a crucial change of direction for the genre – as the first strong, independent, and sexually active young heroine who formed a literary role model for P. D. James and others writing thirty years later.[41] The Vane–Wimsey trilogy (*Strong Poison* (1930), *Have his Carcass* (1932), and *Gaudy Night* (1936)) marked a move into the more novelistic trend of investigating psychological and emotional states, violating Sayers' own high-profile objections ('the less love in a detective story the better'), voiced in her introduction to the *Omnibus of Crime* (1927). Both Sue Ellen Campbell[42] and Gayle F. Wald[43] have documented this generic shift: Wald identifies how the presence of desire in the narrative disrupts the detective hermeneutic of pure reason, revealing its weakness and demystifying the Golden Age detective as a metaphor for order. It is this way in which Sayers blended the two genres of crime and romance together which inaugurated a new direction in the field:

> whereas classic detective fiction contains a single problem, the novel exposes the problematic . . . The love interest in *Gaudy Night* is but one step on the way to this novelistic universe, opposing the static unreality of the 'pure' detective world.[44]

Wald posits how although 'the murder mystery has a solution that can be arrived at through careful reasoning, the love story remains dangerous because unsolvable';[45] it is this idea, prefiguring the anti-crime novel, which accords Sayers with such a significant genre shift, via the quintessentially feminine intervention of romance. Valerie Pitt has similarly argued how in the character of Wimsey, 'Sayers breaks away . . . from the unquestioning neutrality, the usual moral simplicities of the genre'.[46]

The period of formative expansion branded the Golden Age occurred in a time of change and modernization for women's roles, the inter-war years providing women with greater work and leisure opportunities which led to a rapid growth in middle-class women writers,[47] including those trying their hand at detection. Two further examples from the Golden Age then, take up the incipient feminist strain within the genre.

When Miles Franklyn wrote *Bring the Monkey* in 1933 she was 52 and had been a feminist for many years. The book reflects her politics on several levels. First, it is a satire of the country-house whodunits elevated by the Ronald A. Knox fold. Tattingwood Hall is a Gothic mansion, replete with white-sheeted ghosts roaming windy midnight corridors, and sinister family secrets. The evil deed is performed in an apparently sealed room, with a commemorative dagger, by the scheming sadistic patriarch, a stereotypically jealous husband. The narrator is a Watson figure, a friendship forming the centre of the novel, in which Ercildoun Carrington is overshadowed by the glamorous Zarl Osterley. Both typical fictional crimes are represented – murder, and the theft of a fabulous Eastern jewel – indubitably a parody of Wilkie Collins' *Moonstone* (1868). Both women are suspected and ultimately Zarl admits to the theft, which she had performed as a 'lark' (168).

In contrast to Holmes, Zarl is unconcerned about detection, and indeed turns out to be partially culpable herself. The traditional form is broken by having this female friendship at the narrative centre; it legitimizes this intimacy and accords it with literary value. This structure is not inherently new, but represents a development in a genre characterized by male friendship.[48] Further, it allows many expressions of illicit cynicism regarding men and romance. Conversely, this primacy of female friendship is problematized by a central deceit in Zarl/Ercildoun's relationship: Zarl lies about concealing the diamond, leaving the police's suspicion to rest on Ercildoun. Her insensitive negligence in this, her general acerbity, and her domination of Ercildoun combine to destabilize the simple notion of 'heroine'. Franklyn's feminism is healthily unsentimental, presenting female friendship as a complex alliance constituted within a predominantly individualistic milieu. Zarl is the more conventionally attractive, but it is Ercildoun who provides a moral centre, as nurturer and harbinger of resolution within the novel's hermeneutic.

In spite of its upper-class setting the novel critiques social privilege, by using a classical device: natural justice. Lord Tattingwood is killed by cancer. His vicious misogyny, handcuffed to a bloodthirsty militarism, are two aspects of violence ideologically combined with contemporary resonance. *Bring the Monkey*, despite its pronounced racism, contains strong criticisms of masculinity and dominant forms of sexual exchange. Suffragism, and women's post-war independence, provided the cultural space for 'New Woman' heroines; Franklyn has taken the idea and presented the protagonists realistically, pinpointing serious concerns, and managing simultaneously to defrock the high seriousness of the conventional form. The timbre of the novel is acutely reflective of the cynicism of the inter-war period.

Second, *The Port of London Murders*, published five years later in 1938, is a strikingly different novel. Set in dockland, London's 'human backwaters',[49] working-class poverty and despair thread through the novel. Josephine Bell's two careers as a doctor and a writer lend credibility to the text's many observations on the social context of ill-health. Her first book *Murder in Hospital* (1937) presents Dr David Wintringham as the central figure who appears in later works as an amateur detective. The victims in *The Port of London Murders* are generally working class, the villains exclusively middle class and moneyed. Its radical social criticism extends to a clear indictment of the way men often manipulate women for sexual and financial gain, using the characters Pamela Merston, Mary Holland, and Martha Kemp. June Harvey, the text's leading female, is saved from a similar fate at the hands of a sadistic salesman Gordon Longford, partly through her own spunky self-preservation, but ultimately thanks to the knightly intervention of jilted lover Harry Reed. Despite its romantic closure and unsophisticated characterization the novel reveals an important structural transgression, principally in that the detective is killed off half way through. This leaves the novel bereft of any clear unifying figure or pair of figures in the heroic tradition.

The Port of London Murders opens and closes with a hostile and malevolent Thames, and London is a constant, symbolic backdrop. The city motif owes much to the American hard-boiled school, and even developments within the wider literary and cultural scene, evoking Joseph Conrad's *The Secret Agent* (1907), for example, or Graham Greene's *Its a Battlefield* (1934). As Gary Day has already suggested, the changes in the detective story during this period

> arose as a response to a new perception of the city as a place of darkness and poverty, in addition, it was felt to be undifferentiated and inhabited by swarming masses.[50]

The legacy here is also strongly Dickensian: the fog of chapter 4 is highly evocative of *Bleak House*, the stock scenes and characters borrowed from Victorian melodrama, the deaths gruesomely gothic in execution – the atmosphere conspires to create a satire similar in intention to *Bring the Monkey*, but with a stronger reliance on political realism. Both novels evidence a swing away from the country puzzle and its commonly perceived cozy conservatism, the quintessentially English crime formula. Raymond Williams in his literary mapping of *The Country and The City* (1973) described the familiar nostalgia for an ordered and happy past which the pastoral setting evokes. Lately, critics of the crime novel such as Alison Light,[51] have deconstructed this image of benign passivity, reminding us of its contained violence. Employing an urban setting though, and invoking a Dickensian London,[52] allows for the metaphorical exploration of the city as 'a destructive animal, a monster'.[53] Describing a dense black cloud hanging over London in *Dombey and Son* (1848), Williams comments on it as

> the obscurity, the darkness, the fog that keep us from seeing each other clearly and from seeing the relation between ourselves and our actions, ourselves and others.[54]

It is the desire to comprehend the unknowable, malevolent *irrational* force which drives the detective story in its urban setting, rooted in nineteenth-century fears of degeneration,[55] and twentieth-century fears of anomie and alienation. It is somewhat of a critical cliché to locate the 'country cozy' as a feminine and the urban nightmare as a masculine form. Josephine Bell's evocation of the city as menace has a specifically gendered interpretation, after all, if Man is so decentred by this alienation, how much more so is Woman? Bell has written on the territory of male writers and reinscribed the special sexual dangers of the city from a women's point of view. The structure becomes disseminated throughout the feminist crime novels of the 1980s, dovetailing with that decade's simultaneous fascination with, and denigration of, urban capitalist culture.

During the 1930s and 1940s there was a significant increase in the number of female investigators. Dozens of these are documented by Patricia Craig and Mary Cadogan in *The Lady Investigates* (1981), including Patricia Wentworth's Miss Silver, Gladys Mitchell's Mrs Bradley, the North American 'she-dicks' such as Susan Dare, Gale Gallagher, and 'girl detective' Nancy Drew.[56] Two World Wars shook the domestic morality exemplified in early detective fiction, with its clear-cut metaphysical binaries. The Great Detective, figure of refined reason, was an insufficient paragon for the rapid social change of the war years. Julian Symons[57] describes how the figure gradually became humanized, accessible rather than exceptional, and how authors such as Allingham and Marsh contemporized the form. He continues:

> Nothing is more indicative of the changed atmosphere in which the new writers worked – writers, that is, who produced their first books near the end of the Golden Age or later – than the abandonment by most of them of the series character . . . The reaction against the pre-War Superman detective was partly political, prompted by distrust of all Supermen, and partly based upon the writers' feeling that they had something of interest to say which would be hampered rather than helped by the development of a single character . . .
>
> The new writers were inclined to ask Why rather than How and their Why was often concerned with the psychological make-up and social background of killer and killed.[58]

Symons explains the breakdown of the symbolic hero, the deployment of multiple and female characters, and the growing psychological depth of the genre in social terms. I would argue, however, that the pervasive influence of women writers upon detective fiction strongly affected these changes, their structural incursions being assimilated by, and irrevocably changing, the mainstream genre. Even the fact that many of these women chose a satirical approach forced a growing critical self-awareness upon male and female writers. Symons' in many ways admirable historical survey of fictional *Bloody Murder* is persistently dismissive of women authors. His masculine critical bias is partly a result of the re-presentation of this perceived rigid gender divide in which women create inferior imitations, only reflecting, never directing, the generic development.

By the 1940s many novels, by men and women, were breaking the form and reconstituting it with new priorities. Two Pandora Press reprints, the British Christianna Brand's *Green for Danger* (1945), and the North American Hilda Lawrence's *Death of a Doll* (1947), are centrally concerned with women's psychological and social oppression. *Green for Danger* is set in a Kent military hospital during World War II, and figures professional, hard-working and efficient nurses. Their military superiors, the male doctors, are seen to wield considerable power over their female staff. The pressure on these women to marry in order to achieve social credibility and 'happiness' is unrelenting, reinforced by the ridicule accorded to older single women such as Sister Bates, and VAD Woods; 'single-minded devotion to the opposite sex' (8) is obligatory. The most eligible virgin, the feminine ideal, the pure and lovely Esther Sanson, is, significantly, the murderer. Thus Brand implicitly criticizes, by using the 'least likely person' device, this frenetic desperate coupling. More are seen to suffer from this expedient social exchange than benefit, even the one stable relationship (between Dr Barnes and VAD Linley) has perceptible cracks. The novel ends not with moral or romantic closure, but with malcommunication and frustrated desire, which quintessentially re-presents the novel's disillusionment – with the war, an old order has gone.

The key atmosphere of claustrophobia[59] is both part of the narrative suspense structure, and the psychological rationale for the murders – Esther's neurotic mother fosters an unreasonable guilt on her daughter, and she murders to escape this legacy from her dead parent. There is a strong case for relating this textual claustrophobia to the more material social and psychological position of women, caught on many sides by expectations they cannot fulfil. This textual metaphor pervades not just *Green for Danger* but also *Death of a Doll*, a chilling psychodrama set in a New York women's hostel, which without a single narrator or protagonist, functions itself as the unifying structure. Women's financial insecurity is again at issue: Ruth Miller, a 29-year-old saleswoman is alone and poor, a victim of disabling circumstance and few social choices. It is her dependency on cheap accommodation which results in the coincidence which leads her to her murderer. The ruthless lesbian villain, a paranoid psychotic, sadistically clubs her victim to death. We want to know, in Symons' words, why? Angela Weir and Elizabeth Wilson in their essay 'The Greyhound Bus Station in the Evolution of Lesbian Popular Culture'[60] describe how in the period after World War II increasing mobility for women meant the growth of single, independent female sub-cultures within larger metropolitan areas of which *Death of a Doll* is a literary example. Drawing attention to the concomitant growth in urban lesbian identities, Weir and Wilson examine the prevailing constructions of lesbianism in the novels of the period, of which *Death of a Doll* is sadly representative of the pathologizing tendencies of the new psychology.

Death of a Doll was preceded the year before by *Blood Upon the Snow* (1946), which is a perfectly horrible gothic tale, replete with the metaphorical chill of the thick, enclosing snow which envelops the looming 'small castle' whose architecture calls for 'dogs, loose and chained' (5). The terrible secret of the menacing house reveals a woman made mad by the sexual jealousy and avarice of a tyrannical husband. Years before the woman had married again, mistakenly believing her first husband to be dead. Through years of blackmail, she has endured, her second 'husband' being made to butler for the family. Number two is a gentleman surgeon, with delicate hands and a domesticated nature – in short he is a feminized man. Lawrence displays the violence in masculinity, preferring a model of quiet aptitude, a man who has been *subservient* to the woman in order to prove his love.

Lawrence is particularly fond of the gothic form, and her short novella *The House* has all the classic functions blended with an explicit use of horror motifs. Published together with *Composition for Four Hands* as *Duet of Death* (1949), the two draw on aspects of Charlotte Brontë's *Jane Eyre*. In *Composition for Four Hands* the victim is paralysed and trapped within her own head; robbed of speech and on the verge of madness, the man/beast murderer is revealed to be her own husband. Lawrence's indictments of marriage and masculinity, together with Brand's cynical rendering of romance, reflect the anxiety and disruption over gender conventions induced by the war. The traditional Georgian marriage had become untenable when the fiction that 'ladies' married 'gentlemen', for eternity, if not fifty years, broke down.

Christianna Brand's novel *London Particular* (1952) was also republished in the 1980s. Recreating the smog-ridden London of the time, the text is similarly enclosed by metaphorical weather. By centring this murder around an unwanted pregnancy Brand foregrounds both female sexuality and abortion. The guilty party is a man obsessed with an idealized female. Having fallen from grace the idol must be shattered, but although Ross is a victim, Brand makes clear that her coquettish flirtatiousness, her promiscuity, and her habitual lying discursively conspired to confirm 'femininity's' responsibility for her death. Brand critiques the excesses and tragic effects of both masculinity and femininity, clearly a contemporary agenda for feminism.

As women were increasingly confined to the role of wife and mother during the 1950s, due to the 'returning heroes' of World War II,[61] crime fiction by women returned to the home. At least three novels exploited the particular fear of women for their children: Charlotte Armstrong's *Mischief* (1951), Celia Fremlin's *The Hours Before Dawn* (1959), and Josephine Bell's *Easy Prey* (1959). Set in a New York hotel, *Mischie*f concerns newspaper editor Peter O. Jones and his wife Ruth, who leave their 9-year-old daughter with a babysitter, apparently a psychotic. She lures young, cynical anti-hero Jed Towers into the hotel room in a passage prophetic of Hitchcock's *Rear Window* (1954). When Towers discovers the presence of Bunny O. Jones in the adjoining room he threatens to leave . . . the babysitter will do anything to make him stay. *Mischief* plays on maternal fears; it is a woman's horror novel in its subject and claustrophobic structure. When Ruth returns (she intuits the danger) and discovers Nell about to kill Bunny, she attacks Nell and there ensues a fierce fight. Armstrong's description defies the iconolatry of female passivity – the disturbing and radical inference from *Mischief* is that we are all animals. *The Hours Before Dawn* painfully and realistically recreates the trials of the young mother, whose exhaustion alone is enough to induce mental instability. In a Brontëan gesture Fremlin places a madwoman in the attic, in the form of schoolteacher-lodger Miss Brandon, who plans to kidnap the baby and murder its mother. The text explores 'real' mother love, and as the heroine ruefully observes:

> Take away the pride; take away the possessiveness; take away the physical contact; the jealousy; the selfish pleasure; and you are left with Love. Wasn't there a philosophical problem that went something like that? What is a chair? Take away the back, take away the seat and the legs, and you are left with Chairness – the essence of a Chair. But not, one would suppose, with anything that you could actually sit on. (181)

It is appropriate, perhaps, that in a decade variously prescribed and contained by a conventional political climate and its concomitant cosy morality, the 1950s produced texts by women crime writers expressing conspicuous dis-ease with the family. Critical work on these writers, in relation to the prevailing conservatism of the period, is thin on the ground, and a revision of these literary resistances, coupled with an investigation of why these writers chose the crime form, could constitute another book. The Cold War had commenced, and McCarthyism had pressed the search for the 'Enemy Within'. It is no coincidence that this movement inwards – towards the family, and even the self, in a growing psychological imperative – evinced feelings of claustrophobia which fundamentally informed the work of the 'Second Wave' Queens of Crime from the 1960s to the present day.

One writer who has consistently foregrounded and refined the claustrophobia of the psychological crime novel is Patricia Highsmith (1921–), according to Symons 'the most important crime novelist at present in practice'.[62] Her first novel, *Strangers on a Train* (1949), depicts that pattern of peculiar psychological imprisonment between two people which she was to continue as her personal motif. Instead of an absolutely moral Holmes/Watson type of reassurance at the centre of the novel there is the subversive, explicitly homoerotic and tortured obsession of two murderers for each other. Although Bruno is the acknowledged 'psychopath',[63] the careerist and misogynistic Guy is hardly an attractive hero.[64] Bruno's erotic possessiveness over his mother, his vicious hate of any of her lovers, especially of his father whom he has Guy murder, is suggestively oedipal. The novel is also concerned with the crisis of individuation between Guy and Bruno:

> And Bruno, he and Bruno. Each was what the other had not chosen to be, the cast off self, what he thought he hated but perhaps in reality loved. (162)

One strong, radical aspect of Highsmith's writing is her firm integration of good with evil, no longer cast out as 'other', but slipping undifferentiated into the totality of human behaviour. The rejection of a Manichean morality disturbs the expectations and pleasures of the reader, who is made more and more uncomfortable.

Kathleen Gregory Klein's treatment of Highsmith's novels argues that she has gone as far as creating a new fictional form, citing her introduction of the cult figure Ripley (*The Talented Mr Ripley*, 1955–) as a new type of criminal super-hero, Highsmith's deliberate violations of realism, and the psychological directive as indicative of the novelistic;[65] as another critic, Deborah Philips, put it, 'her novels are nearer whodunits . . . but much more about how and why people can become murderous'.[66] The way in which Highsmith's work is tabulated in relation to the crime fiction canon is an issue about how the popular hard-boiled action text is gendered as masculine, and the soft-boiled, emotion/psychological-centred text is gendered as feminine. Attempts to locate Highsmith within the traditionally perceived masculine canon fail because the *image* of the archetypal text is so selective. Thus Symons' comment that Highsmith is the best can be understood in terms of the elevation/denigration type of evaluation which maintains the masculine form as normative. As I explained earlier, the intent of this study is to describe the impact of feminism upon this commonly conceived masculine canon, and so to question the construction of the paradigm itself. As we examine the historical trajectory of the female-authored form, the discrete categories of masculine or feminine texts, canons and counter-canons begin to crumble under critical scrutiny, as we understand how feminine and feminist models are implicated in the construction of both dominant and oppositional texts; to express this another way – the female author and detective has shot through and feminized the man in the mac.[67]

The three authors chosen to close this chapter and bring us into the present day all write within the historical context of the Women's Liberation Movement, developing particularly during the 1960s and 1970s an explicitly political ideology: modern feminism. This Second Wave of 'Queens of Crime' signifies another era of female achievement. It is important, though, to examine not just the fact that women became dominant figures in the field, but also the texts they produced. Patricia Highsmith, for example, has been criticized in her stereotyped attitudes to women:

> Highsmith validates the concept of women as appropriate victims of murder or violence: they are presented as having deserved punishment for being too available or unavailable sexually, too domineering or insufficiently independent, too loving or too hateful. The short-stories collected in *Little Tales of Misogyny* with their stereotyped titles ('The Fully-Licensed Whore', 'The Wife', 'The Breeder', or 'Oona, the Jolly Cave Woman') are the most openly anti-women. Inasmuch as women are easy victims, violence and crimes against them are easily justified and rationalized.[68]

Is Highsmith being ironic? Tom Paulin thinks not:

> It would be wrong to read these stories as indirectly feminist satires on dependency because the real centre of their inspiration is the delight Patricia Highsmith everywhere shows for the brutal ways in which these unlikely women are first murdered and then 'thrown away'.[69]

This issue of intention and interpretation focuses the debate on to readership and perversely I think the argument can be made both ways, which conveniently introduces my ambivalence towards two other key contemporary authors, Ruth Rendell and P. D. James.

A dissolving sense of reality; lack of self-perception; reticence in moral pronouncements; obsessive, pathological characters; the narrative privileging of complex, tortured, relationships[70] – all these features of Highsmith's writing are similarly to be found in Ruth Rendell's (1930–), and can conceivably, along with an acute sense of domestic detail,[71] and intricate plots, be annexed as 'feminine' tendencies within the genre. But Ruth Rendell is held to be a mainstream crime writer sympathetic to feminism; she is most certainly aware of its concerns. Her novels contain single mothers, lesbians, feminists, and major issues such as rape (for example, *Live Flesh* 1986).

In *From Doon with Death* (1964), Rendell's first novel, a lesbian relationship is the central mystery. One woman is the active, beautiful, cultured, hysterical middle-class lover, the other a passive, plain, fearful, introverted, working-class loved; in this 'infatuation that had warped a life' (181), lesbianism is seen to lead to insanity and death. The three main women characters in the novel perform three iconic functions: Helen Missal is a bitchy whore, Fabia Quarant a violent madwoman, Margaret Parsons a mystic siren. The reader identifies with the stolid, conventional Inspector Mike Burden, and through him his Chief Inspector, Wexford. The traditional Holmes/Watson structure is enhanced by the antipathy felt towards all the other characters. The novel is strung with sexual ambiguity: a camp chemist and its salesman who prices in lavender ink, the 'landgirl' whose 'big pitted fingertips were more like a man's than a woman's' (43), and the giggling and slatternly women at Nectarine Cottage[72] with their intimated lesbianism. Sexuality is a constant presence which is foregrounded but not developed beyond simple clichés. Women's symbolic status is inferred through an absence: Burden's nameless wife is a shadow on the first few pages whose brief presence provides a corrective background to the others' deviance from the unspoken norms of marital monogamy. *From Doon with Death* is deeply indebted to the lesbian pulp novels of the 1950s and 1960s which I describe in Chapter 6, cheap imprints often written by men using female pseudonyms[73] which represented lesbians as immature narcissists tormented by warped passions.[74]

Twenty-one years later, in *An Unkindness of Ravens*, Rendell focused intently on women and sexual violence, covering assault, rape, incest, bigamy and paedophilia. In one sense it is her 'feminist' text. Feminism is a constant and explicit presence represented by the militant girls' club, ARRIA (Action for the Radical Reform of Intersexual Attitudes). By identifying the Women's Liberation Movement with five hundred fervent adolescent schoolgirls, led by their lesbian games mistress and her man-hating fanatical love, Edwin Klein,[75] Rendell implies feminism is merely an immature stage which hysterical minors may undergo if subjected to the influence of perverted authority figures. 'Lesbian teacher corrupts schoolgirls' is a tabloid storyline; Rendell imbues this with a more sinister dimension: one suggested initiation rite to ARRIA is to kill a man.

Rendell is superficially hostile to organized feminism. At a more subtle and equally effective level, she rejects an important feminist concern. The murder victim Rodney Williams is vilified as a promiscuous paedophile who rapes one daughter and attempts to seduce his other. Sexual assault permeates the novel as the major theme. In the final ten pages we learn that the supposed incest was merely the girl's paternal seduction fantasy, *à la* Freud. In the whodunit structure the reader anticipates a final twist which lays bare misplaced assumptions, revealing 'truth', and re-establishing order. Thus incest is relegated to the imaginary, an adolescent wish-fulfilment, product of an unstable and dangerous sexuality.[76]

An Unkindness of Ravens was first published in 1985, and can be seen as part of that decade's hostility towards the feminist activism of the 1970s. But, it is also a reaction against radical and lesbian feminism specifically, which was expressing itself in the form of cultural feminism in the early 1980s, when the manuscript was being written. The act to expunge 'extremes' from the Women's Liberation Movement was an attempt to make the message palatable to the masses; it is a mechanism common to liberal feminism. Ruth Rendell herself has commented on *An Unkindness of Ravens*, that 'it was just anti-militant feminist',[77] and as Cora Kaplan has observed:

> she is better at suggesting the ways in which modern feminism has changed the ambitions of her women characters than in her attempts to deal with self-identified feminists.[78]

Although the Wexford series is Rendell's most popular form, she also writes psychological suspense which one reviewer has dubbed 'chiller-killers'.[79] One of these recent novels, *Heartstones* (1987), is self-consciously gothic, set in a haunted house replete with two young virgin victims. One, however, is a murderer. The domestic claustrophobia is enhanced by the protagonist's obsessive self-absorption. An isolated anorexic, she apparently disables her father with sexual possessiveness. The young female psyche is represented as sinister and violent. Despite this, the novel does cast the house as a malevolent force, a sympathetic metaphor for women's domestic imprisonment.[80] In a comment on this structure in her novels, Rendell aligns herself with her gothic foremothers:

> I'm fascinated by domestic detail, what people are eating, drinking, wearing . . . especially what it's like inside their houses – that's the stuff dreams are made of.[81]

Finally, Rendell's third series is written under a pseudonym, 'Barbara Vine', an alter-ego device employed by many women crime writers enabling them to write out of a different (usually more empowered or violent) self. Symbolically these are the most 'feminine' of her texts, the material has been described as 'gentler',[82] more domestic, and yet in terms of the crime form I found them most disturbing. Five books to date – *A Dark-Adapted Eye* (1986), *A Fatal Inversion* (1987), *The House of Stairs* (1988), *Gallowglass* (1990), and *King Solomon's Carpet* (1992) – are testaments to the psychological torture of human relationships and the latent pathology of the mind. Helen Birch comments on how Rendell has been compared to Highsmith, but adds that Rendell's writing lacks the latter's misanthropy, how it is 'offset by irony' with 'flashes of black humour'. That these thrillers have been read as 'close to farce or parody'[83] positions Rendell in that same self-conscious tangent to the high seriousness of the genre which undercuts moral and mythic absolutes.

P. D. James (1920–) is Britain's best-selling living crime novelist. Her novels of the 1960s – *Cover Her Face* (1962), *A Mind to Murder* (1963) and *Unnatural Causes* (1967) – portray women in a somewhat brutal light, for example the scheming and selfish Sally Jupp; the sterile and obsessive Enid Bolam; the avaricious Mrs Bostock; the sadistic and sanctimonious Sylvia Kedge. As Norma Siebenholler has observed, they are a

> fussy, neurotic, sadistic, simple, scheming, or evil . . . on the whole, a depressing lot.[84]

These books, together with those of the 1970s – *Shroud for a Nightingale* (1971), *An Unsuitable Job for a Woman* (1972), *The Black Tower* (1975) and *Death of an Expert Witness* (1977) – observe classic structures enriched with a novelistic emphasis on characterzation, realism, literary allusion, and the employment of diverse points of view. The major generic themes are represented: alienation, death, retribution, and the effects of murder upon all concerned.[85] James combines these with gothic motifs, claustrophobic atmospheres, and tortured alliances.

She is self-consciously aware of the form, as *The Skull Beneath the Skin* (1982) suggests. The *Guardian* described this novel as 'baroque' (back cover); many other reviewers failed to see the essential tenor of the text, pastiche. This hideously macabre Victorian melodrama overlaid by gothic horror and the most enduring clichés of the detective genre gives the novel an aura of playful excess, in the humorously self-reflexive tradition of the early women detective writers. The characters even ridicule their own role in the recreation of a formula:

> This is a story-book killing: a close circle of suspects, isolated scene-of-crime conveniently cut off from the mainland, known *terminus a quo* and *terminus ad quem*. (187)

> The butler did it. Even in fiction, so I'm led to believe, that solution is regarded as unsatisfactory. (296)

The metafictionality increases with the knowledge that the Websterian play they have all gathered to re-enact is a

> highly stylized drama of manners, the characters, mere ritual personifications of lust, decadence and sexual rapacity moving in a stately pavane towards the inevitable orgiastic triumph of madness and death. (90)

The stable point for the reader's identification is Cordelia Gray, heroine of *An Unsuitable Job for a Woman*.[86] Although Cordelia is apparently an admirably capable, honest and perceptive investigator she can only operate with the validation of the law establishment, in the form of policeman Adam Dalgliesh, James' serial hero. This dependency on male intervention is complicit with the novel's ending, when Cordelia is saved from drowning by a passing sailor:

> She was dimly aware . . . of being carried ashore, of his hands under her breasts, of the strong sea-smell of his jersey, of a heart beating strongly against her own. (363)

Cordelia's autonomy is usurped by this romantic pastiche; it is a conventional generic closure that female operatives are rescued from a violent death in the final few pages by a protective man, often a potential suitor. Sadly, many readers miss James' satiric intention, including Julian Symons, who commented that in *The Skull Beneath the Skin* James 'returned to orthodox detection'.[87]

A Taste for Death (1986) is a straight crime novel, concerned with the murders of a Conservative minister and a local destitute. Social issues specific to women are highlighted: abortion and reproduction, career choices versus domestic responsibilities, ageism and older women. For the sake of 'realism'[88] James introduces a major new character: Inspector Kate Miskin. Youth and inferior rank ascribe Miskin with less prestige than her male colleagues; she functions in an intermediary role, providing an emotional centre for the reader. Significantly, the only home the reader is allowed to inhabit is hers. This too is violated by the murderer. The myth of the invincible detective is temporarily ruptured, and symbolically restored by the timely intervention of Dalgliesh. Kate is hard, deductive, ambitious, taciturn, private, principled, honest and loyal – a model hero. This is tempered by an unequivocally heterosexual femininity; Dalgliesh observes:

> He wouldn't have chosen her if he had found her disturbingly attractive, but the attraction was there and he wasn't immune to it. But despite this pinprick of sexuality, perhaps because of it, he found her surprisingly restful to work with. She had an instinctive knowledge of what he wanted; she knew when to be silent; she wasn't over deferential. He suspected that with part of her mind she saw his vulnerabilities more clearly, understood him better, and was more judgmental than were any of his male subordinates. She had none of Massingham's ruthlessness, but she wasn't in the least sentimental. (354)

Kate Miskin's expedient independence is intended to service her senior officer. It may be that this is a microcosm of how feminism was assimilated by late 1980s culture, reproducing the New Woman as sexy and strong, and still essentially feminine. Kate Miskin, however, has not lasted long – P. D. James' later novel *Devices and Desires* (1989) returns Adam Dalgliesh to centre-stage.

Although thematically critics[89] have sought to establish James' commonality with earlier women writers such as Sayers, Marsh, Allingham, and Christie, once again, it is at the level of form that her writing is most transgressive. In 'The Formula Challenged: The

Novels of P. D. James' Erlene Hubly[90] charts the movement towards realism in James which challenges the basic premise of the commonsensical form – that the world cannot be known, and neither is it basically a good place. In confronting us with chaos and destruction, James' fiction refuses the myth that order can be restored by reason. She is not beyond imposing morality though – as Dennis Porter observes, her novels of 'bad manners' posit that some things are more important than the edicts of 'truth' or 'justice'. But even as James, according to Porter, tries to offer instead 'a religion of love, of devotion and sacrifice of self', yet

> this is precisely what is lacking in the world projected in her fiction.[91]

Porter argues how her detectives, in the hard-boiled tradition, are to carry the cultural load of the purifying discourse, as a damage-limitation exercise. His deconstructive reading interprets these attempts as failures, and on reading *Devices and Desires* again, a deeply ritualistic text, it is an evaluation with which I must concur. Perhaps P. D. James, despite her own authorial intent, has proven the ultimate ineffectuality of the detective hero as a redemptive force, a theme clarified in her subsequent science fiction thriller *The Children of Men* (1992).

Highsmith, Rendell and James are implicated together by the literary worldview they share; the explorations into the effects and motivations for murder are expressed as psychological investigations into the darkness of the human psyche for which there is no effective guiding moral principle. This, together with the strongly ironical strand coursing through the novels when confronted with the spoors of the 'cosy canon', situates them in an evolving relationship with their predecessors. They write, however, in an era when feminism has become an explicit discourse. Whilst distancing themselves from its overt manifestation, and any type of 'extremism',[92] they do in fact include forms and issues of interest to a feminist reading of their works. Thus the 'feminine' and much more so the 'feminist' content of these texts is rather implicit. Sexual violence is an area of *crime* explored with little analysis of its social or institutional contexts, and often representations of sexual deviance replicate common-sense, *status quo* attitudes. The genre's historical development, however, has ensured feminism's muted presence even in this appropriated and anaesthetized form.

Anyone wishing to reconstruct critically the classic form could do worse than to read Marion Mainwaring's *Murder in Pastiche: Or Nine Detectives All at Sea* (1954/1987), a satiric investigation which succeeds better than any serious academic piece in destabilizing the excesses of generic machismo. In this text I hear the echoes of the 'Laugh of the Medusa':[93] an eminently murderable journalist supplies the corpse, the RMS *Florabunda* a floating village of likely suspects, and nine famous detectives the investigation. Mainwaring encapsulates each sleuth by a prismatic enhancement of their individual idiosyncrasies, so that, for example: Trajan Beare's (Nero Wolfe) four-hundred-pound pyjama-clad body never stirs from his bunk, Atlas Poireau (Hercule Poirot) is so offended by the untidiness of murder that he resolves clues with mathematics, Sir Joh. Nappleby (Michael Innes' Sir John Appleby) insists it is 'rather a matter of pursuing certain themes from Wordsworth and Gray' (64), Miss Fan Silver (Miss Silver) – finds her answer in a knitting bag, and Spike Bludgeon's (Mike Hammer) answer is to kill everyone in sight. The cameos are quintessentially veracious but sufficiently distorted by the prism into colourful parody – each peculiar predilection enriches the pastiche ensuring the reader's affectionate criticism of these generic totems. Riddled with *double entendre* along the lines of 'he ejaculated inwardly' (18), 'Tourneur felt himself go suddenly taut' (87), 'He accepted thankfully Mr Waggish's subsequent invitation to have a quick one before dinner' (89), Mainwaring subtly criticizes the historic phallocentricity and homo-eroticism of the genre. The novel may be subtitled 'Watson's Revenge'; the traditionally disenfranchised and frequently feminized helpmeet gets away (literally) with murder, confounding the detectives with irrelevant conundrums, and afterwards departing the vessel for his island retirement paradise, parting with the shot:

> 'To have seen such heroes walk the deck, I count the World Well lost!' (181)

In choosing to invoke parody as holding up the mirror of recognition to crime fiction and masculinity I know I am in danger of arguing for a reflective aesthetic. But it is precisely this structural mutability of the form to parody which substantiates my claim that these writers are implicated within it, not adjunctive to it. The intention of this study is to describe the impact of female and feminist concerns upon the popularly conceived masculine canon, and in demonstrating the extent of that work contribute to disturbing this construction of the paradigm.[94] The categories of masculine/feminine texts and canons and counter-canons are not so conveniently watertight as our literary guides would often have us believe. Despite the huge amount of published work on female detective and crime fiction, the genre continues to be perceived as a masculine one, despite, or perhaps because of, the impossibility of this paragon hero. Why, then, did feminist writers take up this supposedly antipathetic form in the cultural explosion which followed the Women's Liberation Movement? When Rex Stout declared on 31 January 1931 that 'Watson was a Woman',[95] was he saying something profound about the genre itself, destabilizing its masculinity, revealing its self-parody, and paying homage to the structure of femininity disseminated through it, or was he suggesting that women could only be part of the genre if they cross-dressed? The difference invoked to contrast between 'hard' and 'soft' crime fiction is implicitly gendered, with the former retaining the semantic loading of 'original' or 'ground'. The serious stuff is 'softened', and by associated implication, weakened.

Feminist fiction of the 1980s concentrated on continuing the development of popular literary genres which burgeoned in the 1970s with the publication of, typically, conversion novels dependent on realist conventions ('I was an unhappy housewife until I met Fran the Feminist'), romantic lesbian novels, and science fiction, which spoke to the utopian imaginings of a hopeful counter-culture. In the mid-1980s a smattering of feminist crime novels appeared, and began to proliferate into *the* feminist book to be reading. The sub-genre flourished. Back in 1986, embarking on my Ph.D. thesis, I became engaged with the question 'Why these? Why now?' in the Cultural Studies tradition of examining popular literary production in relation to its hegemonic context. There was a superficial connection to be made – that feminists had retrenched into a reactionary genre for reactionary times. We were in the middle of Thatcherism and Reaganism, political activism had seemingly transmogrified into oppositional cultural production. Certainly feminists of the 1980s spent more time reading than marching. These were the easy points of analysis. But it was also important to examine what *possibilities* these novels offered the feminist or proto-feminist reader. Women were enthusiastically consuming these books – there had to be something in it for them. Were these pleasures revolutionary or reactionary, or a contradictory combination of both?

'Feminism' is a problematic term here. There are different divisions and slides between different feminisms, and the taxonomies which follow do not describe discretely bound interest-groups or philosophies. For the purposes of coherence I have had to be schematic in order to show broad thematic tendencies. How these ideological agendas and restraints then relate to formal textual conventions can tell us something about the relationship between popular cultural forms and resistance. At the point of first conceptualizing the project, feminism was interpreted by academia as an adjunct to other more important and prestigious ideologies, namely 'liberal feminism', 'socialist feminism', 'Marxist feminism', and so on. In part this reflects the way feminism structured itself during the 1970s, building upon the campaigning traditions of the former; in the 1980s the identity politics of race and sexuality came to the fore; latterly, the critical theories of psychoanalysis and postmodernism have stimulated the feminist imagination. The chapters respond to this metamorphosis of interests over time. The book, therefore, has two concerns; earlier, contextual chapters primarily focus on a historical survey concentrating on the more ideological and cultural implications of these novels; the second part of the book pushes further into the textual complexity made evident between feminism and crime fiction which provokes new questions about identity and power, discourse and subjectivity, both for the 1980s and into the 1990s.

For thoroughness, a complementary study is needed of male writers and the influence of female writers and the feminist discourse upon their texts, but this falls beyond my present scope. Similarly, my treatment of mainstream women writers has been cursory, introduced as a necessary contextualization for the more avowedly self-conscious feminist products which came later, in order to demonstrate their location in, and debt to, previous traditions. Just as one cannot ultimately isolate various feminist agendas, however, similarly there is some ideological crossover between self-identified feminist texts produced by a feminist publishing house, and mainstream texts which are open to radical readings. Generalizations have had to be imposed which do not do justice to the paradoxical nature of texts. What I have provided, though, is an overview of a series of structural relations, applying genre and reader reception theories, in order to expose the tension and explore the compatibility between a counter-cultural ideology, and a popular literary form. Accordingly, I have trodden a pathway between the two traditional approaches to perceiving popular culture either as unproblematically 'folkloric' – 'of' the people – or as mindless mass programming – 'for' the people. These naive, common-sense assumptions have been discredited by the kinds of work in Cultural Studies which have tried to draw out the contradictory, sometimes conflictual, reading positions available to the active consumer. Because of this more open approach to interpretation, however, a single judgement regarding feminist crime fiction is not appropriate and will not be made. My interpretation of these novels has sometimes focused on the prescribed or dominant reading, and sometimes on the way a text could offer a different, deconstructive reading. To borrow a phrase of Eve Kosofsky Sedgwick's,[96] to illustrate how these books are 'kinda subversive, and kinda hegemonic'. What follows weaves through a method for understanding the delivery of that contradiction.

2

The New Woman – a sheep in wolves' clothing?

Liberal feminist crime fiction

When a woman first identifies as a feminist in western culture, it is most often as a liberal feminist, 'asserting her claim to the equal rights and freedoms guaranteed to each individual in democratic society'.[1] Twentieth-century liberal feminism has absorbed strands from the liberal tradition defined by male philosophers such as John Locke, Jeremy Bentham, and the contemporary liberal John Rawls, who argue that all men (*sic*) are equal before the law, and should enjoy the same rights. Historically, the liberal feminism of Mary Wollstonecraft, Harriet Taylor, and John Stuart Mill has argued that in a democratic society women must be similarly endowed, expressed in the campaigns for Suffrage they endorsed. Hence the liberal feminist campaigns of the 1970s were typically around equal pay for equal work, access to abortion on demand, childcare provision for working mothers, and an end to sexual discrimination in the form of the adoption of equal opportunities policies. Implicit within liberal theory is an optimistic belief in reform, a strategy seen as extendable to all areas of social life, including cultural forms such as crime fiction, commonsensically held to be a masculine genre.

Since the inception of the genre female protagonists have been usurping male heroes, and as a liberal strategy of equality the instigation of female heroes persists in being popular, even a hundred years after Mrs Herlock Sholmes. As part of a policy of deploying positive images of women, it remains pertinent within a society still clutching to male dominance in nearly all areas of public life.[2] Despite tendencies during the 1980s to trash pre-Modernist icons of authentic agency, positive images of women continue to accrue readerly acclaim.[3] As fantasy figures, these heroines facilitate a politicized vision of Woman. Female agency is assumed as these super-sleuths sally forth, suitably sanctioned by the literary institution, to strike down crimes committed against humanist definitions of society. Functioning within a fantasy environ of post-feminist opportunity, these powerful detectives resolve three unstable forms close to the liberal feminist heart – the individual, the family, and the state. The reworking of these three pillars confers upon liberal crime fiction a radical charge constrained within an overall conformity.

The ambiguity of this position reflects these texts' generation out of the juxtaposition between feminism and the bourgeois institution, the structural self-interest of the conventional middle classes. By assuming a reformist standpoint, feminism becomes assimilable by unreconstructed egalitarian notions of gender, framed by basically functionalist attitudes. Arguably, even the premise of bourgeois feminism is contradictory, at once struggling for social change whilst concomitantly wishing to maintain certain social privileges. Another way of conceptualizing the political positioning of these novels is to imagine a structure of two texts, the surface text – which is progressive – and the depth text – which is conservative. I am intentionally using a hierarchical model because I would argue that it is largely the latter which prevails, or is dominant, in signification. If we are to infer from an analysis of liberal feminist texts that oppositional cultural values are formed within the dominant shadow of mainstream ideology, and that these values can become virtually disconnected from the radical impulses that provoked them, we might concur with Tony Bennett that

> It is no more possible in the past than in the present to locate a source of popular cultural activity or expression which is not, at the same time, shot through with elements of the dominant culture and, in some sense, located within it as well as against it.[4]

As a result, these texts strain between ideological allegiances, and are difficult to place as either 'mainstream' or 'liberal feminist'. Despite the fact that most are produced by the huge multinational mass publishing houses such as Penguin, Pan, Arrow, Ballantine, Macmillan, Collins, and Faber, feminism is still foregrounded – in its liberal form – as a central narrative structure, self-consciously articulated in the character of the detective hero herself.

This unstable positioning between dominant and subordinate cultural locations can be illustrated by the way the radio adaptation of Sara Paretsky's novel *Killing Orders* (1984) was publicized in the *Radio Times*, the programme magazine of that great British liberal institution, the BBC. The front cover of the weekly edition of 2–8 November 1991 proffers star and 'sex-symbol'[5] Kathleen Turner as V.I. Warshawski, Paretsky's serial investigator, who acted the role of the eponymous hero in the 1991 film production.[6] The choice of Turner for the role of Warshawski was a contentious one, deeply unsatisfactory to those readers of the novels who saw this as a 'sell-out' to the screen imperative of glamorous femininity. Face to camera, Turner sports a low-cut black dress, and highly decorative dark glasses, pulled down from her eyes. Rather than conceal the active gaze of the detective, the glasses have the effect of alluring the (masculine) viewer into a sexualized spectatorship, which is reinforced by the direct linguistic address 'LOOK GUYS, I'VE NEVER DONE THIS BEFORE'. The role of female investigator is located as new, naive, transgressive and *sexualized* (the virgin/whore binary is implicated and then collapsed within the same image). The symbolism of the dark glasses she wears shifts from impenetrability to availability, further suggesting impersonation, disguise, and artifice where before there was moral authenticity. (Reflected in the dark hero's lens is the image of oneself.)

Inside this same issue of *Radio Times* is a three-page feature article on Kathleen Turner graphically headed 'Kathleen TURNS UP THE HEAT',[7] a sexual innuendo made explicit by the caption in the centre of the third page:

> 'On a night when I'm really hot, I can walk into a room and if a man doesn't look at me he's probably gay'.[8]

This supports a photo of Turner lying on a bed. Visually central to the whole caption/image composition is Turner's cleavage. Contrary to this dominant construction of Turner as sexual object is a second strain, however, captured by two smaller captions on the previous double-page spread: the somewhat patronizing 'Kathleen Turner hopes to strike a blow for women' (Andrew Duncan), and the rather overreaching 'This role is my chance at a quiet revolution for women' (Kathleen Turner).[9] The *Radio Times* reinforced the message in its 23–9 January 1993 edition[10] with its repeat feature on Kathleen Turner who returned to play Warshawski in *Deadlock* for Radio 4. This full-page photo of Turner has her face to camera wearing what resembles a négligé and a seductive smile, lying on a bed, with a gun pointed at the viewer. The block caption on the opposite page enjoins *double entendre* with reference to the previous text's risqué form of address. Turner says:

> 'I enjoy doing it on the radio. I can close my eyes and get a better performance.'[11]

Quite.

Despite the limitations of these statements, they are an attempt to vocalize the liberal feminist idea of the liberated woman, who is equal to the male role but still retains femininity – strong *within* her gender role. The way the 1980s literary figure of Warshawski is adapted and appropriated for this 1990s mass media construction is dependent on the figure of the New Woman, a creature of reformed convention disseminated throughout the novels. A level of parody threading through the literary texts to be examined in this chapter, though, does not traverse the divide, and even that limited radicalism becomes lost in transit. For example, the literary Warshawski is primarily an agent of narrative momentum, a figure of action, whose femininity, at times, is ironically constructed. In the film treatment Warshawski is played by a star who is herself an icon of glamour. The specularity of the form enhances this interpretation so that the agency which is a given in the literary text becomes the transgressive curiosity in the visual text. Still, that the 1980s Warshawski is recuperable as a sight in the 1990s text supports the argument that the image of feminism presented is unstable.

During the latter part of the 1970s and most predominantly in the 1980s a particular type of woman crime writer gained ascendancy. Typically white, professional, and middle class, often holding a Ph.D. from a well-known university, this intellectual has integrated liberal feminism into her texts as political discourse. Her novels are often self-consciously literary, and employ standardized settings from both the British and North American traditions. According to the liberal tradition outlined by Mary Wollstonecraft in *A Vindication of the Rights of Woman* (1792), education is the key to social improvement, allowing a woman to develop her rational and moral capacities. Ratiocination is of course the key skill of the conventional detective, in a genre ostensibly committed to moral enlightenment. An ideal combination of these three elements appears in the campus novel, a modern equivalent of the country-house murder. T. J. Binyon has observed that 'academics form by far the largest group of amateur detectives',[12] and whilst outlining a large cast of male protagonists he concedes that the female author Amanda Cross' heroine Professor Kate Fansler is 'undoubtably the most convincing'.[13]

Amanda Cross, published by the American giant Ballantine Books, is the pseudonym of Carolyn Heilbrun, Avalon Foundation Professor of Humanities at Columbia University, and author of *Towards Androgyny* (1973), *Reinventing Womanhood* (1979), and *Representation of Women in Fiction* (1982). In my analysis of Cross's fiction, I am aware of the danger of conflating the separable identities of Heilbrun, Cross, and her heroine Kate Fansler (indeed, Heilbrun comments on the generation of identities Cross and Fansler as empowering alter-egos resultant of her own 1960s middle-class-American history[14]) thus creating an unproblematic chain of identification communicable to the reader. But I do think there is an argument for connecting (not conflating) them through an analysis of the common trajectory of liberal humanist feminism. Cross's first detective novel was *In the Last Analysis* (1964), which was followed by *The James Joyce Murders* (1967), *Poetic Justice* (1970), *The Theban Mysteries* (1971), *The Question of Max* (1976), and the three novels of the 1980s which I have chosen to examine in this chapter, *Death in a Tenured Position* (1981), *Sweet Death, Kind Death* (1984), and *No Word from Winifred* (1986). *A Trap for Fools* followed in 1990.

Death in a Tenured Position was released in Britain as *A Death in the Faculty* in 1988 by Virago Press; in the USA it won the Nero Wolfe Award for mystery fiction. It concerns the death of Janet Mandelbaum, the (fictional) first woman professor appointed to Harvard's English department, a highly reluctant pioneer whose antipathy to feminism is commensurable to her colleagues'. Harvard's residual misogyny is exposed and provoked by the direct intervention of Professor Kate Fansler, Cross's own serial detective, at first called in to clear up an embarrassingly contrived incident: Mandelbaum is found compromisingly drunk, in a bath in the ladies room, with a local lesbian present. Her reputation plummets. When Mandelbaum is subsequently found dead, suspicion falls firmly on Harvard itself. As her ex-husband puts it:

> 'She was murdered because of what she was and where she was and what she represented.' (147)

In a sense Harvard is guilty; Mandelbaum's death is ultimately revealed as suicide, and the text clearly and painfully makes explicit the hostility which caused it. This central hermeneutic can be read as a microcosm of women's incursion into the academy; in the form of content or executors, women are concertedly ridiculed or reviled. In common with *Sweet Death, Kind Death* (1984), the novel foregrounds the progression of feminist studies, a self-confessed concern of Heilbrun's. Kate Fansler tells the formidable Professor Clarksville that women's studies are about

> 'Shifting your emphasis because of feminism . . . just as you have doubtless shifted some emphasis because of Marx and Freud.' (136)

This argument is clearly situated within a specifically North American socio-historical frame: the late 1970s and early 1980s when feminist scholarship was becoming an established margin within the Humanities. British feminist literary historian Janet Todd, writing in 1988, reminisces of this same period of relative expansion:

> Working by now at Douglass College of Rutgers University, I had at one time or another such colleagues as Elaine Showalter, Adrienne Rich, Domna Stanton, and Catherine Stimpson. Nina Auerbach, Nancy Miller, Patricia Spacks, Carolyn Heilbrun,[15] and Ellen Moers were more or less down the road. I might be forgiven for thinking for a while that feminist criticism, riven with contradictions as it was, various in its modes and aims, had in large measure arrived in the academic world.[16]

Fansler's appeal, locatable as Heilbrun's similar concern as critic, that feminism be assimilated by the liberal pluralism of North American popular criticism inevitably consolidated its bourgeois roots. Whereas in Britain feminism has been historically aligned with a class-based critique of society, which strongly emphasized the economic nature of oppression, having a degree of theoretical sophistication lost on much North American criticism,[17] there feminism of the 1970s and early 1980s was criticized as a limited reformism improving the lot of an already relatively empowered selection of White, middle-class, heterosexual, female individuals. Arguably, a structure of incorporation defused the more radical feminist critiques of the diverse operations of power.

Kate Fansler seems to epitomize certain characteristics accredited to this American bourgeois/liberal privileged form of feminism. Most obviously, she has impeccably élite class credentials: 'Born to wealth and position', she is married to Reed Amhearst, who operates 'in the higher reaches of the police world' (5). Kate's wealth is frequently mentioned in the text; although employed as a university professor (highly respected in her field of Victorian literature – traditionally not a subject for academic activists), she has no need of its remuneration which thankfully releases her to detect at will. Her relationship to – in her own words – 'dear' Harvard is ambiguous: 'your relations have probably given Harvard millions' (120), one character accurately asserts.

Fansler is in the tradition of aristocratic sleuths such as Lord Peter Wimsey, and as such could be read as parodic, although evidence for this rests more with the text's self-conscious literariness (in the tradition of Sayers, who also came in for criticism for her class prejudice[18]), rather than with the character construction itself. Her response to this key lesbian feminist character however, (stereotypically working class and poor), seems to illustrate on a personal level a political referent: the interactions that were problematic in the national feminist movement of the 1970s. Joan Theresa, presented as a naive purist, named for two legendary extremists, is irrevocably Other; Kate is synonymously patronizing, unnerved, rejecting and fascinated. *Death in a Tenured Position* is a book of its epoch in the sense that it defends feminism from 'extremists', whilst firmly maintaining bourgeois security. It also depicts that contradictory pull heterosexual feminists have shown towards the mythic lesbian Romance, revealed in Kate's response to the ironically entitled women-only coffee-house Maybe Next Time. Described as 'reassuring', 'humble' (65), 'in its air of tenuous hope', and 'wistful' (121) it makes Kate uneasy, feeling as she does that it is 'Hard to stay away, impossible to join' (66). Her ambivalence articulates the limit between what is and what is not acceptable. Despite a flavour of irony, and the hint that Kate's conventionalizing is ever so slightly over the top, there is never any real doubt that Kate actually will become a lesbian, since the text's conflation between lesbianism and a strong revolutionary position precludes such a fundamental ideological shift. Kate casts lesbian lifestyle as an exotic diversion to be indulged and tolerated, rather as one would a persistently yapping puppy. Implicit within the liberal idea of toleration is a disguised distaste and disapproval. Inevitably 'toleration' becomes tiring: when Kate is asked to testify in a lesbian mother's custody battle she confides her irritation to a male ex-lover:

> 'We don't want another victim of this mess. But though I would admit it to no-one else, I'm a teeny bit tired of pulling Harvard's chestnuts out of the fire, particularly when I'd rather see them all, and especially the English Department, slowly roasting. And not a word of thanks of course.' (160–1).

Luellen's struggle is rather separate from Harvard's, despite Kate's collapsing gesture. This violent image consigns all her troubles to an undifferentiated realm in which only the privileged can afford not to discriminate. Whether this generic homogenizing is in the author's intention, or at the genre's insistence, is not possible to identify, but even if Fansler's irritation is parodic, the device fails because the rest of the text does not support a more radical interpretation. *Death in a Tenured Position* reflects a bitter and long-standing concern – to deflect any discreditable whiff of lesbianism from academic feminism; as Bonnie Zimmerman once stated:

> feminist critics have felt that they will be identified as 'dykes', and that this would invalidate their work.[19]

That Janet Mandelbaum is set up in this way can be argued as intentionally ironic – the episode in the ladies room tips her over into despair, and her consequential suicide could be read as a covert representation of the pressures on actual lesbian academics. Instead of confronting the prejudice directly, however, the relentlessly conventional posturing of the protagonist in *Death in a Tenured Position* as interpretive authority (*Professor* Kate Fansler) introduces and reinforces a positionality of homosexuality-as-irredeemably-Other, which I intend to develop as a deep structure of the liberal text, common to many of the novels discussed here.

Sweet Death, Kind Death, written three years later, continues many aspects of Cross's style, the constant literariness now privileging feminist 'foremothers' such as Virginia Woolf, Jane Austen, Stevie Smith, Charlotte Perkins Gilman, and Sylvia Townsend Warner. The exclusive college is now a women's – Clare College – and Kate is ostensibly hired to a task force to report on Gender Studies. Her objective is to investigate the suicide of the course's principal defender, famous woman writer and critic, the evocatively named Patrice Umphelby. The book conflates two investigative structures, straightforward detection in the manner of applied ratiocination, with the search for woman-as-enigma, thematically a structure appropriated and problematized by many 'Second Wave' feminist fictions. Patrice dead has significant symbolic value: being consistently described as saintly, she is 'just this side of the angels' (145). Kate self-consciously (and somewhat pretentiously) describes her one meeting with Patrice as having 'taken on all the significance of synecdoche, metonymy, and the force of the paradigmatic' (38). Patrice functions as a symbol of the feminist search for literary mothers, an icon of elevated genius, a fictional figurehead in the historical canon instigated by the early North American critics such as Patricia Spacks (*The Female Imagination* (1975)), Ellen Moers (*Literary Women* (1976)), Elaine Showalter (*A Literature of Their Own* (1977)), Sandra Gilbert and Susan Gubar (*The Madwoman in the Attic* (1979)). Janet Todd comments perceptively on Heilbrun's part in this critical nostalgia:

> At a time when literature was losing its humanistic rationale, Heilbrun tried to co-opt the humanist position for feminism, announcing ringingly: 'feminism, able to combine structuralism, historical criticism, New Criticism, and deconstructionism, reaches into our past to offer, through fundamental reinterpretation, a new approach to literary studies. Moreover, it offers vitality to counter what threatens us: the exhaustibility of our subject'.[20]

Patrice's heavily symbolic death by drowning is in fact no suicide; she has been killed by a fellow academic for reasons of professional jealousy. However implausible this may seem, it too must be intended as a symbolic caricature. Geddes' fears are palpably ridiculous, an example of the dominant's fear of its own 'underside': it is difficult to see how women could take over the Academy, even if Gender Studies are now here to stay. Even as the book asserts 'when an idea's time has come, not even those whose reactions are the most impassioned can stem the tide forever' (132) – consigning the rise of Gender Studies to fate – it is significant that Fansler has proselytized the assimilative Gender Studies instead of the more politically combative Feminism.[21]

No Word from Winifred contains many comments on teaching literature and women's writing, unemployment in the Humanities, and the specific vagaries of the Modern Language Association (of which Carolyn Heilbrun is a former President). Like *Death in a Tenured Position* and *Sweet Death, Kind Death*, the novel is self-consciously literary, and similarly foregrounds women's literary history in the form of a fictional central character/mystery, Winifred Ashby, honorary niece of Charlotte Stanton, principal of an Oxford college and popular novelist. The novel recalls three other literary women – Dorothy L. Sayers, Mary Renault, and Muriel St Clare Byrne – and concerns the unravelling of Winifred's past. Her diary and letters are key, and in examining these Kate Fansler partakes in the same symbolic search for literary foremothers. Kate's niece, Leighton, finally decides to look for Winifred in India, unwittingly partaking of the 'new colonialism' of wealthy White westerners:

> 'And when I've found her – if I find her – who knows? Probably I'll write a book called *In Search of Winifred.*' (216)

It's all very cozily self-reflexive . . . the Amanda Cross books, often imitating in style and political intention the Golden Age writers, support many of the important aims of feminism. But despite the recent developments towards a more articulate and cohesive feminism, they continue to contextualize these aims within a universalizing humanism. Cross seems to limit her own best intentions, as is aptly illustrated by her alter-ego's own comments on women, men, and the academy:

> Men have long been members of a profession whose masculinity can, particularly in our American society, be questioned. I suspect that the macho attitudes of most English professors, their notable male bonding, can be directly attributed to the fear of female dominance . . . These male fears are profound, and no less so for being largely unconscious. Meanwhile, the old familiar habits of male dominance and scorn of female interests in the profession make these attitudes appear natural and right. Women students and professors, in a tight market and cruel economic situation, are in no position to fight those who control jobs. While willing to benefit, passively if possible, from affirmative-action programmes, they accept the fears induced by their professors and eschew feminism, particularly as an academic study. If to this we add the burden of anxiety borne by all women who confront the male power structure, we have a situation in which there are few inducements to either sex to undertake feminist studies. Why then not ignore the whole thing? Why not let the question gracefully disappear?
>
> The answer, I believe, does not lie in the political rights of women, who are half the students, who earn half the doctorates (or more), and who comprise, in their sex, half the peoples of the world. *The answer lies, rather, in the political situation of English studies today, in the threatened state of literature.* [My italics][22]

The temptation to refer to Heilbrun when discussing Cross is too seductive, since both rather seem to put the cart before the horse, illustrating a fundamental weakness in the liberal position, which is single-issue-based and not willing to encompass the meta-dimension of the ideological, a criticism one can equally level at the crime fictions. Resorting to the literary, which Cross does in the novels by deploying devices which foreground fictionality, though parodic, is not sufficient to disguise the disappointing lack of radical insight into the complex relations of oppression. A case of form without the content, perhaps.

Amanda Cross's fiction itself sits uneasily between the high/low cultural divide; published in the USA by the massive Ballantine Books, in the UK it appears in the quality imprint Virago, a company characterized by a liberal feminist publishing identity. Similarly, most of the texts discussed in this chapter fall into two categories according to the country of publication – USA texts being located in the popular market, UK texts being placed with quality publishers, regardless of whether the detective is an amateur or professional. Rosemarie Tong has identified new directions for liberal feminists, a number of whom

> are willing to concede that individual actions *and* social structures prevent many, if not most, women from securing *full* liberation.[23]

There is a temptation to read this difference of emphasis as being the reason why USA texts are marketed by the established mainstream popular publishers, possibly being more palatable to the dominant order, and seeing British texts as more disruptive, 'contained' within the more exploratory high-culture domain. I think this model is too simplistic, operating on the assumption that popular culture is intrinsically more conservative than high culture.[24] Another issue arising from the British-centredness of this study is the extent to which the unconscious allocation of value operates to demonize North American popular texts. Partly in order to resist this denunciation I would propose the view that the buoyancy of the enterprise culture prevalent in the USA can respond to political changes with relative rapidity – a potentially progressive mechanism of change. Ultimately, though, the ease by which liberal ideology is disseminated through different types and levels of culture illustrates the way in which the dominant discourse of democracy in the West is amenable to and inclusive of liberal pluralist aspirations. The extent to which these liberal feminist crime novels can be read as 'radical', or 'oppositional' is circumscribed by this assimilation.

I have not been able to resolve satisfactorily this question of the allocation of literary value, but I have a further observation: that on the whole there is a related split between two historically distinct forms of liberalism – in the North American texts there is represented classical, libertarian liberalism, whereas in the British texts there is a preponderance of welfare, or egalitarian liberalism.

Classical liberalism is disseminated throughout the USA texts within a doctrine of rights, as epitomized by the American Constitution.[25] According to recent libertarian philosophy 'right' takes priority over 'good', the autonomy of the individual being most important. Classical liberal feminists believe that a woman can

> liberate herself 'individually' by 'throwing off' her conditioning and 'unilaterally' rejecting her traditional sex roles.[26]

This self-determining agent is then free to pursue her own ends as a right. The detective hero is, perhaps, her apotheosis. A discourse of rights harmonizes with the myth of individual endeavour, within the textual construction of this popular hero. Her (somewhat arrogant) self-sufficiency was reinforced during the 1980s by the cult of enterprise and opportunity common to Reaganomics and Thatcherism. The pioneer frontier mentality being implicated here[27] is also reflected in the profile of the female investigator, whose visionary androgyny is manifested in skill, but not appearance.[28] Hence masculine agency is married to heterosexual femininity.

This New Woman of the 1980s has manifested the aspirations of ordinary women readers to control their social environment and to defuse its masculine threat. For example, the presence of potential or actual male lovers in these narratives who are represented as a danger to the detective's independence, or further, a physical menace, can be interpreted as a mechanism whereby the threat of an external masculinity can be defused by the appropriation of masculine structures of agency and aggression by the heroine. In the liberal notion of androgyny as 'balanced' she no longer needs the external man, as she has incorporated him, or at least his 'best aspects', thus he can be excised by the narrative – and almost always he is despatched. It is a limited political vision of autonomy.

Using a very different formula from Amanda Cross, the Chicago-based writer Sara Paretsky (Ph.D. in History) chooses to place her heroine squarely in the hard-boiled tradition. V. I. Warshawski is half-Italian and half-Polish, a professional private investigator in the high moral tradition of street crusader. Paretsky once commented in a *Guardian* interview on the forthcoming film tie-in:

> 'I'm under contract to Tristar, the people who made Rambo . . . My dream is that they'll get Sylvester Stallone to play V. I. in drag.'[29]

There are more than cursory similarities. Warshawski does much to uphold a major North American myth. Taking on corrupt institutionalized crime – insurance frauds, the Vatican Bank, medical malpractice, industrial poisoning, Lloyd's of London, pension frauds – she tackles white-collar crime in a way which is intentionally critical of the 'state's' intrusion into the private sphere:

> 'I feel strongly about billions of things, and on most of them I'm impotent. If I was being realistic about crime I'd be writing about the really common crime – murder. Shooting is a tragedy, but it doesn't affect thousands of people. Fraud can. We don't know how many people commit suicide or die in poverty because their savings have been embezzled . . . My books give me the chance to nail the bad guys who ordinarily get away with it in the courts.'[30]

This laudable critique is firmly constrained within an established mode of cultural protest which Jerry Palmer has coined 'kerygmatic':[31] the hero enters the conspiracy (the two fundamental units of the thriller) in order to 'save'. Warshawski is the bearer of good news, she has what it takes to redeem the world, but for this scenario to be enacted, the reader must implicitly trust the individual's capacity, through her own moral agency, to

> save society from conspiracy: in other words, in each novel *he* [*sic*] *refounds the state*.[32]

To elaborate: Ms Warshawski has no problem with the liberal worldview, summarily that we are a collection of essentially rational agents whose mandate to the state is that it must protect persons and property, and simultaneously guarantee the maximum freedom from interference by others. A paragon of individual competition, Warshawski's social Darwinism ensures her survival through multifarious beatings, arson attempts, car accidents . . . (and there is more than a hint of parody in this picture of a breathless desperado) in defence of a 'private' sphere embodied with a quasi-familial symbolism. Her real parents are dead, but they hover like angels of conscience and protection. Forever desired and forever out of reach, her Italian mother as moral mentor, her Polish father as principled policeman, their hyphened-American ethnicity signifies an individualism built on the myth of urban multicultural assimilation. In the books *Indemnity Only* (1982), *Deadlock* (1984), *Killing Orders* (1985), *Bitter Medicine* (1987), *Toxic Shock* (1988), *Burn Marks* (1990), and *Guardian Angel* (1992) Warshawski's closest relationship is with Dr Charlotte Herschel (Lotty), a top obstetrician who operates a street clinic for the poor. A Holocaust survivor, Lotty too is an immigrant, an outsider, whose chosen profession/mission is intended to 'cure those injustices she'd suffered as a child' (*Bitter Medicine* (272)). To Warshawski she is 'my refuge' (*Killing Orders* (181)):

> 'First she filled in for my mother, and then we became – friends is a weak word for it.'
>
> (*Bitter Medicine* (183))

Picking her up and patching her back together, Lotty is her emotional port in a storm. Warshawski's investigations are usually stimulated by some real or metaphorical family connection – in *Indemnity Only* she is hired for one dollar by Jill Thayer, daughter of a corrupt banker:

> Something about her pierced my heart, made me long for the child I'd never had. (138)

In *Deadlock* the murder of a close friend and cousin Boom Boom necessitates an investigation in the medieval tradition of 'knight avenging family honour'. In *Killing Orders* Warshawski is reluctantly hired to clear her aunt's name, and perseveres with the case to uphold her dead mother's honour – she appeals to local Mafia Don Pasquale:

> 'I made a promise to my mother, you see, a promise as she was dying . . . I appeal only to your sense of honour, your sense of family.' (169–70)

In *Bitter Medicine* the teenage victim is 'almost family' (13), and her stillborn daughter, named after Warshawski, haunts Warshawski's subconscious as her own baby. In *Toxic Shock* the antithesis good family/bad family is used to site child sexual abuse and incest within the biological (bad) family. The alternative family in the form of quasi-sister Caroline, and her dying mother Louisa, is a paragon of loyalty. Warshawski's closing words to her (pretended) sister are 'Till death do us part, kid' (320).

In *Burn Marks* Warshawski's aunt's homelessness provides the impetus for an arson investigation, but the narrative actually closes with another non-traditional family member, her dead father's friend Lieutenant Bobby Mallory (Head of the Violent Crimes Unit, Chicago Central District). She presents him, symbolically, with her father's police shield. In the five previous novels the two are constantly antagonistic, in perpetual struggle over Warshawski's professional autonomy. This resolution of Bobby as the new father is at once reformatory (a non-biological figurehead accepts her independent sphere and agrees to treat her more equally), and reactionary (she reinstates the Law – and the father).

In *Guardian Angel* (1992) her primary relationship begins to crack, as Warshawski realizes she cannot always depend on Lotty being there for her as the 'good mother'. I find this a positive development as it is an attempt to demystify female selflessness, and represent the way real friendships can change over time. On a more sceptical level it renders Warshawski back to being the lone private investigator of traditional hard-boiled fiction, and as the series enters the 1990s it reads as an expression of political disillusionment, particularly since the new intimate in her life is Police Sergeant Conrad Rawlings, a potential conflict of interest she dismisses:

> Of course, on principle a private investigator should discourage close entanglements with the cops. On the other hand where would I be if my mother hadn't climbed in bed with a police sergeant? If it was good enough for her, it ought to do for me. (236)

Maybe Warshawski is just still looking for her mother, a pervasive quest in women's writing. On the other hand, the fact that Rawlings is Black allows for the introduction of a race theme which may be positively developed in subsequent books.

The significance of 'family' may be interpreted in a number of ways: (i) in that women's social sphere is often the domestic, the defence of this unit is more likely to be represented by a female writer/protagonist than by a male; (ii) the domain of the isolated 'hard-boiled dick' has been invaded by obligations which demand overt emotional engagement and responsibilities; (iii) the fact that kinship is unconventionally extended to include non-blood relations suggests a progressive definition of family; (iv) this unit is valorized and protected from the anonymous corruption of corporate enterprise, reinforcing big business as the popularly perceived folk devil. The family is a crucial site of interest for liberal philosophy, straddling as it does the individual and the state. The ambivalence towards retaining the family model for the reproduction of democracy is rendered visible in that classical liberal text by Betty Friedan *The Feminine Mystique* (1963), where the advocacy for reform, not rejection, as with Marxist feminism,[33] is strong. Within the structure of the novels, the threat to the family is always removed by Warshawski, the enigma resolved, and order restored. This effectively re-forms it (in both senses) and perpetuates a mildly revisionist status quo, so that Warshawski is complicit with its continuing hegemony.[34]

Popular conceptions of liberalism have been criticized as being ahistorical for assuming the universalizing changelessness of human nature (in relation to economic behaviour and the essential conflicts that circumscribe human interaction), irrespective of differences like class, race, or gender.[35] Hence 'truths' specific to a late capitalist White western heterosexual masculine culture are indiscriminately mapped on to 'people' in general, who are interpreted in relation to dominant frames of understanding. The liberal vision of equality has been accused as a chimera for the assimilation of difference into dominant cultural formations. There is in liberalism a perceived deep structure of common humanity, a notional centre, which all of us supposedly share, irrespective of cultural diversity. Humans are distinctly defined by their essential capacity to reason, and their ability to identify their own interests. Warshawski, in keeping with her fervent individualism, clearly colludes with these liberal ideas on the subject. In *Indemnity Only* she advises Jill:

> 'Lots of things in this life happen to you no matter what you do, or through no fault of your own – like your father and brother getting killed. But how you make those events part of your life is under your control. You can get bitter, although I don't think you have that kind of character, or you can learn and grow from it.' (132)

In *Killing Orders* she informs her lover:

> 'we all have to listen to the voice within us, and how easily you can look at yourself in the mirror depends on whether you obey that voice or not. Everyone's voice gives different counsel, but you can only interpret the one you hear.' (83)

Alison Jaggar[36] points out that within this tradition there is a conceptual confusion: she refers to John Stuart Mill's claim that 'the capacity to act on moral principle belongs only to "cultivated" adults',[37] and Locke's assertion that reason is, on the one hand, 'the common rule and measure that God has given to mankind [sic]',[38] and on the other, only fully present in those who own property. She concludes that the liberal conception of reason is

> normative as well as descriptive. This means that individuals who fail to develop their capacity for reason are not just different from those who succeed; instead they are regarded as *deficient* because they have failed to fulfil their uniquely human potential.[39]

There is a strong sense of this in Paretsky; hard-boiled detectives always have reason on their side in their grapple with the forces of irrational malevolence. The enemy is consistently inconsistent, as Palmer explains:

> In the thriller, the conspiracy replaces the wilderness [of the Western]. It is the wilderness within, as it were; it is what makes the world into which the hero plunges an opaque, radically uncertain world. It is a wilderness which is wild . . . because it is inhabited by dissemblance: the conspirators hide between disguises; things are not what they seem.[40]

It is a small step to connect conceptually irrationality/malevolence/duplicity together within a paradigm of animality, or sub-humanness, and this the novel seems to do in a way which is disappointingly Manichean. To take the stock street kid figure in *Bitter Medicine*, the *stand-up cat*,[41] Sergio Rodriguez, leader of a gang called the Latin Lions: Sergio is paid to murder a doctor, effected in such a way that Lotty remarks:

> 'Whoever did this was mad with rage or inhuman.' (54)

His 'dazzling smile' is a duplicitous façade reinforced by cunning charm – ostensibly a community officer, his good looks conceal a vicious sadism; in one scene he slices Warshawski from the eye to the neck:

> 'Now, Warshawski. You stay out of my face.' (80)

A 'sociopath' (110) and persistent liar, Sergio is linked to the variously denoted nightcrawlers, derelicts, punks, muggers and buggers of Paretsky's novels which constitute the ubiquitous 'them'. Sadly, the text falls prey to the classism raddling the bourgeois history of liberalism, which extends the hand of democracy only to those endowed with certain means.

However, there are many sympathetically feminist aspects to Paretsky's novels: she presents a heroine empowered by her own volition,[42] engaging with the real and metaphorical mean streets successfully; she represents succinctly certain liberal feminist issues – in *Bitter Medicine* she ridicules the hysterical hypocrisies of the anti-abortionist lobby; she is sexually independent; her closest alliance is with a woman; the effects of male crime upon women are frequent issues. There is also one particularly curious feature of Paretsky's work which calls for more interpretation: Warshawski's constant changes of dress (I counted sixteen in just *Bitter Medicine*). To allude to its significance is to preclude a gendered reader: for the heterosexual male reader, or the lesbian reader, she may function as a glamorous spectacle (the outfits are often silk and almost always are expensive); for the heterosexual female reader the function may be more aspirational, her style metonymically suggesting a bourgeois fantasy of empowerment. As a fantasy of empowerment, Warshawski's style reassures the female reader that 'dressing up' enables you to do the job. The fetishization of clothes in Paretsky's work implies the 'draggish' imperative of femininity, signalling its artifice. Or is the reason perhaps more mundane – could Warshawski's constant need to change her clothes be a reflection of the many identities necessary to her survival as a woman in a multi-roled and predominantly masculine environment? Women, conditioned to efface their own personality through dress, are expediently adept at that Holmesian skill, disguise. The paradox in this conspicuous consumption is parallelled by observing Warshawski's eating habits, which swing from cavalier disregard (she never shops, her fridge is a parody of bachelor spartanism), to gourmet dinners ingurgitated with gormandizing gratification. Averting the dangers of gluttony, Warshawski inevitably jogs after said ingestions, as though female excess always exacts a price.

Fellow North American serialist Sue Grafton's private investigator Kinsey Millhone, however, eats junk food and is 'completely ignorant when it comes to clothes' (*'G' is for Gumshoe* (146)). Whereas Warshawski exudes class, Millhone appears artless:

> My usual practice is to crop my own mop every six weeks or so with a pair of nail scissors. This I do because I'm too cheap to pay twenty-eight bucks in a beauty salon. I have hazel eyes, a nose that's been busted twice, but still manages to function pretty well I think. If I were asked to rate my looks on a scale of

> one to ten, I wouldn't. I have to say, however, that I seldom wear makeup, so whatever I look like first thing in the morning at least remains consistent as the day wears on.
>
> (*'G' is for Gumshoe* (2))

Warshawski offers a fantasy of femininity, whereas Millhone offers relief from femininity. In the ten books to date – *'A' is for Alibi* (1982), *'B' is for Burglar* (1985), *'C' is for Corpse* (1986), *'D' is for Deadbeat* (1987), *'E' is for Evidence* (1988), *'F' is for Fugitive* (1989), *'G' is for Gumshoe* (1990), *'H' is for Homicide* (1991), *'I' is for Innocent* (1992) and *'J' is for Justice* (1993) – Millhone's image as an investigator is constantly being remade. She often makes mistakes, rejecting infallibility as a *modus operandi.* The narrative momentum involves her constantly reasserting her right to the role of private detective. For a woman, being a private detective involves work; Millhone does not fit seamlessly into the male model. A female colleague at the insurance company California Fidelity, where she checks claims in return for free office space, asserts:

> 'You're cute, you know that? You think you're such a hard-ass.'
> 'I *am* a hard-ass,' I said defensively.
>
> (*'G' is for Gumshoe* (146))

In *'G' is for Gumshoe* Millhone is resentfully dependent for protection on a male private investigator, Robert Deitz. He shadows her to prevent a contract killer from executing her. His superior knowledge, particularly of guns, saves her life at least twice. As Kathleen Gregory Klein has pointed out, her professional and personal ties to conventional sources of law and order (she even has an – admittedly intermittent – police officer boyfriend) ultimately reinforce the positioning of the traditional male detective. Unlike in Paretsky, where individuals can be taken to represent social crimes, notions of justice are also enacted at the personal level:

> her latent feminism is individual rather than communal; she sees both problems and solutions in personal rather than systemic change.[43]

This discourse of individualism is reflected in the classical liberal view that women and men compete equally as candidates for criminality or insanity. Disregarding social practices which are more likely to categorize women as mad or bad, Grafton's fictions have a preponderance of crazy female villains. The perpetrators are dehumanized, as they are deprived of rationality, serving to reinforce the primacy of the central, stable, rationalist hero.

A lonely hero: as Maureen Reddy observed of the five creators of female private investigators in hard-boiled fiction – Sara Paretsky, Sue Grafton, P. D. James (Cordelia Gray), Liza Cody (Anna Lee), and Marcia Muller (Sharon McCone) – they all

> begin by deliberately establishing their female heroes as cut off from their families of origin.[44]

Given that for women 'identity' is so bound up with relationships, as they are defined socially and psychically as a self-in-relation, this mechanism can be understood positively as proposing independence as an ideal. Relying on the liberal myth that solitary individuals can select and reject social roles at will, it has a limited political expediency as a vision of autonomy, of vital use to any group structured as a servant class.

Each of these detectives is free to choose non-traditional intimacies in order to reformulate as 'pretended' family units. None go as far as Grafton though in vilifying the biological nuclear family, regarding which she is unrelentingly nihilistic.[45] The pain, abuse, and sickness depicted at the centre of this liberal tenet give her novels a radical edge, refusing the romantic reinstatement of the family at the epicentre of Reagan/Thatcherite ideology. By exposing this model as an extension of the selfish ego, of the individual (male's) domain, Grafton's deconstructive ploy at once hails the convention of the lone hard-boiled hero, and undermines it. Further, in *'H' is for Homicide* Millhone is kidnapped by a violent Hispanic gang and during her time in a Los Angeles barrio commits car crime in order to assure them of her credibility. In a number of instances the detective becomes the felon – in order to solve the case assuredly – not only in her actions but also in her shift in perspective that intractable moral divide is clouded, so that by the end of the novel simple formal oppositions become questioned.

Liberal academic Robert B. Parker[46] has a Ph.D. in English from Boston University, has been a professor at the prestigious North-eastern University, Massachusetts, and has written literary critical texts. According to the *New York Times*, his serial hero, Spenser, is

> Tough, wisecracking, unafraid, lonely, unexpectedly literate – in many respects the very exemplar of the species.
>
> (*Looking for Rachel Wallace* (1987), back cover)

He also eats organic ham, washes dishes, makes the bed, cooks, goes to the toilet, and cries. The feminization of this hero must be laudably attributable to the influence of feminism during the preceding decade. Previously I have examined female hard-boiled heroes who have incorporated masculine attributes. His assimilation of traditionally feminine behavioural habits validates a notional androgyny which is founded on (questionable, binary) precepts of 'balance'.

Looking for Rachel Wallace (1980) is deeply disapproving of any kind of political extremism, from the Ku-Klux-Klan and Christian fundamentalism to 'man-hating' radical feminism. The story is amusingly parodic though: Spenser, self-cast as Sir Gawain, searches for a fairy-story maiden, imprisoned in a tower by a symbolic wicked step-mother. After a stereotypical shoot-out, Spenser picks up and carries his lady through waist-deep snow to his waiting carriage, which transports her safely to his bed. But, Rachel is a lesbian, and Spenser loves his girlfriend and foil Susan, a strong woman whose narrative function is frequently to mock Spenser's misplaced chivalric posturing. So, whilst Susan and Spenser celebrate Christmas on the couch, Rachel requisitions the bedroom for her recovery. The end is very touching:

> Much later we heard Rachel cry out in her sleep, and I got off the couch and went in and sat on the bed beside her, and she took my hand and held it until nearly dawn. (223)

The novel appeals to the liberal citadel of political tolerance. Whilst this can occasionally degenerate into conceptual simplifications and popularisms such as 'we're all the same under the skin', its testimony to friendship's victory over polemic is a hopeful altruism amongst a genre overwhelmingly committed to individual competition. Nevertheless, by rendering Rachel passive in the final scene, the liberal text can be understood as acting to expunge radicalism, by defusing its active force, removing the threat and stabilising the status quo.

In Britain there is one private investigator comparable to her recent North American counterparts: Liza Cody's Anna Lee, whose serial transition to television (initially in *Headcase* broadcast on ITV on 10 January 1993) also resulted in an enhanced 'glamour job' being performed on the screen version of the heroine. In line with the British accent on welfare, or egalitarian liberalism, Ms Lee is not a free-wheeling loner, but operates within the constraints of a very concrete social structure – an employer.[47] Brierly Security is a bureaucratic, tight-fisted detective agency, owned by grand patriarch

Martin Brierly whose efforts to govern his foot-soldiers are exacted even more vigorously over Anna. Her ability to negotiate her own investigative trajectory is circumscribed by these social conditions which demystify the detective as quintessentially autonomous. In two instances, in *Bad Company* (1982) and *Head Case* (1985), however, she breaks the masculine code of silence disobeying her employer and privileging female solidarity – inferring that the code is to be negotiated, not imposed. Taking these two novels and the four others to date – *Dupe* (1980), *Stalker* (1984), *Under Contract* (1986), and *Backhand* (1991) – there is something indefinably British about the books (apart from the obvious – that they are set in London). Anna Lee is beaten up much less frequently and then less ferociously; she does not carry a gun; her cases are usually small, plausible affairs; the plots are more 'realistic'. The fantasy of the hard-boiled hero is exchanged for a figure fraught with mundane problems, petty tensions, modest aims, his moral high seriousness undermined with ironic humour. The issue of violence is fraught for feminist authors. Sarah Dunant reminds us how 'terrorised, battered, sexually assaulted, mutilated, even dismembered, [female] bodies have become part of the grammar of the form'.[48] She points out that since classic private eyes narrate in the first person, these feminist protagonists are allowed to become subjects, as well as objects of violence, making gratuitous voyeurism less permissible for the reader.

Writing in 1988 Maureen Reddy observed that, like the Americans 'Anna Lee investigates cases that always return in some way to the family'.[49] Family still fills a privileged place: in *Bad Company* fellow private investigator, friend, and father figure Bernie finds Anna's downstairs neighbours Bea and Selwyn, inhabitants of the ground-floor flat, in order to inform them that Anna has been abducted:

> 'And then, there's her mother and her sister', Bernie ploughed on. 'One of them might ring here if they can't get an answer upstairs.'
> 'We'll tell them as little as possible,' Bea decided, 'Anna hates them fussing unnecessarily.'
> 'That's why I haven't told them so far. It's not as though they're a close family . . .'
> 'Bea and I are more of a family than they are,' Selwyn said.
> 'I know, Mr Price,' Bernie said, 'that's why I'm here.' (90)

In *Backhand*, however, there enters an undertone of disintegration. Their landlord is selling the building over their heads and the tenants face eviction. Anna's replacement family, Bea and Selwyn, are separating. Anna is increasingly antagonistic towards Quex, her partner, implying a potential split. Her job at Brierly is becoming untenable. Impending homelessness means relocation:

> Just around the corner from the garage and not far from C and H was an estate agent. Anna parked her car. A few hours in the neighbourhood had told her that it was seedy enough to be cheap. And suddenly, upwardly mobile was a direction she did not want to take. It was a treadmill. She wanted one of those dirty little pockets of London where you could put your car up on jacks without the next door neighbours raising their well-groomed eyebrows. She wanted a pub not a wine bar, a betting shop and a café where you could get sausage, bacon egg and beans with two slices, not tofu and bean sprout flan. She wanted a local shop where a woman could go for her breakfast pint of milk in slippers and curlers. (137)

This indictment of 1980s gentrification, enterprise, designer fads, style, and family life – real or re-created – marks a new move. Anna's disillusionment catches her looking to the USA, to Florida, where the case has taken her. Working with private investigator Rule Suarez, she also sees his role as inapt:

> Rule took the gun out of the glove compartment and stuck it in his jacket pocket. Anna turned away as if he were doing something obscene. (255)

> Anna was thinking about the handgun and American detective books. Maybe one man's fiction was another man's reality. If that was so she was in the wrong place at the wrong time with the wrong company. (170)

Caught between pining for an irretrievable and nostalgic working-class past positioned as realism, and the unrealizable dream of the paradigmatically masculine hard-boiled dick, Anna is stymied. At the end of *Backhand* she enters the 1990s having sluiced away her fictional antecedents, only to be left as the self-determining agent of liberal fantasy, reinstating the quintessentially liberal myth of independence so precious to the private eye.[50] Even in her rejection of the form, she becomes contained within it. It remains for Cody's next novel to show how intransigent the genre is.

Excepting Anna Cody, most liberal feminist writers have chosen the female amateur as their series detective. A favourite choice has been the investigative journalist, of which key figures have included Antonia Fraser's Jemima Shore (first novel *Quiet as a Nun* (1977)), and Lesley Grant-Adamson's Rain Morgan. There were many other 'one-offs' during the 1980s, crime novels executed with stultifying self-consciousness and sesquipedal political platitude. Lesley Grant-Adamson's six novels to date – *Patterns in the Dust* (1985), *The Face of Death* (1985), *Guilty Knowledge* (1986), *Wild Justice* (1987), *Threatening Eye* (1988), and *Curse the Darkness* (1990) – emulate classic crime scenarios, but never seem to recreate the claustrophobic intensity of a Highsmith, James, or Rendell, despite tackling more overtly feminist themes. *The Face of Death* chillingly represents male psychological violence; this 'horror on a housing estate' (back cover) is an indictment of suburban married life, a kind of working class *Rebecca*.[51] It depicts an amnesia victim who is claimed by Peter Dutton to be his wife. He has murdered his real wife, who lies buried in the back garden. 'Carol's' complete subservience to Peter Dutton almost kills her too, and the feminist lesson is clear.

Self-consciously literary authors also published by Faber include Maggie Gee, an established experimental writer whose *Dying, in Other Words* (1983) is a Chinese box novel full of self-reflexive styles and structures focusing around the brutal sex-murder of Moira Penny, victim of pervading neighbourhood misogyny. The novel takes the central hermeneutic whodunit and twists, plays, confuses and frustrates this desire for knowledge and closure, re-presenting and asserting the real horror of the victim-as-object over and over, exposing the prurient pleasure/narrative indulgence of the armchair investigator. Andrea Dworkin has described Deborah Cameron and Elizabeth Frazer as 'exposing the convergence of masculinity and sexual murder' in their fascinating study *The Lust to Kill*.[52] They draw particular attention to the absence of women as sex-killers, and address a gender-specific theory and practice of murder, as the eroticization of power, violence and death. In their own words: 'what turning persons into objects is all about, in our culture, is, in the final analysis, killing them'.[53] Whilst personally being wary of this view's potential reductionism, the idea that structures of representation have real physical effects certainly has been central to feminist debates about pornography and the definition of harm, throughout the 1970s and 1980s. Many of these novels are investigating *masculinity* as a violent threat to women, and the links are often common-sensically made – many fictional killers are avid readers of violent pornography, and the link is assumed to be causal. Gesturing towards this idea in *Dying, in Other Words*, Gee's narrative circularity and repetition connects this sexual murder with the amorphous and hostile domain of masculinity, which circumscribed Penny's life and death.

Emma Tennant's three experimental novels – *The Last of the Country House Murders* (1974), *The Bad Sister* (1978), and *Two Women of London: The Strange Case of Ms Jekyll and Mrs Hyde* (1989) – are all complex, polysemic, playful attempts to problematize the thriller, placing emphasis on the psychological, and executed with pungent parodic insight. The most perfectly articulated liberal politic in a crime novel, however, is found in another Faber title *The Eye of the Beholder* (1988), by Minette Marrin. Essentially a spy thriller it involves an amateur sleuth whose job as a television producer for the BBC locates the tension between the individual and bureaucracy succinctly. Her desire for individuation is solidly undermined by the final scene: under threat from a homosexual Russian spy dealing in Nazi art treasures she contacts her godfather, who just 'happens' to be the First Sea Lord. He rescues her. The recent changes in eastern Europe render this Cold War mentality already arcane and obsolete, but although now out of date, the text is interesting for the way its own liberal and feminist agendas are defeated.

Two recent British novels bear further examination as examples of self-conscious contemporary efforts to 'modernize' and 'liberalize' the detective novel; first Joan Smith's *A Masculine Ending* (1987), significantly another text chosen to cross over into dominant culture, in a BBC Drama adaptation shown on Sunday 14 April 1992, accompanied by a feature article in the *Radio Times* of that week.[54] A short feature on Smith in the *Guardian*[55] asserts her socialist roots in Hammett and Chandler, where Smith observes herself that 'crime fiction is attractive to feminists because it is a political form'. Whilst wanting to reserve judgement on the utility of this evaluation, it is interesting to view it in relation to *A Masculine Ending* itself. Smith employs the conventional unifying structure of a central detective, this one an amateur of the woman professor ilk, the stylish serial sleuth Dr Loretta Lawson, who reappears in *Why Aren't They Screaming?* (1988) and *Don't Leave Me This Way* (1990). A university lecturer in English, and founder member of the feminist literary review collective *Fem Sap* (Femina Sapiens), Loretta makes frequent casual reference to the contemporary critical debate concerning gender and language. Post-structuralism is particularly slandered:

> Deconstruction was the literary fad that had succeeded structuralism, and she considered it even more pretentious and silly than its predecessor. As far as Loretta was concerned, the purpose of the movement was to state the obvious in as convoluted a way as possible, thereby creating a mystique. The trick was . . . never use a short word when a long one would do. (17)

> The very name of the movement offended her. She imagined the English departments of various American universities converted into huge breakers' yards in which was being dismantled the edifice of world literature. (46)

Like the Cross novels, this text re-centres humanist criticism and English as 'world literature'. Symbolically, one of the movement's prime exponents, Hugh Puddephat, is murdered and left decomposing in the altar of a French church. Shown to be a manipulative, egocentric, preying, pompous, unscrupulous, duplicitous, misogynistic, hypocritical, promiscuous, priadic pederast killed in revenge by a boy described as 'pretty', and cruel, with 'long fingernails', in a 'frenzied attack' (70/129/89), the author seems concipiently to conflate gay male sexuality with anti-feminist, anti-social behaviour. Dr Lawson's shocked contempt is most manifest not in response to the murder, however, but in a story concerning Hugh Puddephat related by his estranged wife, Veronica. Hugh has fallen for one of his students, in an unrequited fashion. In Veronica's words:

> He didn't tell me anything about him, except to say he wanted to live with him as soon as he was old enough. He said it was what he always wanted, but he'd been afraid to face it. He even apologised for marrying me, said it had been a terrible mistake. He seemed to think living with this man would make everything alright. And then he . . . He said he wanted to have a baby, and he wanted me to be the mother . . . Hugh would move in while I had it – he said he was fonder of me than any other woman, so he'd like me to be its mother – and eventually he'd go off to live with his lover, baby and all. (166)

Loretta's response is 'appalled silence':

> Of all the things she had ever heard about Hugh Puddephat, this was unquestionably the worst. She had never encountered selfishness on such a grand scale. He must have been mad . . . For what Hugh Puddephat's wife had just told her *amounted to*

> *an excellent motive for murder* . . . Puddephat's behaviour had been far, far worse than abandoning his wife for another woman. (166–7). [My italics]

Having constructed a character of consummate unpleasantness, Smith concludes that 'It was in his sexuality that the clue to his death lay' (169). It is in fact his homosexuality which causes his death; it is an old theme. The novel contains an explicitly conventional condemnation of gay male sexuality and an implicitly pro-family message. The reader is expected to concur with her revulsion both of Hugh as a character, and his 'perverted' sexuality. Interestingly the BBC adaptation of *A Masculine Ending* omits this motivation entirely, choosing instead to rewrite Puddephat as a promiscuous bisexual whose spurning of a female student leads to her suicide and a tit-for-tat revenge killing by her cousin. The gay pregnancy angle, even in this very camp, melodramatic reproduction of the novel, is obviously too off-the-wall for the BBC.[56]

Exploring alternatives to the heterosexual monogamous family is a feminist concern first advocated by Marx and Engels; Smith, 'brought up on Marx',[57] seems more enamoured by the *status quo*. *A Masculine Ending* contains a certain amount of self-conscious intervention by phenomena I shall name 'feminist scenarios', for example the collective meeting, the fight for gender studies, the lecherous male rebuked, but these do not seem significantly to challenge the underlying premises of the text, which support a socially privileged feminism hardly reformist of existing mores.

In *Candyfloss Coast* (1991) by Barbara Crossley, which is published by the feminist press Virago, the structure of homosexuality-as-threat is made even more explicit, by linking it to the paradigm of Green politics. Amateur sleuth/reporter Anna Knight (read saviour), stumbles upon a German multinational's secret intent to dump nuclear waste in the Irish Sea. Two men are crucial in executing the deed, both homosexuals: rent-boy Sammy and his client Giles Hurt (read damaged victim), council executive and upper-class fop. The narrative uncovers their 'sinister other life' (114), the 'seamy underworld' of a 'shifting society of prostitutes and their prey' (17). These 'feral creatures [who] prowl around to take advantage of . . . vulnerability' (21) are living

> 'on a knife-edge as it is – one twist, and you'll find they're sticking it in you. After all, if they're going to be destroyed what have they got to lose?' (15)

The AIDS panic of the 1980s is being invoked, operating discursively to conflate homosexuality with disease, decay, death, and self-destruction. The fear that 'you'll find they're sticking it in you' is paranoid fantasy, a phantom rape which can be explained as a projected fear from the heart of the unstable, heterosexual, nuclear family. This fantasized bodily rape is woven in with another contemporary cultural anxiety, the 'rape of the wild', fears about which were expressed during this decade in growing ecological activism and the 'Green' movement. As the two threats gain momentum in the narrative it is a small step to connect them, signifying homosexuality as the threat to the Earth.

Homosexual characters are 'liberally' spattered throughout the majority of these novels. Optimistically, their presence could be read as a positive images strategy. Because their narrative function is so often to connote deviance, however, I think this interpretation is naive; I am more pessimistic. Jonathan Dollimore[58] has explored the way homosexuality, though perceived as marginal to our society, and denounced by it, is actually an integral part of it. This structure is reproduced in these liberal feminist texts. Homosexuality is the threat that must be expunged by a heterosexual hero. Its persistence and repetition is certainly a testimony to the 'return of the repressed', and significantly of the failure of heterosexuality to achieve dominance. Further, I think it is important to understand the fascination for homosexuality these texts reveal – to pinch Stuart Hall's rather compatible model of racism:

> 'I think we've been mistaken about racism, in imagining that racism is powered, is driven, exclusively by the need to hate. I think that we don't understand racism until thc degree of envy and desire that there is in there for a kind of something lost in white culture.'[59]

The liberal ideology of individual rights, of the permissiveness of the private, allows for the expression of difference. But it positions that difference as other to itself, and eroticizes it, endowing it with projected sexual power. The question of whether homosexuality is being named and contained, whether the centre is being upheld or destabilized is, as far as these texts are concerned, an issue of reader response and difficult to assess. Has the heterosexual reader been thrilled by the forbidden, in order to be returned safely back to the norm, or has s/he been reminded, once again, of the very precariousness of that norm?

The decision about the role of homosexuality in these liberal fictions is similar to the one regarding how feminism is placed. Feminism is injected in order to enrich, temporize, and affirm the literariness of detective fiction, and its roots in a notional politics of liberal humanism. The tendency is to rebel within an overall conformity, and in this I am reminded of the historical interrelation between liberalism and capitalism, the one emerging with the other. Traditional values of justice, privacy, the individual, and the state, coupled with the desire for human fulfilment (curtailed completely by murder), cohabit comfortably with the concerns of the detective novel. Whilst supporting the view that feminist criticism must partake of a wider critique of society, these writers endeavour to foreground strands of feminist thinking which are often tokenistic and circumscribed by a universalizing humanism.[60] Without wishing to castigate these writers for colluding with masculine forms, the production of these counter myths does not sufficiently analyse the myth-making process: what must be called into question are those literary constructs like the subject, or the idea of the humanist self.[61]

In sum, I have discussed the various ways in which radicalism is expunged, in its different forms, from the narratives. The threat is defused by being spoken for, and assimilated. Despite the presence of parody in several of these novels the radical content is derailed by the deep structures of conventionality undermining it. The issue of intention is a contentious one, but my impression is that this act of containment is structurally imposed by the predetermination of the genre, which may be working against the reformist aspirations of the authors. For example, in *Looking for Rachel Wallace* Spenser acquires femininity, but Rachel (the lesbian feminist) is rendered passive, child-like, and dependent, in his *bed*, for it. Thus, in Tania Modleski's conception, can they have produced 'feminism without women'?[62] It is the ideological complexity, revealed in the textual structure, of these novels which retains most interest for the critic in assessing their signification in the cultural field. They are clearly pleasurable texts, as sales continue to testify. Why is explained very succinctly in a recent review of Sarah Dunant's *Fatlands* (1993):

> The pleasure of *Fatlands* – as in so many of these thrillers – is not so much the competent plot but the excavation of an independent woman's domestic life, which is both mundane and in crisis. Why is it so particularly satisfying to find out what Hannah eats for breakfast, what clothes she flings on, what flowers she wants as she lies in her hospital bed, how she

remembers her childhood and manages her lovelife? Is it that we recognise and *identify* with her; not superhuman or stunning, but a bungling, touchy, anxious, ageing, not-so-modern modern woman? Aha – who wins in the end![63]

3

A case of 'death by political correction'?

Socialist feminist crime fiction

The ideal reader of the feminist crime novels of the 1980s[1] is a woman familiar with the problematization of the western feminist project which took place in the late 1970s. The tendency of the early Women's Liberation Movement (WLM) to reduce the variety of different women's experiences to a conceptual category Woman, in an expedient but essentializing totalizing moment, induced by an activist prerogative, had been displaced by a burgeoning socialist feminist critique of various cultural formations of dominance and submission. This socialist feminist analysis of women's everyday experience, their 'ordinary lives', depended upon a complex set of connections being made between interweaving societal structures and divisions taxonomized as 'class', 'race', 'sexuality', 'age', 'ability', and so on. The reader of these novels would already be informed by the way feminism in the 1980s had extended its interrogation of gender into a 'politically correct' embrace of diverse counter-cultural projects. These alliances led to something of an identity crisis within socialist feminism itself (questioning what might be specific about *gender* oppression). The spatter gun campaigning agenda of some of the feminist crime novels of the period frequently produced narrative incoherency; in an effort to say something about everything, the most worthy attempts were, flatly, boring. The formal sympathy between the (predominantly urban) crime novel and social comment became collapsed into a crude didacticism which failed to find fans beyond the already converted.

The site of utterance for these texts was specifically counter-cultural. Because the modes of production and the intended reader were both located oppositionally, the articulation of anti-hegemonic utterances steeped in the discourses of post-1968 protest movements now dates them considerably. There is a thematic tension between the typically 1970s utopian vision of social transformation set against a fledgling recapitulation, pessimism, and retreat into individualism. These texts represent that knife-edge political sensibility permeating feminism in the mid-1980s. The more successful of these novels fielded a critique of patriarchal society[2] usually through a strong female hero who is *relatively* whole and centred. Fractured and fragmented *yet* authentic and autonomous, this fantasy figure provides a re-entry for the marginalized into society in order to regain power.

There is a danger that socialist feminism is delivered in this chapter as globally indistinguishable. Certainly, to collapse together the socialist feminisms in Britain, the USA, and New Zealand does not do justice to the ways in which feminists have inflected their fight with the specificities of their own culture. There is a lack of published theory on these differences. In this chapter, points of concordance have been stressed at the expense of dissimilarities, so that a notional 'socialist feminism' can be temporarily assumed by the reader for the purposes of discussing the novels more thoroughly. Treatments of socialist feminist concerns within the fictions are not readily differentiated. One slight divergence occurs in the way USA (as opposed to British) texts continue to invoke individualist solutions with an enduring reliance on 'self', despite the socialist impetus towards collectivism.

By undercutting the totemic split between the public and the private these narratives uncover patriarchal 'motive' (of keeping the female body as private property), and expose the 'crime' of masculinity, of men's control of women's sexuality. Indeed, the paradigm of deviance sets up a sympathy between masculinity and exploitative sexual behaviour which in a swift syllogism positions male sexuality as intrinsically oppressive. Socialist feminist Iris Young[3] sees campaigning about women's sexuality as a struggle which encompasses an opposition to both capitalism and patriarchy at the same time, whereas earlier feminist Juliet Mitchell in *Woman's Estate*[4] saw sexuality as a limited focus for the liberatory struggle, arguing that change here may be more apparent than real. Nevertheless, these novels take the representation of sexual politics to be a key feminist agenda. Crucially they appropriate the Marxist concept of alienation to express women's relationship to capitalism: from her labour, from her body, from her sexuality, from her intellect, from her self – women's experience of alienation can only be transformed by a reintegration which comes through self-knowledge, collectivity, and social alliance[5] – a process which presumably, must start in the imagination.

Valerie Miner's first novel, the thriller *Blood Sisters* (1981), was first published by The Women's Press in London, although most of Miner's fiction, like herself, is North American. Four of her novels, including *Murder in the English Department* (1982), were republished by Methuen in 1988. Perhaps *Blood Sisters*, by problematizing IRA mainland 'terrorism' as a political semanticism, could only have been written by a North American, given the diverging sympathies held between the mainland British and the ethnic Irish community there. Miner, like her protagonist Liz, presents the outsider's view, using the crime form to connect with political concerns seen as concomitant with feminism, a structure to be repeated in subsequent texts such as Hannah Wakefield's *The Price You Pay* (US intervention in Central America) and Barbara Wilson's *Murder in the Collective* (US repression in the Philippines). *Blood Sisters* concerns two Irish sisters and identical twins Gerry and Polly, and their two daughters Beth and Liz, both named after their maternal grandmother Elizabeth Mooney, a (fictional) legendary Republican activist. Although Polly emigrated to California, and Gerry to London, the two sisters' lives mirror each other in a dialectic of poverty, class, immigration/alienation, and vicariously through their daughters, whose separate commitment to the WLM/IRA constitute the text's most overt political tension.

The novel, through the use of structured pairs – Gerry/Polly, Beth/Liz, Gerry/Beth, Polly/Liz – is concerned with identity in the sense of female connectedness versus individuation. Feminist texts have variously exalted, explored, and deprecated familial ties, often romanticizing mythical foremothers and political sisters at the expense of real ones. *Blood Sisters* foregrounds 'finding oneself' in relation(s): when Liz mets Beth she

> looked up to find herself watching herself from the sidewalk across the street. This was herself, an endomorphic self, with the same auburn hair, small green eyes, freckled face. (15)

> it was fun to pretend they were sisters, even twins. (24)

Gwen, Liz's lover, spells it out:

> 'I see you as mirror images.' (88)

She thus paints them both as one figure. Liz falls in (unrequited) love with Beth, and this causes a rupture as another opposition intervenes, homosexual/ heterosexual, a distance causing some apparent change of identities (103). But the secular trend is towards integration, as the four women plan their symbolic return to the family bosom – Ireland (always a woman, Dark Rosaleen or Kathleen ni Houlihan in Irish folklore). Consequentially, then, in contradiction to Jerry Palmer's unequivocal exegesis of thrillers,[6] *Blood Sisters* is potentially anti-individualistic.

Our moral sympathy is engaged, not with a single hero, but with the complex social and political involvements of all the Flannigan family women. The ideological links are made through the lives of Polly and Gerry, Liz and Beth. According to Palmer the hero must save society from conspiracy, and ultimately refound the state. These women are in active opposition to that state – Beth is manipulated by her Provisional IRA cell-group into bombing Whitehall, her mother's employer. Gerry is secretly working late, to raise money for their Irish holiday; Beth breaks into her office just as the faulty bomb explodes.

In *Blood Sisters* both the conspiracy, the threat and the hero(es) are manifest in one homogeneous group. The generic conventions are turned in upon themselves in the manner of the *negative thriller* – 'the hero's local success is insufficient radically to purify the social order' – or the *anti-thriller* – 'conspiracy dominates the entire genre: competitive individualism has been eliminated, and the individual is reduced to solitary inadequacy'.[7] Through associating this violence with the male impulse – Liz's brother is maimed by mishandling a bomb, Beth is blackmailed by ex-boyfriend Bruce into the Whitehall plant – Miner advocates the non-violent struggle which formed the centre of the pacifistic feminism of the early 1980s. The family unit is blown apart:

> It should not end here. It did not make sense. It could not end here. 'We're all on the edge of breaking through', she had told Polly. 'You and Gerry are (were) finally coming together after all that time. Beth and I are (were) doing well on the book. We are (were) going back to Ireland together'. (204)

Their shocked solitary inadequacy is imposed by the state. Beth will be imprisoned for many years, and Liz is left to the isolation of authorship. She will write, significantly, of Irish women, and the Irish struggle, and their words will be their weapon, locating this ending within the vision for feminist publishing which generated the massive surge of creativity in feminist culture in the 1970s and 1980s.

Murder in the English Department (1982) was also first published by The Women's Press, although entirely set in Berkeley, California. Home to Professor Nan Weaver, Berkeley signifies both the progress and impediment of a feminist cultural practice. Nan, divorced and in her forties is a tired, untenured departmental token feminist,[8] alternately ostracized or patronized by her male colleagues. The faculty has a famous Milton scholar, Angus Murchie, notorious with women students for his inebriated lechery. Inevitably the two are at odds, increasingly since Dr Weaver has steered the student sexual harassment campaign. In keeping with convention, Murchie is an eminently murderable man. On New Year's Eve Nan overhears a violent argument emanating from Murchie's office; on exploration she discovers Murchie, terminally expiring with three deep gashes in his stomach, pants down and penis 'like a purple magic marker' (45) obviously spent. Knowing that her favourite student Marjorie Adams has fled from the room, she erases fingerprints, and picks up Marjorie's incriminating scarf. Nan is not pocketing a clue, but protecting a woman and sister. When Nan is subsequently charged with Murchie's murder, she maintains a mute defence of Marjorie, believing, despite imprisonment, that the lack of clear evidence will get her acquitted.

Not only then is Nan an uncharacteristically reluctant investigator, she is also an accessory to the crime; concealing evidence is a criminal act, and her uncompromisingly conscientious incarceration clearly confounds the conventionally strict demarcation between the law breaker and the law enforcer. In violating this code, Miner disrupts the conventional myth that institutional law is apolitical, choosing to break the law in deference to a principle she perceives as morally superior. In problematizing and spreading 'guilt' away from the traditional malcontent of crime fiction, the inherently rotten villain, the anomalous bad apple, Miner contravenes the thriller's regulatory structure legal = good (us), illegal = bad (them). She highlights the obscuring veil of 'objectivity' which is coercively disguised in all legal discourse. This detective is no neutral arbiter of a transcendental Law. Appropriating the convention of the 'law of the outsider' from the hard-boiled school of thriller-writing, feminist heroes utilize an established literary structure, that the hero, although surrounded by corruption, remains stoically decent, to legitimate their particular ideological opposition to dominant forms of male sexuality.

Sexual politics underpin the whole narrative of *Murder in the English Department*, whether concerning Nan herself, constantly threatened by unemployment if her political stridency is perceived as impeding her 'academic objectivity'; or Nan's sister Shirley, so archetypally the all-American mother, martyr to modern maternity; or Nan's niece Lisa, made ill by parental protection, imprisoned by patriarchal parochialism; or Marjorie Adams, nearly raped through her naive blindness to sexual power, discarded by a father too appalled by her disgusting licentiousness. Miner makes explicit the pervasion of institutional sexism. Effectively this becomes the *real* crime of the novel, and Murchie's murder a justifiable retribution:

> Momentarily, she contemplated whether murder would be the perfect climax to every rape. (45)

And indeed, Adams is acquitted, by a female judge who rules:

> 'rape is an act of such physical violence that it warrants substantial use of force in self-defence.' (166)

The 1988 television documentary *I Shot My Husband and No-One Asked Me Why*[9] showed how many women who killed their husbands or boyfriends after years of terrible physical and sexual abuse are summarily sentenced to life imprisonment with pleas of self-defence reaping negligible clemency. The slight precedents set by feminist attorneys are now becoming offset by a rallying array of 'pro-male' jurisprudents, contriving to suffocate any mitigating leniency in its early stages.[10] Thus we may discern that Miner was describing not what she saw, but what she *wants* to see. Whilst this wish may be seen by some as utopian, allowing some readers a pleasurable revenge fantasy, the structure is constrained by the conventional wisdom of divine retribution so common to the crime novel. Sadly deterministic, – rapists do not drop dead and their victims are not vindicated by the courts – Murchie's exemplary execution does not solve the problem of patriarchy or male sexual abuse, even though it may provide a therapeutic release for readerly outrage.

That feminist novels murder a patriarchal victim/villain is a somewhat inevitable structure to be repeated in several texts. It is a crucial aspect of these particular crime novels that all acts of violence are given a social context, and not seen as isolated individual idiosyncrasies. To be (mis)judged according to a perpetrator's predilected politics is partially to delineate the domain of ideology. Since the crime novel depends so pivotally on individualism and individual responsibility, though, one must consider how far this may be incompatible with a feminist analysis of society.

In common with many of these feminist texts, *Murder in the English Department* does posit a socialist critique. Nan Weaver is a working-class hero, her position within the institution is hard won and insecure. She is intimidated by the suave and articulate Marjorie Adams, with whom she argues defensively for a feminist literary criticism. By contrasting Amanda Cross's privileged professor Kate Fansler with the academic underdog Nan Weaver, critic Cranny-Francis argues convincingly that:

> Miner's careful placement of Weaver in terms of gender and class enables her to operate as a detective, uncovering the narrative of bourgeois patriarchal culture and subjectivity.[11]

In keeping with the Amanda Cross novels, Smith's *A Masculine Ending*, Bryant's *Killing Wonder*, tangentially *Blood Sisters*, and several more texts to be discussed, the narrative of *Murder in the English Department* is set in a site in which, as Anne Cranny-Francis has noted, knowledge is produced, fabricated, accumulated, reproduced and communicated. They are, she elaborates:

> sites primarily concerned with linguistic representations of the 'real', with books, pamphlets, magazines. They are sites concerned with the fictions by which societies represent themselves to themselves, by which the socio-economic organization is exposed, justified, reinforced. They are sites concerned with the strategic function of language and of fiction . . . all challenge the conventions of detective fiction to some extent, all suggest an awareness by the writer of the ideologically strategic function of these conventions.[12]

In certain respects Miner does attempt to break the form, in deploying a reluctant and 'criminal' sleuth, politicizing the operation of the law and dispensing with the myth of the objective investigator, but ultimately there are two disturbing aspects to *Murder in the English Department*. First, although Marjorie Adams is released from the charge, and the campus consciousness has been duly raised, Nan herself has withdrawn from the institution. In the final scene she drives off into the Sacramento sunrise in what seems a curiously anachronistic individualism: figuratively, she walks away, in a quintessentially 1970s counter-cultural rejection of the 'rat race' in favour of a journey of self-discovery. (Although this could also be read as a radical feminist gesture of separatism, I prefer to read this, with the benefit of 1992 hindsight, as defeatism.) Second, a query regarding suspense: as the reader knows from the beginning that Marjorie murders Murchie, this essential element of the classic whodunit is missing, thus the novel's status as crime fiction is open to interpretation – arguably the feminist trajectory in this case broke the form completely.

Hannah Wakefield's *The Price You Pay* (1987) is a hybrid in two senses: featuring a North American expatriate practising law in London, the novel is set here and in California. The author's name, Hannah Wakefield, is the pseudonym of two American women working in London, the one a former editor and writer, the other a partner in a 'well-known firm of solicitors' (inside front cover). One would anticipate, therefore, some textual/discursive reflexivity: the solicitor spends the story pursuing a duplicitous just-dead journalist. Semiotically speaking *The Price You Pay* recollects the canonical readings of Edgar Allan Poe's 'The Purloined Letter'; elusive documents are pursued by the law in order to establish truth. Ultimately it is not these that divulge meaning or power, though; the proper object of attention is the signifying chain itself. The relationships within the chain contain a microstructure of social order and the human subject. To contextualize: in keeping with the allusion to 'The Purloined Letter', it is progressively clear to the reader/investigator (as Dupin) that the journalist Amanda Finch was a CIA informer; her incrimination, like the letter, is in 'full view'.

The novel opens with resignedly celibate solicitor Dee Street (the surname undoubtably evoking Chandleresque urbanization) resisting her romantic fantasies for radical psychiatrist Dr David Blake. He is married. After drafting his connubial will, which involves a brief meeting with famous feminist feature journalist Amanda Finch, David's wife, Dee shelves her fantasies. When Amanda is murdered, along with Chilean refugee Carlos, Dee can tastefully substitute herself as David's partner. Whilst framed by the conventions of the crime novel, *The Price You Pay* combines these with elements of romantic fiction. In supplanting Amanda, Dee must spend the rest of the narrative expunging the image of Amanda as David's rightful partner, exonerating herself in the process. David is a reconstructed romantic hero: his 'lean, angular' (2) looks, deep blue eyes and dark features are tempered by an occasional retrogressive bout of sexism. Depicted vaguely endearingly as the worried, protective male, David's naive foolishness enhances his perceived dedication to Dee, and stresses her superior discernment. He places them both in severe danger by indulging in some self-pitiful male-bonding with Amanda's brother Craig, capitalist ideologue and paragon of patriarchy. Craig is disclosed as the real villain, having destroyed their parents in defence of profit, deceiving Amanda and manipulating her into lifelong dependence. Discovering Amanda's documents merely leads the reader to deduce the obvious; it is Dr Alan Dexter, an academic, who describes the 'signifying structure' of Amanda's family relationships, the deceits which dictated her treachery. He redesignates her as victim, not villain. Dr Dexter also becomes the arbiter of justice, shooting Craig and saving Dee's life. In *The Price You Pay* the corruption of the social order is manifold – in reparation to the harm done to Chilean revolutionaries by Craig/Amanda, Amanda's estate donates £60,000 to the Campaign for Socialist Chile. The gesture is palliative; the symbols of hope, David and Dee, really only personalize an ineffectual skirmish with syndicated capitalism. As Dee puts it:

> We'd been outmanoeuvred and I knew it. (216)

What pleasures are in this text for the feminist reader? First, the structure of Amanda-as-enigma: initially she co-opts our sympathy and admiration, vicariously through protagonist Dee, and we desire her interpretation and vindication. Second, Dee's romantic fantasy of David demands some narrative closure and fulfilment. Third, through identification with Dee, the reader shares her status and momentum. Fourth, by operating a Britain/USA axis the novel indulges a binary around realism/political nostalgia. By describing and trivializing a romantic nostalgia for 1960s protest – symbolised by Berkeley – 1980s relatively comfortable conformity is valorized as 'realism'. Geographically, historically, and ideologically (for the British reader), revolutionary politics are 'over there'. In some respects, *The Price You Pay* is less to do with a galvanizing political vision than with narrative device: the text admirably creates the aura of conspiracy so integral to the thriller. Once the mystery is clarified this threat is not assuaged; in this, like *Blood Sisters*, lies its formal interest.

The Price You Pay provides a useful crossover between North American and British feminist novels. Despite its partial setting in London, the text lacks the more reticulating social criticism of British feminist fiction. Indeed, the narrative voice of *The Price You Pay* is firmly white, middle class and heterosexual: Juan Diego, Chilean resistance organizer is obsessed by offended honour, irrationally and paranoidally anti-American, an autocratic husband who exacts wifely obedience – in fact every inch the red-blooded dago of Caucasian mythology; Dee's response to her best friend's rape and subsequently declared lesbianism is 'half anger, half sadness ... I felt my eyes dampen' (132), the intimation perhaps being that if only she'd met the right man ... Thankfully:

> Paula's decision about her sexuality wasn't going to turn her into a social separatist, [read *man-hater*?] the way it had a number of my other women friends. On the contrary, it seemed to me that, freed from the pressure to flirt with men, Paula had become much more easy about herself and saying exactly what she felt about the world men had made to a man more directly. (139)

That lesbianism is seen only in relation to masculinity and heterosexuality casts it as a negative and inferior shadow of dominant 'natural' sexual order. Implicitly, Paula must measure up to Dee's social imperatives.

To turn to Britain, during the mid-1980s the socialist feminist crime novel was visibly represented by Gillian Slovo, a South African born journalist and film producer. Her three novels *Morbid Symptoms* (1984), *Death by Analysis* (1986),[13] and *Death Comes Staccato* (1987) feature serial detective Kate Baeier, a Jewish freelance journalist and Portuguese immigrant. Whereas her male predecessor may have had a wife at home, Kate has her 1980s equivalent: an indecisive ex-mathematician turned poet and single parent Sam. Sam and his son Matthew represent the domestic sphere in Kate's life, thus inverting one gendered sacred cow. Kate Baeier breaks another more literary convention: whilst in *Morbid Symptoms* she is a journalist turned reluctant amateur investigator, by *Death Comes Staccato* Kate has turned professional due to her success. Like V. I. Warshawski, women proving their competence and economic viability in such a masculine field valorizes their patronized amateur female forebears.

Morbid Symptoms, 'set in the London of Citroen Dyanes, Marxist astrologers and muesli' (back cover), is sited in that ideal small circle of suspects, a collective;[14] this time African Economic Reports (AER). One of its members, Tim Nicholson, is murdered. The classic red herring device is employed to mislead the reader that the South African police have murdered Tim. It is highly plausible: he has uncovered a secret agreement between Argentina and South Africa to manufacture nuclear weapons. Using a pro-Boer British front organization, International News Limited, a double agent, David Munger, has infiltrated AER. Whilst efficaciously educating the reader into the tactics used by totalitarian states to control dissent, for Slovo the narrative must not be so predictable. Tim is murdered by another member of AER, Michael, whose masculine temper kills to protect his own pride and reputation. Michael is

> 'somebody who's not the enemy in the sense that the South African security police is.' (138–9)

As Kate puts it:

> This isn't the revolution; just one of those hiccups probably caused by the frustrations of all our lives. Gramsci called them morbid symptoms. (139)

Morbid Symptoms escapes the simple Manichean morality of many thrillers, which disperse culpability and responsibility firmly on to the Other; rather the text attacks the male Left's values and working practices. Franco Moretti declared that in detective fiction 'criminals are *never* members of the bourgeoisie',[15] but in the socialist agenda of Slovo's fiction the villains are usually just that – 'us', rather than 'them'. Whilst in sympathy with AER's work, Kate Baeier, as a female, is apart. Although she identifies the murderer, she gives the men the knowledge and withdraws, with no attempt to arbitrate justice. Her friend Anna observes:

> 'I wonder if you, if we, would have felt differently, if it was a woman who had been killed.' 'I wonder', I said. (140)

In some sense *Morbid Symptoms* is a characteristic socialist feminist swipe at the patriarchal Left, reflecting the political tensions of the time. Months later when AER phone Kate and ask her to join them ('Ron and I both feel that an all-men collective can no longer function in this day and age' (147)), Kate turns them down flat – she'd rather tidy her room. The clearly symbolic implication of this is that these men should get their own house in order.

In *Death Comes Staccato*'s vituperative sub-text Slovo excoriates the culpable deceit of capitalist Gordon Jarvis in his dangerously exploitative work practices and safety negligence which leaves one employee dead and another seriously injured in a factory fire. Thus, on the one hand we have the crimes of the rich, which are visited upon the poor and children. By constantly offsetting one environ against the other, self-indulgent corpulence against the dingy scratchings of the poor, Slovo continues to make her socialist points, that structural oppression causes individual casualties, and that the personal is the victim of the political.

Another British serial detective novelist writing socialist feminist fiction is Val McDermid, author of lesbian sleuth Lindsay Gordon of *Report for Murder* (1987), *Common Murder* (1989), *Final Edition* (1991) and *Union Jack* (1993). As Paulina Palmer has already pointed out, McDermid attempts to rewrite the representation of femininity in detective novels as a source of problems and disruption.[16] In the first paragraph of the first book Lindsay Gordon describes herself as a 'cynical socialist lesbian feminist journalist' (3). If this isn't marginalized enough, she is also Scottish. Despite the allusion to 'truth' a journalistic detective inevitably invokes, her investigatory projects are classic crime fantasy. Her social positioning is exploited to reveal the complex negotiating Lindsay has to do in order to straddle the upwardly mobile divide. Having a rich middle-class lover exacerbates the personal sphere of this enquiry. The books are not loaded with suspense, and the characters are often formulaic, but McDermid manages to depict the minutiae and ordinariness of class perspectives and in this way I found the narratives touching. McDermid also produced *Dead Beat* in 1992, and *Kick Back* in 1993, both with mainstream publisher Victor Gollancz. Her new hero is a professional, and heterosexual; the murderer in *Dead Beat* is a journalist, cast in a gesture of playful mockery which is also an ironic reflection of changing concerns.

Television crime series seem to have engaged more overtly with female protagonists than mainstream literary fiction – emanating perhaps from the accepted convention of woman as spectacle. From Emma Peel in the 1960s, replete in her fetishistic leather machismo, the woman investigator/enforcer has fractured into a spectrum of liberated women, from series such as *Hill Street Blues*, *Juliet Bravo*, *Police Woman*, *Charlie's Angels*, *The Gentle Touch*, *Hunter*, *Dempsey and Makepiece*, *L.A. Law*, *The Bill*, *Prime Suspect*, and others. During the 1980s a plethora of major parts have been assigned to women, positioned by the text as variously tokenized or glamorized, and feminist critics have offered both prescribed and alternative readings of these. Julie D'Acci (1987), Lorraine Gamman (1988), and Beverley Alcock and Jocelyn Robson (1990) have all written about *Cagney and Lacey*, the archetypal female buddy team, first transmitted in 1982, conceived in 1974, solidly within the discourses of the liberal women's movement.[17]

Targeted at a working-women's audience, *Cagney and Lacey* has tackled many feminist themes over the years; it has a huge and dedicated following, has received many awards, and has 'provided jobs and consequently a forum for a significant number of women in the television industry'.[18] According to Gamman, the programme engages a kind of Kristevan mockery in order to destabilize the genre's characteristic machismo; engaging in multiple viewpoints

> we witness a deflection of the single scrutinizing gaze.[19]

Traditional realism is rejected, and through pastiche and parody the programme subverts the masculine form of detective narrative. Whereas D'Acci and Gamman present *Cagney and Lacey* as a liberatory text, Alcock and Robson have criticized 'these liberal concerns' in their article for *Feminist Review*, choosing to argue for the

> fundamentally reactionary project at work in the demise of Christine Cagney, via alcoholism and a freewheeling lifestyle.[20]

The authors argue that Mary Beth as a 'true woman' is structured in order to recuperate Christine as a woman-who-wants-to-be-a-man back into the heteropatriarchal order, which she has transgressed. They further argue that a lesbian reading of the text demonstrates the erotic charge between the two, and that the relationship is structured upon desire.

These brief remarks are intended to introduce the British buddy series *South of the Border*. First broadcast in 1988, and then in 1990, the two series were anchored by a pair of young women, Finn and Pearl, both positioned as outside the law. Working class, recently homeless (read 'street-life'), paroled for stealing, Finn is a laconic Geordie whose demeanour is definitely anti-feminine. 'Gritty and glamorous',[21] Black Londoner Pearl occupies a more established position as exotic Other,[22] although the attempt is made to refute this by positioning her as marginally more in charge than Finn: her life is scrutinized more, her family and love relationships occupy more narrative space, she is the central stable subject in relation to Finn's more turbulent mystery. Although the casting of Pearl has been criticized for deploying a woman with fairer, European features, her Black identity has facilitated a more explicit, benevolent rendering of race issues than traditionally represented in, say, *Miami Vice*.[23] The number of significant Black characters in *South of the Border* results in the impression of a community, rather than of a single, token exotic, included to jazz up the spectacle. Also, by depicting a law-abiding community, the programme challenged the prevailing stereotype of inner-London criminal ghettos overrun by Black gangsters, muggers and dealers, in which Black is synonymous with criminal.

South of the Border tried to reconstruct the traditional format of a television crime series as a formula fitting for the Left. Race, class, gender, sexuality, ecology, animal rights, alternative parenting, sexual violence – a whole panorama of oppositional politics were presented as plot dynamics. Instead of state-sanctioned investigators *à la Cagney and Lacey*, this text's sleuths worked for a radical legal practice often antipathetic to the law. The audience, although primarily intended as younger people, must have crossed over with Cagney and Lacey;[24] the lesbian viewer could even more explicitly fantasize the lesbian continuum between Pearl and Finn. Finn's clothing is heavily influenced by contemporary dyke fashion: Doc Martens, black jeans or 501s, black leather jacket, checked shirt, short haircut. Lesbian viewers, conditioned to and adept at reading otherwise,[25] were certain that here was their screen dyke.

The writer Barbara Machin produced two episodes out of seven for the second series of spring 1990. The Women's Press simultaneously published her novel based on the series. The fact that the book is published by a feminist press reinforces the series as 'alternative', although as work on *The Color Purple* has shown[26] (published by the same press and filmed in Hollywood by Steven Spielberg), the transition from sidelines to mainstream can be fraught. Indeed, the novel does allow for a more developed, complex discursive base in the way that a fifty-minute single-issue drama cannot. The novel is clearly informed by socialist feminism, its central mystery concerning the corruption of a union and the embezzlement of strike funds. Pearl and Finn locate the perpetrator, with the invaluable assistance of Maureen, the union boss's secretary. A small but significant sub-text could be dubbed 'secretary's fight back', as the dénouement depends on Maureen and her opposite number, Judith, outmanoeuvring their subservience with the shrewd knowledge of underlings. The moment is captured as the union boss John Foxton pours himself a cup of coffee: 'Black for me, please', (214) retaliates Maureen.

Whilst the novel is a clear indictment of capitalism and the profit motive, there are also several secondary themes, of which anti-romance is the most cohesive. John Foxton is an ex-lover of Millie's, a divorced radical lawyer and mother of 18-year-old Laura. The residue of mutual desire is stimulated by the investigation, and the instability of this intense relationship engages the reader's desire for fulfilment. Identification with Millie reinforces the difficulty of being a single professional woman: it is lonely and stressful. In parallel to the Millie/John indeterminacy is the Pearl/Fitz quandary: the insecurity of romance is underlined by the fact that ultimately both men abandon the women for their wives. Resolution, in the form of romantic closure, is denied the reader; in a manifestly feminist gesture Millie looks to her daughter for emotional concordance, and Pearl seeks solidarity with Finn:

> 'I'll tell you something, Finn.' Pearl looked at her seriously, 'Apart from one or two gross little habits, you're easier to live with than any man.' Finn smiled doubtfully. (220)

That these words close the narrative accentuates their importance. The text, in the preceding few pages, has just introduced an attempted rape, and unearthed Finn's sexual abuse by her uncle and guardian.[27] The text becomes overloaded in its heteropatriarchal critique. Perhaps acting to offset the reader's frustration and dissatisfaction with this and the romantic trajectory, the detective hermeneutic, by contrast, is satisfyingly conventional. The villains are cornered, the victims exonerated, and the unions strengthened and victorious by deciding to unite to fight. *South of the Border* is cleverly constructed, coopting the reader into a feminist/socialist closure, rather than an individualist fantasy of desire.

Australasia has produced some feminist crime writers too. The pulp lesbian romance texts of Claire McNab, and the more experimental novels of Lesley Thomson and Marele Day, are all urban thrillers set in Sydney,

> 'the crime capital of the South Pacific.'[28]

Building on the urban thriller, and taking the experimental novel further to embrace the social criticism of realism and the self-consciousness of metafiction, Rosie Scott's novel *Glory Days* is the geographical underdog, set in Auckland, New Zealand. The cultural mix which is Kiwi history also permits the combination of the best aspects of USA and British politics in a clever reconstruction of both individualism and collectivism. According to the New Zealand *Listener*, *Glory Days* (1989) is 'a sprawling Rabelaisan sort of thing',[29] a crime novel containing a cocktail of assorted Auckland lowlifes, a study of a city and the social strata germinated by the exchange of money and power. *Glory Days* is a study of class: a complex interweave of gender, race and sexuality combine to suture the characters within a vexed hierarchy of cultural capital, into which the eponymous hera is positioned as poor, fat, and female, mother of a Down's Syndrome daughter Rina, and a half-Maori mixed-race son John – somewhere near the bottom. However, Glory Days is a figure of resistance: the novel simultaneously indicts the hegemonic mores of late capitalism, and proffers Glory as a symbol of strong, surviving womanhood, without falling for simple heroism. Her name is perfectly ironic.

Glory Days is a rock singer and a painter. She rescues a young junkie from an overdose one night in an act of sisterly solidarity. When the girl dies, Glory becomes framed for murder by her psychopathic model, Roxy. The ensuing investigation is enacted in order to exonerate herself and a fellow 'sister', the transvestite prostitute, Grace. Glory's situation is paradoxical: in every aspect of her life except in her painting, she is subjected to social approbation (the represented is so much more acceptable than the real). As a rising artistic 'name' she is patronized and tolerated by an all-male middle-class artistic establishment. Glory's is a view from the other side, and the narrative neatly deconstructs some serious shibboleths of privilege and conformity, starting with the family, gender, parenthood, heterosexuality, law and order, and profit.

Glory is the product of a vicious father and a wandering, mad mother, both victims of poverty and alcoholism. Her own marriage, at 15, was a shotgun affair which produced John. He is physically abused and given up, Maori style, to her mother-in-law Nettie. Her second husband, Weasel, a con-man and thief, is clearly disturbed by his own family history. Brought up by Jehovah's Witnesses, they instil in him a revulsion towards the body and sex. Although the biological father of Rina, he has never seen her; she is effectively fathered by Glory's lodger, the bald and neurotic Al. He in turn is engaged to Sue, but this does not preclude the secret sexual liaisons between him and Glory, although on a purely friendly basis. Glory's extended family includes the men who live next door, some Maoris and motorcycle gang members among whom their leader Moe is a fearsome greaser. Their symbiotic communality is based on the loyalties of Others.

The text does not romanticize the men's masculinity, but rather represents it as an acculturated imposition, a difficult state of ritual for them to negotiate. Gender demands are those among many, such as when Al announces his impending marriage, which makes Rina distraught; Al cannot cope with emotion or vulnerability, his is a parody of masculinity:

> 'I'll come and visit you, Rina. I'll come and see you, eh?' He patted her severely. 'Don't cry, mate, come on, mate. Don't cry.' 'I want you to stay,' wept Rina. 'I want you to stay. I hate Sue. I want you to stay.' 'It's been a good house,' Al said, giving me an appealing glance. He was thrown by all this, it was the sort of provocation which had him hiding in his room for a week. (214)

> The door of the house suddenly slammed open, Al burst out of it, snatched Rina up and ran inside. (217)

It is Al who is squeamish, who regularly reminds Glory of her domestic responsibilities, and who acts as a supportive home base. The relationship suggests the separation between romance and parenting which has been advocated by alternative family models.

The Marxist-feminist field of argument has been largely stimulated by Michèle Barrett's book *Women's Oppression Today* (1980).[30] Her naming of the 'family household system' has been explained as a 'historically constituted element of class relations'. Authors Johanna Brenner and Mari Ramas go on to say:

> The role of male as breadwinner (a) locks men effectively into wage labour, (b) has deprived them of access to their children, and (c) oppresses them by imposing a rigid definition of masculinity.[31]

This system 'divides and weakens the working class and reduces its militancy'.[32] Socialist feminism sees class, gender, and the family as interrelated ideological constraints which operate in the domestic sphere to weaken women. It is fitting, therefore, that the novel *Glory Days* constantly interweaves these mandates, undercutting them with images which defamiliarize the norm. Al's masculinity, for example, is maintained almost at the level of hysteria:

> 'Thanks,' I said. It was a mistake. Al hated being thanked for anything. That kind of intensity threw him off dangerously and with his usual paranoid acuteness he knew I was moved by his clumsy offer. He got up abruptly, his skull flaming. 'Well, I'm just going down to the shed.' Mutter mutter. (160)

The physical transition from kitchen (feminine space), to shed (masculine space), is effected through the threat of emotional vulnerability. This satiric image is a distillation of thousands of domestic disputes, and is represented through the eyes of Glory, the stable centre. The text's presentation of masculinity, whether as Al's neurosis, or Moe's lumbering protectiveness, is controlled by Glory's reaction to it. She maintains status:

> On the way out, one of the grizzled old derros raised his glass to me. 'Good on you, lassie. Good on you, lassie. I've always liked them well stacked. Plenty to get hold of, heh, heh, heh.' I bent down on impulse and kissed him as I went past. (116)

Simply to respond with indignation to this sexual harassment would be to ignore the complex relations of power between them. Glory defuses his action with good humour, affirming their mutual alienation rather than sealing their gender antagonism.

Gender is an unstable commodity: the transvestite prostitute Grace parodies to excess the artifice of femininity. 'Hollywood on high heels' (56), the spectacle of Grace is a biological male, referred to throughout as 'she':

> Teetering over the grass in her high heels, trailing perfume, came Grace all done up to the nines. She looked very angry. I glanced at her face with affection, it was such a relief to see her. She stopped short, taking it all in. 'Well, who are you now?' Such a poisonous purr. (153)

Lesbian and feminist writers interfacing with masculine genres tend to estrange through using parody, which accentuates the reader's sense of superior distance. Parody addresses a highly knowing audience, through the use of style; it is closely connected to pastiche, its sceptical, deflationary intention highlighting the presence of ambiguity in its target. It is analogous to that perversion of bourgeois norms, camp, an expression of the 'gay sensibility'.[33]

Both women writers and lesbians, positioned as Other, have facilitated a subversive awareness of the real, and this has often been through playful disruption and mockery. Grace's presence in *Glory Days* is both as the stock queen of hard-boiled lowlife, and a distillation of textual attempts to deconstruct gender.

> The queen was wearing a blue sequined dress which caught in the streetlight, and cruel stilettos. Her leg muscles were thrown upwards and out with the strain. She looked stunning . . . Forgetting herself for a minute, she spat into the gutter. (17)

The passage reflects the cruelty of gender's masquerade; the effort required to maintain a credible image; the ease of forgetting one's 'self', displacing into the gutter, in one metaphorical move, femininity.[34]

Rather than exploiting the exotic figure of a kind-hearted queen in order to boost the reader's comfortable conformity, the text uses the figure of Grace as a critique of the hypocrisy engendered in social hierarchies, and the violence required to maintain them. Grace is brutally beaten by the police, a regularly repeated liberty she is resigned to, since

> Queens were even lower in the scale than street kids and they always rated a couple of smacks at least. (5)

Law and order is imposed by a suspicious and unregulated force antipathetic to individual freedom and rights. *Glory Days* follows the conventional structure us/them in which an inverted Other – the establishment – are the villains of social crime. The self-interest of the bourgeoisie is underpinned by the profit motive; when Glory was a child she would imagine people who lived in glass towers, high above her, in an image evoking Fritz Lang's *Metropolis*:

> Their flesh was aglow with the good food they'd just eaten. They looked down on us with a smile of indifference – they were up there, under the eye of God, they were taller and whiter than us, and glowed with the holy light of money . . . Out of our mean lives, from furnaces which never scorched them, people like me forged the artefacts which they took as their own, embalming them in art galleries and museums . . . The creations of outsiders like myself were the food of the rich. (224–5)

Glory's agent, Nigel, comes in for the most attentive criticism. The epitome of artistic patronage, he

> 'was used to bohemian, working class even, but genuine underclass was going too far.' (37)

At her opening, Nigel ingratiates a gallery buyer from Sydney, a man who turns art into finance. They wheel and deal over Glory's head, and her presence is inconsequential:

> Bob was looking after me, startled, calculating, bemused. 'Well, I see what you mean about her size.' It was obvious that they'd already come to some understanding, with Nigel selling me down the river, right, left, and centre. Men's talk it was, I could tell by the faintly contemptuous expression. I'd see to it all later. (227)

Patriarchy is spliced to capitalism within a conspiratorial contract. The hierarchy – with working-class women being disenfranchised from their own labour – is disrupted by Glory's defiance. Glory is no victim; she retrieves a sense of control and resists the representation of Woman as voiceless object of exchange, her body merely a commodity.

By adopting a Marxist perception of artistic production as labour, *Glory Days* resists the romantic tradition which idealizes it. The series of paintings completed by Glory depict a parody of romanticism, with one set on the family and a second on violence intended to

> 'forever [strip] it of its false glamour.' (39)

The kind of social realism preferred by mimetic artists is rejected too, as her art intertextually intersects with the progress of the narrative. The text is self-conscious about its literary and aesthetic heritage – neither accepting the apparently depoliticized, endless parody of post-modernist frames, nor blithely promoting the problematic classical realism.

Replete with hard-boiled textual signifiers, *Glory Days* is very reminiscent of Dashiell Hammett, who, as Raymond Chandler said

> gave murder back to the kind of people who commit it for reasons, not just to provide a corpse.[35]

Continental Op, like Glory, is fat, middle-aged, and critically disposed towards the managing classes. Hammett was a communist, and his novels, particularly *Red Harvest* (1929), and *The Glass Key* (1931), are replete with social criticism. Like Rosie Scott, Hammett conflated corruption with city life. In *Red Harvest*, for example, Personville is dubbed 'Poisonville' by the Op.[36] He, in contrast, is a figure of justice; similarly Glory's sense of justice is

> 'part of my bones.' (197)

Glory is also the alienated investigator:

> I'd prided myself on a few things, attaching myself to someone wasn't one of them. (213)

Yet, the socialist feminist imperative of communality and responsibility stretches the masculine role, representing what can be seen as a development in the genre, incidentally also moving away from the profound misogyny of the 'tough guy' novel. Glory's relationship to her daughter Rina is one of the most touching and unsentimental attempts to represent motherhood in fiction I have read. Walking the streets, Glory wants to

> 'keep my feet firmly placed in the mud and slime of it all.' (90)

Woman is not free to elevate her morality, like the conventional dick. The text also firmly rejects the othering process of conventional fiction by locating Glory's first husband as a murdered victim, and her second husband as the murderer. The family itself is the seat of violence, a theme threading throughout feminist crime fiction.

Glory has been framed for murder by her model, Roxy, a woman who is so obsessed with Glory that 'she's flipped into thinking she's me' (144). Roxy's room is papered with Glory's reviews, pictures, interviews, articles, each photocopied several times in a kind of Warholian montage. Since Andy Warhol, according to Robert Hughes

> did more than any other painter alive to turn the art world into the art business,[37]

the visual intertextuality aptly supports Scott's socialist aesthetics. The device is also a perfect rendering of the feminist fractured subject, a spectacle upon whom Roxy is constantly rewriting: the sheets are covered with 'scrawled comments in Roxy's tight little handwriting' (107). The image-maker is being made into an image, in an endlessly metafictional mirror. Roxy herself

> had moved in and out of so many games and deals and characters for so long that she was gone, lost in them permanently. (120)

She is driven insane, finally stabbing her mentor and Ideal Woman, Glory. The subject is undoubtably 'unstable'; the text clearly indicts the system which implements this violence.

The tension between maintaining the formula in its historic authenticity, and developing it to encompass feminism, at times results in a mismatch. The urge to represent social causality is occasionally at odds with the fictional frame: Glory deploys the convention of motiveless malice to explain the thriller function of the threat:

> I only knew that this malice beaming down on me for whatever reason had to be stopped by an act of will on my part. (105)

The idea of a distilled Nietzschean will, bent on battling with a metaphysical malignancy, has frog-marched across the genre, following Holmes, since the genre's beginnings. This exalted individualism is incongruous with a socialist feminist hera, and may be indicative of the way intransigent, literary conventions can undermine even the most self-consciously oppositional text.

The ending of *Glory Days* is prosaic, and to some extent recoups the feminist intention by rejecting the hard-boiled closure in favour of an image of sisterhood – a tactic recurring in many of these texts, which reflects a utopian impulse and feminist praxis. Glory is lying helpless and dependent on a hospital bed. A very unidealized, unromanticized nurse – 'a professional dag' (244) – is washing her down. The atmosphere is vibrant with female intimacy: pragmatic, efficient, and unsentimental. Female solidarity is seen to emerge from the hard cracks of human existence.

Already certain textual patterns are emerging in the content of these novels, their political concerns, and the way these are articulated using (or abusing?) the generic conventions of the crime form. Most of the novels published by feminist presses contain an element of socialist feminism which draws on historical strains within the genre itself. However, this social criticism does not necessarily encompass a critique of subjectivity – a crucial aspect of the feminist project to deconstruct the Ideal Woman. These same strategies are recognized and developed to include the foregrounding of sexual identity in the lesbian crime novel, which I deal with in Chapter 5.

One important way of understanding the novels in the sub-genre discussed here is not to confuse the self-conscious agenda of socialist feminism with 'authentic' working-class culture,[38] which has its own traditions. Although there is some inevitable crossover, there is also a distinct difference in readerly effect between the more intellectual intentions of socialist feminist crime novels, which seem to enforce an analytical distance whilst seeking to 'explain' (sometimes rather pedantically) the mechanisms of oppression to an implied middle-class reader, and those texts which resist the construction of the working classes[39] as victims to be saved by political enlightenment. The operation of this patronage is often subtly enforced, but it still has the effect of alienating some readers.

Ken Worpole has argued that working-class writing comes out of 'a politics that addresses itself to people's felt difficulties, hopes and aspirations, [it] actually needs to know what these are rather than assume them from some preconceived programme'.[40] He points out that the major traumas thematically dominating the twentieth-century working-class novel are not the 'structural' issues such as strikes, but the domestic, personal (one might say 'female') problems such as pregnancy, abortion, and enforced marriage. Where the process of identification is successful in these feminist crime novels then, the characterization is more than one-dimensionally reproducing the despairing cliché of poverty – in *Glory Days*, for example, which provokes the *feeling* of satiric survival which empowers the underclass's subversive strength.

This piece of research is informed by approaches in Literary and Cultural Studies in recent years which have argued that popular texts, as part of dominant culture, can also be read as containing elements which can be appropriated by self-consciously oppositional ideologies. Some of the novels in this section test the limits of that designation 'literary entertainment'. They can more properly be read as didactical narratives. The reader is not disappointed if she can discriminate between the two. Shards of political insight are often dulled and blunted by the cover-all moral lesson these texts propound – they fail because they are *too* serious, and their lack of self-conscious parody becomes a formal weakness. The pleasure in reading popular literature is dependent on its ability to be escapist and diversionary. For some readers, trawling around in the desperation of an imagined dystopia does just that. Many of these novels, by trying to depict a cornucopia of deprivation, became, quite simply, prurient. Yielding to the tentacles of political correctness has foreordained that they be consigned to the bin of literary curiosities. Now no longer in print, their radical edge has been blunted by time. Those few still selling succeed because story is not subsumed into consciousness-raising. Writing from the perspective of the 1990s, it is sobering to recognize that by the beginning of this decade socialist feminist crime fiction had begun to peter out, subsumed by other cultural imperatives. *Glory Days* (1989) marks a shift from the proselytizing and earnest politically correct texts seen earlier in the 1980s to the more self-consciously literary products of the 1990s, whilst still managing to integrate a socialist vision. The demise of the campaigning socialist feminist crime novel provides a clear example of how cultural forms alter in response to fluid political contexts.

This chapter, perhaps more than any other, is influenced by the prejudice of my own reading. On reflection I see that my frustration with these novels is at least partly a result of my own trajectory through time. As a young feminist in the mid-1980s I read them avidly, with excitement. They addressed my rapidly changing consciousness and were experienced as conversion narratives. Nearly a decade later my personal and the broader political climate has been transformed – in my academic job and in the security of my own more settled identity I feel that I have less need for such changes.[41] It is difficult to retrieve that periodic flavour of radical optimism which fueled such a frantic exchange of ideals. Perhaps, to be fair, there should have been two such readings here, one for 1985, and one for 1994. Executing this part of the study has been a personal reminder of how retrospective evaluations are so circumscribed by our present sensibilities.

4

'A change is gonna come'?

Race politics in crime fiction by women[1]

Consider these words of Lord Cromer, colonialist master of Egypt from 1882 to 1907, reprinted in Edward Said's *Orientalism* (1978):

> The European is a close reasoner; his statements of fact are devoid of any ambiguity; he is a natural logician, albeit he may not have studied logic; he is by nature skeptical and requires proof before he can accept the truth of any proposition; his trained intelligence works like a piece of mechanism. The mind of the Oriental, on the other hand, like his picturesque streets, is eminently wanting in symmetry. His reasoning is of the most slipshod description. Although the most ancient Arabs acquired in a somewhat higher degree the science of dialectics, their descendants are singularly deficient in the logical faculty. They are often incapable of drawing the most obvious conclusions from any simple premises of which they may admit the truth.[2]

Taking first Cromer's description of the European mind, this may be said to represent the quintessential detective, a man whose deductive objectivity makes him a paragon of narrative knowledge and hermeneutic presence. On the opposite side of this dualism is the Oriental, a man who treads the maze-like streets slip-shod: the gum shoes do not fit. He is incapacitated by race, his apparently illogical, unevolved (and further degenerating[3]) mind is biologically restricted and, therefore, as a detective, he cannot legitimately exist, he is an absence. A Black female detective is consequently doubly disappeared in this coded conjunction.

In this chapter I intend to examine two types of texts: first, to explore how White[4] female authors represent racial difference in their work, in many cases reproducing an Orientalist perspective. White women writers have fallen into exploiting the easy post-colonialist commonsensical attitudes of functional racism, often by reproducing racial Others as criminal, or exotic, or omitting them altogether. Sadly, having some form of feminist consciousness has not guaranteed any kind of anti-racist presence in their work. Writers have capitalized on a clichéd racism, using exotic characters to reinforce the White reader's comfortable conformity. By using categories of crime novels already introduced to the thesis I will show how in each case Black identity shores up White identity – in Said's understanding, how the Occident defines the Oriental, in order to define itself against an Other. Further, I hope to show how there are differences between Others, as 'Black' as a single category becomes problematized, particularly since the majority of readings are located in North American texts which have a complex genealogy in relation to slave history and its specific representations of the Black Other. Thus the undifferentiated threat of the Other becomes historicized and reinscribed as it breaks down into various versions of the threat to White domination. The crime genre has historically colluded with collapsing definitions of Others together, as Clive Bloom has exemplified in his criticism of Sax Rohmer's mystery series Dr Fu Manchu.[5] Bloom picks up two enduring structures in this schema, that the hero Nayland Smith acts on behalf of the 'interests of the entire white race',[6] collapsing White identity too into a seamless whole under attack from 'Chinaman' who is 'used as a synonym for criminal',[7] and the signifier of all homogenized difference as a threat.

Orientalist discourse locates the Other as criminal, and a threat. This discursive construction of Black identity and criminality is so powerful that even feminist writers trying to write against it largely fail to deliver an alternative because the White discourse and the crime form itself are so resistant to change in this aspect.[8] The centre of the crime novel requires Cartesian rational Man. Black man, because of his construction as non-thinking, non-rational, and non-literate, cannot deliver the denotation 'detective' easily.[9] Black women crime writers are consequently very difficult to find; in six years of research I have only found five, all of them from the USA: Dolores Komo, Rosa Guy, Nikki Baker, Eleanor Taylor Bland, and Barbara Neely. The genre is not a logical choice for those positioned outside the hegemonic institution of law enforcement. Hence, in the second part of this chapter I offer readings of all their texts in order to explore whether this relatively small amount of activity could be construed as a generic shift.

Mainstream author Dorothy Uhnak's crime fiction is marketed

with specific reference to her fourteen years as an officer in the New York Police Department, and this conflation of the author's experience with the verisimilitude of the text frames any dominant reading. Her first novel, *Policewoman* (1964), is classed as a non-fictional representation of authentic procedure. Her novels, which present women investigators in pioneering roles, rely on a feminism circumscribed by a confused (and confusing) libertarianism. The Christie Opara trilogy (1968–70) clearly coincides with the impetus of early Second Wave feminism, fictionalizing an image of the lone woman making it in a man's world. Uhnak's writing has also constantly exhibited a narrative fascination with race, knitting together the two contentious discourses of race and gender.

The series characters in the Opara trilogy are racial stereotypes. The subsequent novels also rely on a 'race element' which can be read as a metonymic attempt to convey both universality and verisimilitude. In his essay critic George Dove colludes with this myth of realism by drawing attention to Uhnak's year of research in preparation for writing *Law and Order* (1973); she was

> studying the backgrounds of the immigrants who came to New York City during the past century, the ethnic groups in the city and the general socio-political-economic history of the period covered in the novel.[10]

Dove's short analysis of *False Witness* (1981) dubs the text's female investigator, Assistant District Attorney Lynne Jacobi, an 'aggressive feminist',[11] and subsequently referring to her 'curious ethnic consciousness', he too connects the two together.[12] *False Witness* is the story of the assault, rape, and dismemberment of television star Sanderalee Dawson, the first Black woman hostess of a live talk show. Both Sanderalee and Lynne were born at the same time, and are astrologically twinned and coupled together in a kind of careerist sisterhood version of the traditional crime pairing of ego and alter-ego:

> each of us had taken her place in the man's world and succeeded and widened the spaces around us for others to follow. (44)

Lynne Jacobi's superior is a benign patriarch whose political ambition will prepare the way for her promotion to District Attorney, backed by his preferment and the Republican Party's endorsement. She is constructed as the exemplary woman who has bested patriarchy by her own efforts. Her success, whilst acknowledging the discomfort of sexism, actually depends on the mainstream American dream of opportunity; Lynne's gritty enduring individualism has ensured it. On the other hand Sanderalee's success is thanks to her (White, male) audience. Coached and marketed by managers, her appearance is her asset. Her fame is the fantasy of an exotic sexuality, a Jezebel, as a Black beauty she is pure representation.

Sanderalee's injuries and shock prevent her from speaking, only making animalistic 'groaning, cackling' sounds, and her words are unintelligible. Her subsequent oral and visual testimonies are recanted, rendering the investigation unstable and the image of her as fickle and easily duped. Her voice is silenced and depicted as unreliable, she is not a speaking subject, she is our 'false witness'. As a silenced, sexualized sight Uhnak is fixing Sanderalee as a stereotype. Sander L. Gilman in the essay 'Black Bodies, White Bodies'[13] identifies how the Black woman has stood for Black sexuality, being supposedly more primitive and intense than the White. Gilman's critique of visual icons, in painting, medical illustration, photography, and anthropological drawings from the late nineteenth century remind us of how the construction of the lascivious Black woman was mapped on to female slave sexuality and used as a justification for rape by White owners. In this construction of Black Woman, 'more sexual' is being attached to White identity as an excess. Her sexuality is seen as pathological and corrupting. Sanderalee is both irresponsibly, inherently promiscuous and unintelligent. The novel evokes the literary construct of the exotic primitive, newly freed, unable to cope with modern 'civilization'. The text is also caught within the

> colonial mentality which sees 'natives' as needing control [which] is easily transferred to 'woman' – but woman as exemplified by the caste of prostitute.[14]

The analogy between Black/Woman/prostitute situates Sanderalee in the position of Other, to be controlled by the White male defining discourse. As Gilman puts it, 'white *man's* burden' becomes his control of the sexualized, female Other.[15] The rape concretizes this operation in one action.

The text foregrounds the political and social context of this violent rape and allusions to race and gender issues litter the novel. Lynne Jacobi is outraged, and is personally committed to finding the perpetrator. Since the text constructs Sanderalee as a pathological masochist, however, the reader is encouraged to collude with Lynne's reluctant resignation – in that 'damn old male cliché: "She asked for it."' (257)

In one of those useful textual slips she then concludes:

'In this particular case, she did. Quite literally.' (257)

Despite the feminist theme, the exception proves the mythical rule, of women's complicit desire for rape. But the exception is coded as Other – would she have reached the same conclusion if the rape victim had been White? The construction of womanhood in this text is White. Black Woman becomes fallen-Woman, non-Woman, or 'something else' – the Other Other. The racial or visible colour difference of Blackness subtracts from the unit Woman so that the identity Woman becomes removed from Sanderalee.

Whereas a Black female may be gazed at with pity in *False Witness*, a Black male must efface his cultural history or risk representation as an inauthentic proselytizer for a race war masquerading as Roots. Sanderalee is a mere puppet for the media machinations of her mentor, Dr Regg Morris, spokesperson and advocate of the Palestine Liberation Organization. The text appears to be indulging the totem that the one thing more dangerous than a stupid nigger is an educated one. Two separate racial groups, Arab and African-American, become obsessed with anti-Semitic vengeance once the alleged attacker is discovered to be Jewish surgeon David Cohen. When Sanderalee identifies a different perpetrator, Regg silences her with:

'We got us our Jew, Sanderalee. Don't mess with this, don't rock it.' And when she said, 'But Regg, the man who did this to me: who did this to me.' And he told her that it didn't matter shit. (248)

The positioning and paranoidal portrayal of these interest groups displays the insecurity of the dominant centring discourse of post-colonial America. Said writes:

European culture gained in strength and identity by setting itself off against the Orient as a sort of surrogate and even underground self.[16]

The racial conflicts in *False Witness* are mainly initiated by Black men, acting irrationally and without provocation. When Cohen is scapegoated by Morris, the refutation is on ethnic grounds: 'Jews don't do that kind of thing' (254), says Bobby Jones, Lynne's WASP boyfriend and investigator, implying a hierarchy of racial difference.

By locating racial aggression as occurring between the diverse racial groups *except* White Anglo-Saxon Protestants, effectively this displaces racism as an issue only for competing Others, absent from the White oasis of reason.

Within *False Witness* there is a growing sense of menace emanating from Morris. His physicality is mesmerizing, and his magical manipulation of women and children, his maniacal ideology, his cunning manoeuvring and ruthless ambition all combine to maintain a permanent sense of threat. Despite his superficial education, he is still the Brute Negro of racist folklore 'underneath'. He persuades Sanderalee to undertake a publicity trip to 'Arafat-land'; populated with the proverbial 'groups of dirty little children with runny noses', Palestine turns out to be the epitome of an hysterical terrorism:

> On her ninety-minute TV special, *Search for Peace in the Mid-East*, we were treated to the sight of Sanderalee Dawson, radiant in the hot dusty sunlight, carelessly dressed in her chique Ralph Lauren Western outfits, dancing and gun-waving joyously with Arafat and his band of forty machine-gun armed thieves; slinging an unwelcome, unholy arm around semi-veiled women, probably damning them forever into unimaginable hells for being photographed over and over again with this strangely vibrant American woman. Willing male teachers, grinning boyishly... helped her to sight her automatic rifle. Painted on the targets were the familiar, graspingly evil, large-nosed, Zionist-Jew thugs, and as she fired her weapon, jumping with the kick to her shoulder, as she slaughtered the enemy of the peoples, there was great joy among the Palestinians. (48–9)

The passage is overloaded with signifiers; again, the racism is deferred, on to the Palestinians, implying the narrator's neutrality. Sanderalee owns the gaze, but significantly it passes through the sights of a *gun*: the Black gaze needs to be masculinized, and made violent. The infantilizing representation of Palestinians as emotional children, in their 'simple' prejudice and passion, is another kind of racial Othering.[17] They are positioned as requiring firm control by the hegemonic 'democratic' discourse of Occidental capitalism. *False Witness* is a novel which paradigmatically illustrates the dominant discourse of race, expressed as an investigation into Otherness. But it tells us much more about the paranoid fantasies of White identity.

As feminism developed during the late 1970s its White, middle-class base became more fragmented as the identity politics of women in more disenfranchised groups forced a recognition of 'difference', a category of political praxis and theory which does not treat issues of race as an optional extra, a surplus, to a centralist feminism, implicitly White. Class divisions were also integral to this critique. Black and lesbian women were highly instrumental in initiating this conceptual change, as feminism became restructured as a diverse set of debates challenging the hegemony and homogeneity of the dominant. Consequently race and sexuality have constituted two major sites of enquiry within feminist fiction, particularly in North American texts.[18] A new tradition of writing has revealed how racially marked characters are stereotyped, how race can structure a narrative, and how it can be foregrounded as a theme.[19]

Many of the crime texts written by White feminist authors have offered a 'positive images' strategy which inverts the traditional binary of the form wherein White equals good and Black equals bad. This strategy can transgress the existing structure but it does not change it as such. Novels which contain racially diverse characters sympathetically reproduced for the reader's regard include: Katherine V. Forrest's *Amateur City* (1984), Hannah Wakefield's *The Price You Pay* (1987), Joy Magezis' *Vanishing Act* (1988), Agnes Bushell's *Shadowdance* (1989), Amanda Cross's *A Trap for Fools* (1990), Maud Farrell's *Skid* (1990); Janet LaPierre's *Children's Games* (1990), Lesley Grant-Adamson has her serial character Holly Chase, Gillian Slovo has her secretary Carmen, and several of Sara Paretsky's novels feature the recurrent figure of Hispanic nurse Carol Alvarado. Treatments progress from a tokenistic smattering of one-dimensional goodies, usually minor, helpful characters, offering little more than a nod to literary equal opportunities, to, in Paretsky, for example, a plurality of ethnic identities which operates to romanticize a multicultural melting pot, excising real conflicts and differences between groups. In *False Witness* the proliferation of racially marked characters results in a reinforcement of the threat of Black disruption. In the liberal feminist text the impulse towards individual equality can engender a less obviously racist approach, but the end result inevitably positions race as a 'prop' to the grand narrative structure of the myth of a coherent, homogeneous White identity. 'Difference' becomes synonymous with the Other.

One strategy of feminist writers has been to adopt the thriller format, positioning the reader against the grain by inverting the central threat: instead of Western (Occidental) stability being threatened by the 'dark' (Oriental) forces of communism, the conspiracy fear is located in the White male establishment. Thus the Intelligence forces, like the CIA or MI5, are represented as unregulated and dangerous, a threat to liberal ideas of individual freedom of expression, a repressive bureaucratic machine operating out of control. The new victim becomes the democratic independence of developing countries. North American colonialist, expansionist intervention in areas such as Central America and the Philippines allows a dialectic on race to permeate such texts as *Murder in the Collective* by Barbara Wilson (which also sensitively engages with class and sexuality), and *The Price You Pay* by Hannah Wakefield.[20] By inverting the terms of the racist dualism White security/Black threat, the literary convention is subverted, resulting in a White villain and a Black victim.[21]

These novels attempt to challenge the racist orthodoxy of Orientalist myth, but are defeated by the narrative worldview of the text, as sited (sighted) in a liberal humanism, as I will attempt to show in my reading of Elizabeth Bowyers' *Ladies Night* (1990). Set in Vancouver, Canada, the novel's geographical location is an area metaphor for its Anglo-American hybridity, containing the former's concern for themes of social class, mixed with the latter's emphasis on race. Single parent and private investigator Meg Lacey uncovers a child pornography and prostitution ring which indentures homeless Vancouver girls via drug addiction. Her name is symbolic, intertextually evoking the feminine mainstream fictional detective and mother, Mary Beth Lacey, of cult crime series *Cagney and Lacey*.[22]

Whereas earlier liberal feminist writers such as Barbara Paul, Amanda Cross, and Ruth Rendell have skimmed over social positioning, Meg Lacey, with the hindsight of the feminist debates of the 1980s, is foregrounded self-consciously as bourgeois and White. 'Once I was a suburban housewife', she begins in chapter 6, who is then raped. This quintessential act of male sexual violence provokes a feminist re-education. At 35 she cynically embraces her membership of a 'very privileged, powerful minority' (64); this raised consciousness has caused the loss of her husband and economic status, her divorce stripping her of respectability and a reliable income. Meg Lacey's feminism is a result of her experience, and thus far the novel is a conversion narrative.

During the period of her political education, Meg displays the patronizing fascination with which middle-class guilt has regarded the Other. She develops a 'terror of complacency' (64) which registers in that resolutely feminine site, her mothering:

> I began to feel that if I didn't show my children that there were other attitudes, other lifestyles, I'd be guilty of raising dinosaurs, incapable of adapting to a multicultural world. (65)[23]

The ideology of liberal pluralism is represented in Darwinian terms of progress, in a kind of updated version of exploration and exposition, encapsulated by tolerance. The difficulty of representing an enlightened liberal position is underlined by the structures of language employed as a vehicle for understanding, intention being displaced by the protagonist's defining voice, or more accurately, sight. The enunciator, Lacey, shows her children the objectified Other. The gaze is in two directions, towards her historical culture, and towards the culture of difference:

> I was getting to know people that did not share my assumptions and values, was seeing my class, my culture, my race from the point of view of those outside it . . . I talked to anyone who seemed 'different'. (64)

In positing a neutral, central position between the two, the text falls into the myth of impartiality. Gazing directly at the Other is all too often about covertly appropriating and enhancing White identity, and incorporating the threat. The traditional role of the detective in crime fiction is deductive and evaluative, a man who can walk the mean streets without becoming mean, an aloof man, a watcher who ultimately upholds the bourgeois order. It is the convention of this authorial/authoritarian gaze which so tenaciously restrains the liberal humanist text from surrendering its cultural capital to the margins.

In 'Scratches in the Face of the Country; or, What Mr. Barrow Saw in the Land of the Bushmen',[24] Mary Louise Pratt examines the genre of travel writing as part of the Orientalist expansionist project in force in Africa during the nineteenth century. The travellers, writing in the first person, narrate 'a descriptive sequence of sights/sites',[25] the language suggesting a fantasy of dominance:

> The eye 'commands' what falls within its gaze . . . At the same time, this eye seems powerless to act or interact with this landscape. Unheroic, unparticularized, without ego, interest, or desire of its own, it seems able to do nothing but gaze from a periphery of its own creation, like the self-effaced, non-interventionist eye that scans the Other's body.[26]

The construction could easily be transposed into a description of the classic investigator. The writers of these travelogues positioned themselves as 'personally innocent conduits of information',[27] evoking the disembodied ratiocination required of the investigative observer. Pratt continues:

> this European is too passive and incapable of intervention.[28]

The characteristics of nineteenth-century travel writing and twentieth-century hard-boiled detective fiction are uncomfortably convergent. The latter even evolved from the frontier romance, the colonialist expansion into the Wild West (land already a home for Native tribes), being transposed through time into an urban wilderness battle on the streets of North American cities.[29] The concept of a Dark Continent, replete with racist signifiers, is unconsciously invoked by the twentieth-century myth of the urban ghetto, archetypally Black. As the nineteenth-century explorers depended on Social Darwinism to justify their intervention, so the twentieth century casts those on the streets as lowlife on the social hierarchy. As Lacey unwittingly comments on the relationship with her friend Johanna, a lesbian prostitute:

> I often feel like a child being taught how to swim; *I keep wanting to touch bottom*[30] to make sure it's still there. (33) [My italics]

I have chosen *Ladies Night* to represent the liberal humanist worldview in feminist crime fiction precisely because of its self-consciousness. The novel strains consistently against being read as complicit with bourgeois norms. Meg Lacey is unheroic; positioning herself neither on the side of the law, nor on the side of the 'criminal', she represents the individualistic equivocation typical of the lone dick. Ultimately her 'gaze from the periphery' is self-effacing and, like the explorers incapable of intervention, constrained by the liberal myths of privacy and individual destiny. The villain of *Ladies Night* is Caesar, king of a drugs/pornography empire, murdered, inferentially, by Johanna – the street people take care of their own. Johanna, although White, is designated as Other; as a prostitute she is a sign of excess, along with her friend Salal.[31] Both are made distinct by their appearance, Johanna being very tall, and Salal being very beautiful. Salal is mistakenly identified as Chinese twice in the text, first by Lacy and then by a policeman (prime definers). As she is a Native American, one may deduce that gazing from 'the centre', 'difference' becomes undifferentiated. As a 'criminal type', the discursive association with 'Chinaman' is hard to ignore, especially as she is also a heroin addict.[32] Her construction as the knowing, controlling, elusive, *inscrutable* mystery is another alternative version of racial Otherness common to crime fiction.

The closure in the novel concentrates on a scene of pure sentimentality, releasing the liberal subject from action as the street people are seen to be self-sufficiently caring for their own. The hard-faced Johanna discloses her secret expression of maternalism, a refuge for homeless kids, into which Salal is safely incorporated, hence: inside every prostitute is a warm-hearted mother, the stock 'redeemable whore' of crime fiction, and inside every Black woman is the 'earth mother' or mammy. Despite its probable utopian impulse, the idea is romantic, and it is significant that a text which so self-consciously tries to escape its bourgeois structuring ends positing an act of charity. Meg Lacey, as an isolated individualist, is alienated from this fantasy of communalized oppression, incapable of anything but observation.

The socialist feminist crime novel has often fared not much better in its treatment of race, despite a committed political intention to expose the complex interface of oppression between race, class, gender, and sexuality. Gillian Slovo is able to explore the dynamics of these hierarchies in relation to two cultural oppositions: employee/employer, and Black/White. Like Holmes had his Watson, Kate has her Carmen. Carmen is the friend of a murder victim in *Death by Analysis*, and Kate employs her afterwards in a burst of good business. The two of them check on companies with Greater London Council contracts, ensuring that they are implementing its anti-racist and anti-sexist policies. Their function seems, in 1988, tied to a short period of progressive British municipal politics we can only now see tinted with nostalgia. Kate had wanted a partner, but

> Carmen left me in no doubt that she wasn't willing to oblige. Instead she got me to agree that I was the boss and she made sure that I never forgot it. (11)

Although ostensibly Carmen's reasons are that she wants a clear division of labour, and not to be 'tied down', Kate tries to equalize the status and responsibility in encouraging her to finalize and present the reports. Carmen replies she doesn't have the wardrobe, accent, or patience for it. Later Kate gets Carmen to talk to a difficult witness – another Black – under the assumption he will more readily talk to Carmen (due to tribal loyalty the reader must assume). When

Kate is wrongfully detained by some unscrupulous police, Carmen angrily responds:

> 'It happens to my people all the time. They've got used to swallowing it and getting on with their lives. What makes your experience so special?'

Kate snaps back:

> 'Okay, so it's hard on you. But just don't start with this crap about our people and your people and swallowing things. I don't believe in that and I don't believe you do either.' (92)

The novel attempts a quite complicated interchange on race relations. I suggest that there is some exasperation being expressed by the character Kate, as she betrays a rather simple syllogism: (a) offer a Black person equality, (b) they'll turn it down, (c) so we're all just as free to make choices. Compound this by telling them what they *really* think, and this has a 'most miraculous effect' (92); Carmen smiles, 'a lovely warm open smile', with only a hint, perhaps, of the Happy Nigger.

Carmen has a Bunter-like competence, performing the groundwork with occasional intuitive digs. Her model strength and efficiency can be seen as the author's attempt to promote a positive Black character. Perhaps we are not *meant* to accept Kate's actions uncritically. Her character can be read as a vehicle for the revelation of unconscious racist processes. Biographical information on Gillian Slovo would seem to support an anti-racist authorial message,[33] but by casting Carmen as a Watson, however, it may be that the enduring generic hierarchy undermines the author's best intentions. Trying to place the politics of race in Slovo's work is difficult as the text strains in two different directions. The form exacts a conventional reading against the presumed radical intent of the author.

As in life, one of the classic roles for women in crime fiction is as the investigator's secretary, and the attempt to promote an 'uppity' Black version has been tried several times – Lesley Grant-Adamson does it in her serial journalist/detective's careerist assistant, Holly Chase. The strategy comes across as a revisionist attempt to redeem an entrenched hierarchy. The strength of the contextual, cross-generic, commonsensical interpretation can and does supersede authorial intent. The most convincing Black assistant I have found is Dr Sarah Chayse's secretary Stanley Livingstone, in Lynn Meyer's *Paperback Thriller* (1975). The fact that he is male and middle class helps, but as part of his function in the novel is to raise the spectre of racism in order for it to be excised, I remain sceptical (see pp. 99–106).

It is not inevitable that White lesbian crime fiction will introduce race as part of the radical textual impulse (see Amanda Kyle Williams' espionage thriller *The Providence File* (1991) for a rather regrettable example). However, being similarly ill-defined, the lesbian does have some investment in redefinitions, and there is good reason to find some strategic mutuality. Her (im)position as an Other can cause alliances, as the recent history of feminism has indicated. Feminist fiction of the 1970s and 1980s explored utopian visions composed of cultural diversity in such key science fiction texts as Marge Piercy's *Woman on the Edge of Time* (1979) or Sally Miller Gearhart's *The Wanderground* (1980). The breaking down of a national movement into identity groups, which transformed Women's Liberation into feminisms during the 1980s, has engendered a number of problematics around identity and culture. Conflicts expressed as antagonistic exchanges over what is to be considered 'politically correct' have had a restraining effect upon experimental fiction. The lesbian feminist reader is often challenged in her reading to embrace a myriad of Others which can consign them all to an undifferentiated experience of oppression. Some narratives, built upon a shared oppression *and* a celebration of difference, both lived as categories of resistance, can contain a progressive dialectic. Writers such as Sarah Dreher have attempted to draw out a respectful symbiosis between in this case, racial and sexual Others, prefaced on mutual estrangement.[34]

Gray Magic (1987) is Sarah Dreher's third mystery novel featuring serial character Stoner McTavish. Stoner, in common with Antoinette Azolakov's serial character Cass Milam, is a feminist lesbian rather than a lesbian feminist. She is the proverbial soft-hearted butch, who battles against homophobia and misogyny, masquerading as a metaphysical evil. *Gray Magic* is unusual in that it explores issues of race in relation to Native Americans, focusing on the conjunction of two cultures, Hopi and Navajo, with White Anglo. The novel opens with Siyamtiwa, Hopi mystic and healer, musing on the thought of Something out of Harmony. She is preparing herself for an elemental spirit battle between good and evil, fought between two elected (by the spirits) strangers. Thus the text starts up the detective story dynamic but in an alternative cultural format: a world of chaos is turned into a world of order by the actions of a hero. The convention of cosy closure has been criticized for its conservatism, but Siyamtiwa rejects an easy resolution, recognizing the endlessly repeating cycle of struggle and conflict:

> To fight once more the battle fought so many times. So many times. (1)

Metafictionally, the thought echoes the reading imperative of detective fiction.

Siyamtiwa is tired and ready to die. Stoner, the stranger and her *ingénue*, must fight the evil personified in Larch Begay, another White. According to Navajo custom Begay is a Two-Heart, a Skin-Walker, or Coyote Man. In his human self Begay is a scheming racist who makes money by illegally trading whisky to reservation Indians, in exchange for valuable jewellery and historical artefacts. As Coyote Man, a construct likened to werewolves or vampires, he transforms himself at night into a coyote using the power that the YaYas, an old Hopi society, took from the animal world. The magic of this clan was a force for good or evil; when it became abused the people decided to gather up the fetishes, pahos and baskets, and hide them in a cave. The collection, or YaYa bundle, brings limitless power. It is Begay's Holy Grail.

The YaYa is used symbolically in the text as an intercultural metaphor for masculinity. Several women on the reservation have died of a mysterious sickness; two White women recovered once they moved away. The Indians' explanation, 'YaYa sickness', is dismissed as superstition by those inculcated by White discourse, but respect for Native American belief nudges the reader into a more pluralistic set of truths. Laura Yazzie, a Navajo nurse, stresses the more complementary aspects of Hopi culture:

> 'According to some of the legends, the YaYa could drain the energy from women and use it for their personal benefit.'
> 'That doesn't sound like sorcery,' Gwen said. 'It sounds like marriage.' (126)

Larch Begay himself is a collage of 'Most Disgusting Men in Fiction', a memoir to masculinity's meanest manifestations:

> His dark hair was shoulder length and greasy. The skin of his face – what little was visible beneath an untrimmed and spikey beard – resembled a lunar landscape of pock-marks. A monstrous beer belly overlapped his belt, the tarnished brass buckle sunk deep into his flesh. He wore cowboy boots with rundown

> heels, jeans caked with something dark, stiff, and mysterious, a filthy undershirt. The hair on his chest was matted and wet-looking. His eyes were tiny, red-rimmed, and unnaturally bright. His eyebrows were ponderous. A droplet of spit or beer had caught on his beard. He smelled like the Celtics locker room after the NBA playoffs. (66)

He leers, swears, sneers, barks, growls and wheels and deals. He is both animalesque and a symbol of corrupted science, of urban decay – he runs a gas station, to cultural feminists he epitomizes 'the rape of the wild'. The equivalence between woman and nature is employed in *Gray Magic.* As Siyamtiwa says:

> 'Mushroom bomb is White man's YaYa bundle.' (196)

Begay's filth and ugliness stands for the destructive force of masculinity, but the text is seduced by the convention that villains must be as repulsive as possible, a reductionist stereotype inhabiting a Keatsian myth that 'Beauty is truth, truth beauty'.[35] Unfortunately, the novel also falls for the cliché of creating Begay as working class.

Stoner McTavish is able to tackle Begay specifically because as a lifelong lesbian 'she was a woman whose spirit no man had ever used' (263). Ignoring the ideological dimension, this constructs the lesbian as a symbolic image of romantic separatism. Begay's animal transformations are fuelled by him tapping women's spiritual energy, and by defeating him Stoner ends his exploitation and achieves a feminist victory. Her agency is effected by working with the Spirits – it is the Kachina Masau (the male spirit of death) who kills Begay and saves Stoner's life. On the one hand this deconstructs the individualist myth of an overdetermined hero who single-handedly restores the order of things. On the other hand it is a metaphysical version of the pattern of 'female investigator saved by the timely intervention of a male expert' who executes the threat leaving her non-violent credentials intact. The ending continues to be problematic:

> In that moment she knew that Larch Begay had been a pawn, as she herself had been a pawn, and Siyamtiwa, and everyone whose lives this thing had touched. They had all acted out their roles in a mystery play that had been written a long, long, time ago. Before anybody's memory. It had been Begay's part to tip the balance, and now the balance was restored. White and Navajo and Hopi, the cultures intersected. Male and female. Black magic and white magic. (276)

Constructed, as it is, with notions of a predetermined universal text being in the lap of the gods, this concluding image of cosmic opposites is a condensed articulation of the crime genre's essential hermeneutic. It is also another instance of cultural appropriation or 'borrowings' in which the White looks to the Other, as closer to 'Nature', to tell it some important spiritual 'truth'.[36] By implementing supernatural elements into an acute political critique of White racism and homophobia, and blending this within two genres (fantasy and detective fiction realism), the text's combination is formally interesting.

The 'other realities' presented in the novel depend on marginal perspectives which together combine to form a reflecting mirror directed at White post-colonialism. Language is perceived as a prime channel for maintaining racist hegemony. Siyamtiwa says to Stoner:

> 'So now you will take out a gun and make me walk a thousand miles to die in a strange place.'
> 'What?'
> 'That's what pahana [white persons] do to Indians who annoy them.'
> 'I know,' Stoner said. 'It was a terrible thing, I'm sorry.'
> The old woman covered her head with her arms. 'You gonna shoot me now?'
> 'I'm not going to shoot you.'
> Siyamtiwa shrugged. 'My great uncle was shot by a white man who stepped on his foot. It's your way of apologizing.'
> Stoner was silent. (45)

The movement, closing with a silent, listening subject, is a pincer-like literary parody. Siyamtiwa comments, 'I test you. See if you have a sense of humor', utilizing the unseating power of a joke to destabilize the reader. There are similarities in style here with the Latin-American fantasists such as Jorge Luis Borges, Gabriel Garcia Marquez, or Isabelle Allende, who also slip through realities and implement satire in this way to expose the violence of domination.

Stoner's position as an Other sensitizes her to the mechanics of racism. The Stoner/Siyamtiwa relationship is not simplified or romanticized, however, but the student/teacher structure can enable the White reader, by identifying with the protagonist, to regard her own cultural history circumspectly, although this is clearly still about the construction of White identity. Siyamtiwa is three women: (a) Maria Hernandez, a Hispanic nursemaid who died, alone, of cancer, (b) Mary Beale Ph.D., author of *Walking in the White Man's Shoes*,[37] and

(c) the one Stoner interacts with in the narrative, Siyamtiwa, wise woman, healer, mystic. The White feminist concept of Woman as a fractured subject,[38] is materialized in Hopi custom and belief. Siyamtiwa also rejects the linear sequentiality of the masculinized narrative often execrated by feminists:

> 'No, Green-eyes,' Siyamtiwa said firmly. 'I am Mary Beale and Marcia Hernandez. Not sometimes, all times.'
> Oh boy. Multiple personality. 'I see.'
> 'You don't see. You want life to be like soldiers in a straight line, first one thing, then the next. It makes you feel safe, but it is not how things are.' (194)

The reader of *Gray Magic*, by voyeuristically partaking in Stoner's pedagogy, is inculcated into a parallel alternative critique of the homophobia which suffuses western society, which is currently spoiling Stoner's life in particular. In the first chapter Stoner's lover Gwen comes out to her grandmother, Eleanor Burton. Her response consists of the worst aspects of bigotry, and the inevitable estrangement constitutes a narrative of disorder running parallel to the detecting impulse. The text sets up four strong older women, Siyamtiwa, Eleanor, Stoner's straight friend Stell, and her aunt and guardian, Hermione. Three of them embrace tolerance, as Siyamtiwa says:

> 'Do you think I have time to worry about what goes on in your bedroll?' (114)

By a textual sleight of hand which owes more to imaginative optimism than reality, Eleanor is constructed in an unpleasant minority. The lesbian reader is thus righteously affirmed in her identity, but the textual disorder is not righted in a romantic final closure – this convention is resisted. By remaining sundered, the character of Gwen enacts the real alienation felt by lesbians ostracized by their blood relatives. When Stell tells Gwen to give her love to those who love her for who she is, she advocates an alternative model of family. The text also encourages the lesbian reader to ally her sense of estrangement with those of different cultures, stimulated into a felt relation to racial difference, an empathy built on a shared otherness and a grasp of alternate realities:

> The old woman chuckled and massaged her scalp. 'The Dineh, you know, they like women like you. Let you bring your friend

> into your mother's clan, even let you be a warrior sometimes. Maybe you oughta think about that, eh.' (234)

It is also a White fantasy of Black culture as an elevated pastoral.

So far all the novels I have discussed by White authors position Black characters as secondary to the White protagonist, their main function being to reflect and enhance the identity of the central investigator. This synecdochal pairing symbolically reproduces the structure of Othering which I see as being implicated within and influenced by the historical discourses of post-colonialism and Orientalism. Said says of Orientalism:

> there is no such thing as a delivered presence, but a re-presence, or a representation.[39]

It is difficult to avoid setting up a meritocracy of those White writers who 'get it right' according to an anti-racist imperative. Orientalist representations are produced by a shifting, contradictory, and unstable process which is discursively overdetermined in the construction of a White subject. It may be possible to see whether this Orientalist, historically *male* gaze may be reproduced differently when the enunciator is female, or even feminist, as Gayatri Chakravorty Spivak has explored.[40] She picks up on the language of feminist individualism which dominates canonical women's writing in the western tradition. So far I think that connection still pertains. Subjects socialized as White almost inevitably reproduce Orientalist orderings;[41] although it *may be possible* temporarily and voluntarily to pervert this positioning (and certain different marginalizations/Otherings may facilitate this), I am tempted to concur with Spivak that

> No perspective *critical* of imperialism can turn the Other into a self, because the project of imperialism has always already historically refracted what might have been the absolutely Other into a domesticated Other that consolidates the imperialist self.[42]

Using Said and Spivak then, we may conject that there is no referent for Blackness in crime fiction, only a representation thereof, according to various conventions. Despite this, Spivak argues elsewhere[43] that for Whites not to take the risk of challenging Orientalist orderings is to hide behind the White privilege of silence, the result of which is to perpetuate Orientalism.

Initially, when first compiling this chapter I was to claim the generic incompatibility of a Black female detective, the subject of this next section, at that point having found only the White British author Susan Moody's anomalous serial Black sleuth Penny Wanawake.[44] Penny Wanawake is a non-presence, an empty sign of Black womanhood, 'signifying nothing', but serving the need of the crime text for exoticism. The front cover of the 1985 Futura edition foregrounds a fair-skinned woman of African descent strewn seductively on a leopard-skin sheet, champagne in one hand, pistol in the other, a clingy corset and fishnet tights signifying a sensuality underscored with the subtitle 'Her days were hectic . . . Her nights were dynamite'. She is 'Nefertiti, Cleopatra. The Queen of Sheba' (12), an exotic sexual symbol tempered by a mixed race origin with impeccable White roots. She is

> accepted everywhere because of her mother, Lady Helena Hurley, whose ancestors had sat in the House of Lords for over six hundred years. (18)

As an aristocrat, Penny's status, money and privilege isolate her from the institutionalized racism the state inflicts upon its dependants. Her position allows the text to treat ideological racism as an absence. As an 'almost-White' the character's Blackness has a restricted function, to operate only as an eroticized fantasy of difference. This is epitomized in an exchange between Penny and her lover Kimbell. Black culture, represented in food, is rejected by the two in favour of a European aphrodisiac:

> 'How come you went to school with the Queen or whatever and you cain't tell a smoked oyster when you see one?' Kimbell shook his head. 'Man, they's real good.' He said it in a high-pitched voice, like someone trying out for the part of the coloured butler in a new comedy series. 'You make it come alive for me,' Penny said. ' I can see it all so clear, way down upon the Swannee River, with the darkies gathered on the porch after a hard day picking cotton. Old Black Joe strumming on his git-ah. The boll-weevils chirruping away on the Mississippi delta. And Mammie bringing out the chitlins and the black-eyed peas, with a side order of smoked oysters. Shit, Kimbell. You got no ethnic pride.' 'Wouldn't know a chitlin if it came up and bit my ear,' Kimbell said. (176)

Although Penny is a 'liberated woman', sexually and financially independent, this is a result of station, not struggle. Her Black culture is represented as a distant, filmic sight, satirized by a silly voice, supplanted by European sophistication. Black culture is signified by a sentimental image, as an inauthentic, artificial tableau, lost to history and irrelevant to the upwardly mobile 'reality' of assimilation. The intention is parodic, and the effect is to reassure the White reader by breaking down Black 'excess'.

It is nearly sixty years since the poet Sterling Brown wrote 'Negro Character as Seen by White Authors' (1933),[45] the classic observation of six archetypes in North American literature: the contented slave, the wretched freeman, the brute negro, the tragic mulatto, the local colour negro, and the exotic primitive. Despite the huge social and political changes since then, such as the Civil Rights Movement, and the creation of a Black canon and tradition in literature and criticism, the same deployment of types proliferates. In some ways there is an inevitability about this study: that reading popular texts results in a regurgitation of stereotypes is a comment on the limitations of formula fiction. Certainly the genre has historically colluded with dominant definitions of Others. Is it possible, given the narrative constraints of the genre, to avoid being racist? A reader-centred criticism must allow for the nuances, inflections and areas of ambiguity within the genre. This approach becomes more viable with an open text.

A British attempt to disrupt racial and gender stereotypes can be found in the last White-authored text I wish to examine: Claire Macquet's *Looking for Ammu* published by Virago in 1992. The cover blurb promises

> A film-noir world where distinctions between saints and sinners become devastatingly uncertain.

This invokes the urban dystopian tradition of hard-boiled fiction in which perception itself, intrinsic to investigation, is at best unstable, at worst morally flawed. *Looking for Ammu* breaks with feminist crime convention by rejecting the model of a super-sleuth. White nurse-tutor Harriet Weston, a prissy, conceited, repressed, self-righteous narrator pursues her iconic mentor Black Dr Ammu Bai, who, in the economy of Othering, represents to Harriet the elevation of everything she is not, a beautiful, selfless visionary. As Harriet tries to find the missing Ammu, the investigative trajectory incisively deconstructs the sign of Black-Woman-as-Mystical-Enigma. In looking for the Black Other, Harriet inevitably finds herself, and destroys Ammu, but in contrast to mainstream Orientalist narratives of this type, the text lays bare the self-interest at the heart of the noble act of discovery through some vicious bits of satire.

Looking for Ammu also brings to the surface the unstated sexual desire which drives this kind of plot structure. That the narrator is in love with her idol is plain from the first chapter. Evoking the classic way White westerners have fantasized the Black Other, the text lays bare the eroticism in this White gaze. The reader guesses that Harriet's denunciation of sex as a 'diseased craving' (149), and her claims that

> 'Sex is disgusting. It makes people do filthy things' (187)

is a prelude to her own, drunken initiation with an endearing young butch named Brucie, who deals in drugs and pornography. The text manipulates the generic certainties of both detective and romance fiction leaving the reader questioning the representation of desire. An extended conversation between Harriet and Ammu's friend, Mauritian Dr Jasbir Ramgulam, on the relationship between consequence, intent, and responsibility in pornography raises discomforting issues. The passage is too extended to quote in full, so I have selected:

> [Dr Ramgulam] 'I remember a picture I saw once, a Victorian print,' she continued, 'it was a delicately executed etching of a line of Indian coolies under a white man's whip. It was made in British Guiana I think . . . That picture gave me, for a second, a surging sexual thrill of power . . . Would the picture have had that effect on you?'
> [Harriet] 'No.'
> 'Is that because you are white and therefore not involved, innocent?'
> 'I don't want to know about this -'
> 'But I do . . . Do you think perhaps my dear, because I am black, in my subconscious mind even if my head feels as international as ICI – that my mind has in it a coolie – a victim?'
> 'Every copy of that print should be rooted out and destroyed.'
> 'But even if it was,' Dr Ramgulam said excitedly, 'the woman under the white man's whip would not get back her innocence would she?' (145–6)

Although Harriet is perceived as 'winning' the argument for the pro-censorship lobby, and it is she who diachronically connects the 'Black bodies, White bodies' reading of racism with sexism, she remembers Ammu saying to her that 'a fanatic will always win an argument, because conviction has so much more force than logic' (147). What the text seems to imply, given the other characters' diverse hookups with pornography, is the lack of any firm truth, or monomorphic moral monologue, which can encapsulate the feminist response to oppression. Recalling the words of Lord Cromer,[46] the 'obvious conclusions' and the 'simple premises' are inadequate when imposed by a White character upon a cross-cultural text.

Experience, as a personal and authentic voice, has been discredited by feminist theory of the 1980s, with the charge of essentialism. White authors do not inevitably construct racist narratives, nor Black authors emancipatory ones. Nevertheless, the author's cultural heritage is still significantly helpful as an aid to understanding the locus of a narrative, particularly when she or he shares a subculture actively writing about its oppression, inscribing an oppositional text within a self-conscious literary tradition. In Peter J. Rabinowitz's article 'Chandler Comes to Harlem: Racial Politics in the Thrillers of Chester Himes' he articulates the conflict between the Chandleresque hard-boiled thriller and the racial realities of North American culture. By looking at the Black writer Himes' two detectives, Grave Digger Jones and Coffin Ed Johnson, as connected to and identifying with the poor Black people of Harlem, he extrapolates the violent contradiction in their position, that is to say between the (Black) people, and the (White) Man. Rabinowitz suggests that this endemic violence and rage is caused in their juxtaposition, and that further:

> the violence is not only characteristic of the novels, but is also directed against them: the very incongruity of the genre and its subject matter produces a violent disruption.[47]

This generic disruption is produced in different ways: resolution and restoration are withheld; individualism and heroism are absent or problematic; objective detachment from the 'criminals' and 'victims' – the street people – is not possible. As Frankie Y. Bailey has pointed out in *Out of the Woodpile: Black Characters in Crime and Detective Fiction* (1991), the gender content of this violence in the novels is explicit. The female characters in Himes are depicted as 'cheats, liars, whores, and betrayers'[48] – echoing earlier texts such as Richard Wright's *Native Son* (1940). With reference to Rabinowitz's analysis then, I now wish to discuss the Black feminist author Rosa Guy's two novels *The Disappearance* (1979) and *New Guys Around the Block*

(1983) as texts which integrate a critique of racism *structurally* within the narrative, using a Black male investigator.

Imamu Jones first solved a mystery in *The Disappearance* (1979) in which he is charged with the murder of his recently acquired foster-sister. He acquits himself, but not before the novel has indicted a brutal police force. A White cop/Black cop team take Imamu in for questioning; that he is a Black street kid is enough to justify a whipping with cold towels and rubber hoses:

> Imamu knew both well. He was born knowing them. He had played cops-and-black-boy games all his life. Their eyes said they'd take a dude apart – particularly if that dude happened to be black or Puerto Rican – for the 'truth'. The truth meant promotions. And they really earned those promotions in the black and Puerto Rican parts of the city. White cops like Sullivan could get a young black or Puerto Rican cat suffering from diarrhoea of the mouth, or dead, in half an hour. It took black cats like Brown twenty-nine minutes; they had more to prove. (107)

Sullivan uses the division between Brown and Imamu to maintain his own superiority. This social division is acted out further in the contrast between Imamu's Harlem-born poverty and the middle-class Brooklyn brownstone existence of his foster family, the Aimsleys. Imamu is a victim of Ann Aimsley's aspirational charity; she takes him on in order to 'improve' him, but is quick to concur with the police as to his criminality once the suspicion is raised. 'You just wanted to feel important' (117) rages her teenage daughter Gail, in a community which depends on displaying one's distance from the *déclassé*. Imamu's travelling from Harlem to Brooklyn signals how class mobility does not neutralize the Man, since he becomes internalized. Imamu's positioning also allows him to recognize the extent to which 'truth' equals power.

Negotiating gender roles in *The Disappearance* is problematic. Key women characters express different aspects of femininity and their discomfort with it. Ann Aimsley and Imamu's real mother constitute a good/bad opposition. But Ann's concern is constrained by her obsession to 'belong' – her antiseptic house, covered in plastic to prevent the taint of poverty, is ultimately 'cold'. Imamu's mother, despite being an alcoholic derelict, manages to cross town to wait for her son's release from custody. Perk and Gail, the Aimsley daughters, show the most spunk and autonomy, but the former is murdered, and the latter's intimations of child sexual abuse are negated by being constructed as a false lead. Perhaps the most disturbing representation is that of the murderer herself; a middle-aged sexual siren Dora Belle, depicted as constantly on heat, kills Perk for discovering she is bald. A slighted suitor whines: 'She mad, true. Mad with pride – a deadly sin' (243). The morality of the text infers that this is the violence of a system which constructs Black women as sexualized predators: they must kill to preserve their commodity status. But an equally convincing reading could argue that Dora Belle, as a sexual threat both to the Aimsleys' family life and to Imamu's emerging feelings for Gail, must be ridiculed and excised, recalling the gender-directed violence of earlier texts. Her demise, therefore, is double-edged.

Previously, within the character of Imamu there is a conflation between the traditional opposition villain/hero, which blurs their distinctive roles. In *New Guys Around the Block* Imamu, a petty criminal, is pulled in by the police twice on suspicion of burglary and assault, and imprisoned briefly. Constructed as a criminal by the Man, Imamu commences once again to clear his name, a symbolic act which disrupts the stereotype. Set in Harlem, centred in the Black community, *New Guys Around the Block* concerns the appearance and intervention of two brothers, Olivette and Pierre Larouche. The operations of a phantom burglar are disrupting the street community in that police surveillance and harassment has increased. The structure of outside/inside is crucial to the crime novel. In *New Guys Around the Block* the feared Other becomes, for the Black community, the forces of law and order – the police. When the phantom burglar is found by Imamu, the fact that it is Olivette reinforces the impression of how White racism brands Black people with rage.[49]

Olivette's speech is differentiated as 'phony' by Imamu, who speaks street-language like all the other characters. Olivette is highly educated, self-taught by reading the walls of books in his apartment, his language being formal and 'bookish' as a result. This appropriation of White culture is sensed by Imamu – 'there always seemed to be more to Olivette's words than he was saying' (31). He senses the unspoken discursive level of the 'word-throwing dude['s]' (34) language. In contrast his own speech is experiential street-talk:

> The dude might have read every book ever written – even the well-known stack of Bibles. He might have known every inner city in the entire United States, but it was sure he had to die and

> be reborn with a halo to know what was being put down around the streets of this most inner city. (56)

Some of Olivette's interpretational skills are lacking though: 'My mind ain't no open book' (50), refutes Imamu. Even though Olivette can articulate the liberal disapproval of racism, his interpellation into White culture sustains his position as an outsider.

The text signifies this complicity with White culture by making Olivette's family mulatto,[50] being historically related to the rich Louisiana French, a class above the Harlem Blacks. The violence of assimilation is represented in Olivette – forced to flee from city to city as his crimes are exposed, he and his family are estranged from Black identity and culture. Significantly, it is being called a 'dirty nigger' which provokes Olivette to murder. Unable to identify in solidarity with other Blacks, he causes the death of Iggy, Imamu's friend. Finally he also tries to kill Imamu's friend Gladys because of her 'aggressive' and 'vulgar' sexuality; this thus conflates White domination with patriarchy. The conflicts in racial identity create a violent subject who is also a victim – of assimilation. The disruption in the genre results in no final restoration: Olivette disappears, to relocate and repeat himself in another city, as another violent victim.

New Guys Around the Block is seduced by the literary sign of the tragic mulatto, victim of a melancholic miscegenation, caught between two cultures, two worlds. In particular the mulatto woman

> could be the only type of black woman beautiful enough to be a popular heroine and close enough to wealth *vis-à-vis* her father to be well-bred.[51]

Olivette's mother Flame is tragically beautiful, sexualized to the extent that flirtatious manipulation is her *modus operandi*. Playing on this faded beauty, as Barbara Christian points out,[52] depends on the internalized historical notion of Black as ugly. She is elevated to another social class through her White ancestors; this too makes her desirable, but unreachable. Flame is a victim of Olivette's obsessional perfection – he is both physically and psychologically violent. Fearful in his presence, she is permanently displaced by his deviance, a transient, never able to find refuge. The women in *New Guys Around the Block* are required to perform a difficult dance between their conventional designation as victims, and the various disruptive resistances they make possible.

Imamu is a Chandleresque anti-hero: he is mean, tarnished and afraid; he is part of a community, not an individual who acts alone; he is not detached from the streets, he is part of them, and reluctant to leave:

> 'But I belong down there. They used to be my boys,' Imamu said.
> 'But you're not down there. You're up here with me.' (129)

Olivette's freedom is illusionary; he too is circumscribed by the streets, as Imamu says:

> 'When a dude goes through a sewer, something's got to rub off on him.' (191–2)

The text firmly rejects the crude individualism of the traditional hard-boiled investigator. It employs, then subverts, the classic Holmes/Watson team. Imamu (as Watson) is in awe of Olivette, the mysterious and disturbed intellectual, the superman who is secretly flawed, and in fact, the murderer. Imamu's vaguely erotic feelings for Olivette gently sexualize the relationship which gestures retrospectively towards all those previous homo-social pairings:

> The surge of gladness within him, Imamu knew, came from having so brilliant a boy to care and show his caring, and having a friend for whom he cared, and to whom he wanted to show caring. (64)

> Then they were running, grabbing each other, hugging – a moment of victory. Complete victory – victory for freedom, for love, for friendship. Imamu had to admit that although he had denied it, tried to put it out of his mind, he had expected this most perfect of friends to find the perfect answer. (101)

The sense of epic friendship is romantic, the young men are inspired. As Olivette says 'Everything is everything' (129), the world is an interrelated fellowship. Ironically it is Olivette who stimulates Imamu's familial responsibilities, by his leaving.[53] By making Olivette the criminal, the text extrapolates from and inverts the Holmesian genre's 'darker' side. By supplanting the homiletic and bourgeois Watson with a petty criminal, it refuses the classic form's tidy moralism.

The lives of the people in the novel are restricted by poverty and the physical manifestations of racism – the law's equivalence between Blackness and criminality ensures that the streets of Harlem are the site/sight of police scrutiny. *New Guys Around the Block* signifies the elements of constructedness conspiring to naturalize the street criminal as another representation of Blackness, as a sight, a perception built upon an historical idea of Black people as objects, not citizens. Imamu's intention to find the phantom burglar is stimulated by a desire to

> 'Walk the streets – *like* a citizen.' (87) [My italics]

He cannot be a citizen, only impersonate one. His street-identity is adopted as a self-conscious representation, interimplicating the White, male gaze:

> Slowly he started up the block. As he neared the corner, staring eyes forced him to turn. He saw the police car parked a few feet away with the two policemen looking at him. Imamu sloped his shoulders, and affecting a long stride and rolling gait, he crossed in front of the car, pretending they were not there. They knew him . . . Not having seen him for days, of course, they assumed he had been somewhere up to some kind of mischief. (42)

Even as long ago as 1903 W. E. B. Du Bois described this split subjectivity in his image of the veil:

> The Negro is a sort of seventh son, born with a veil, and gifted with second sight in this American world. It is a peculiar sensation, this double-consciousness, this sense of always looking at one's self through the eyes of others . . . One ever feels his twoness – an American, a Negro; two souls, two thoughts, two unreconciled strivings; two warring ideals in one dark body, whose dogged strength alone keeps it from being torn asunder.[54]

Internalized as a reverse discourse, Black male youth develops a defensive street knowledge which coheres into a skilled sub-cultural resistance. The fictional categories fracture as Imamu makes a fragile peace with Black detective Otis Brown. Forced into an alliance with Imamu in the mutual pain of their desertion, Imamu by Olivette, Otis by Flame, the narrative prioritizes their cultural simultaneity over the dominant's imposed enmity. Black solidarity is important:

> 'You know, Jones,' Brown said, after a long sigh. 'You ain't such a bad boy.'
> 'I been trying to tell you that, Brown.' (198)

The first crime novel written by a Black woman featuring a female detective is Dolores Komo's *Clio Browne: Private Investigator* (1988), published by the feminist Crossing Press of California. Clio Browne is fiftyish, fat, and folksy. She has inherited the Browne Bureau of Investigation from her father, the first Black investigator in St Louis, possibly the USA. The novel is not thematically concerned with racial issues, although the structuring of two old local families, the working-class Brownes, and the rich White Paschals, forms the social background of the investigation, the Brownes being

> bought and sold on that great block of limestone under the rotunda of the courthouse (8)

possibly even by the Paschals. Wally Paschal is accused of murdering his wife, and possibly two other women. Rich and privileged, Wally's defence is a strange choice for a Black woman detective. He is 'a lush, an overgrown kid, spoiled, but not rotten' (22), a victim himself, mainly of his mother's machinations, a prime crime cliché.

The good mother/bad mother axis is one polarity in the book which resists a pro-feminist interpretation: Clio's mother Thalia is a strong-minded, nurturing and eccentric older woman archetypally obsessed by cooking and cleaning; Wally's mother Serena is a selfish, snobbish and indecently sexual schemer. Both are types, and despite the innovation of Clio herself, the novel is strictly formulaic, the language so clichéd it is almost parody:

> 'Put your hands against the wall,' she yelled again as she fished for the key. 'And spread 'em.' (166)

Seen as a type, Thalia can be read as one of the most dominant and complex images of Deep South literature – the mammy. Some Black cultures regard motherhood highly[55] – in African mythology motherhood and nurturing are linked to the creative power of the earth. The mammy, according to Barbara Christian

> is there as a cook, housekeeper, nursemaid and seamstress, always nurturing and caring for her folk. But unlike the white southern image of the mammy she is cunning. . . Mammies kicked, fought, connived and plotted, most often covertly, to throw off the chains of bondage.[56]

Thalia is a contradictory figure – a mother who certainly serves, but who also has a relentlessly resolute will. The fact that she resists her own daughter in order to protect a White 'son' sorely evokes the mythical mammies who put masser's children first.

Clio falls upon clues in the haphazard and coincidental manner of a Pink Panther; her explorations are amateur and undermined professionally by the patronage of friendly, flirtatious and fatherly Captain Felix Frayne of the police (a firmly fictional figure). Although he is discredited by the more 'intuitive' Clio, his magnaminity frames her field of operation. This permissive is made perfectly clear in her final action, which is to step into a squad car. The parameters of her autonomy are closed by the text. Sadly the sparks of self-consciousness in Clio Browne are sunk by this weight, and the character is complicit in underlining her own impossibility. The consequence of all this trite cliché and convention is a text which suffocates racial politics. Is Komo caught in convention's nets? *Clio Browne* is a passing text, a failed parody, victim to the intransigence of the form.

Sixty years after the publication of the first crime novel by an African-American, Rudolph Fisher's *The Conjure Man Dies: A Mystery Tale of Dark Harlem* (1932), it has been republished. It indicates a new interest in the confluence of Black identity with crime fiction, born out by the simultaneous appearance in 1992 of three new novels written by Black women introducing Black female serial sleuths. Thus, Nikki Baker's *In the Game* (1991), Eleanor Taylor Bland's *Dead Time*, and Barbara Neely's *Blanche on the Lam* (1992) are the last category of texts I wish to examine here – novels which do signal some attempt to disrupt the form. Mainstream crime fiction's overwhelming cast of secondary sexualized, subservient, suffering, or savage Black stereotypes had been slightly offset in the White feminist crime fiction of the 1980s by a spattering of one-dimensional positive images. The racism of the former, reflecting dominant White attitudes, has produced a reactive reverse discourse of 'Black is beautiful'. These three novels, in diverse ways, challenge the binarism of that myth by offering three primary, developed characters each engaged in an integrated offensive against institutionalized prejudice.

Dead Time, published by the mainstream St Martin's Press, is formally the most radical innovation, a result at least in part of the limited reform of vocational opportunities in 1980s North America. It is a police procedural fronting Black female Detective Marti MacAlister, a widow and single parent with working-class origins, ironically ticked 'Big Mac'. Utilizing the realist conventions of the urban crime novel, Marti's move from city cop status in Chicago to the small-town 'cozy' setting of Lincoln Prairie, Illinois, allows the reader (by identification with Marti) to confront the cramped parochialism of its local inhabitants. By teaming her up with a White male partner, Vik Jessenovik, the text offers a 'new for old' antithesis of the model of investigator; the securities of the past wistfully exhorted by Vik are deconstructed as fanciful nostalgia, his paternalism is old-fashioned and out of touch. Police station bandinage gets *risqué*:

> 'Want an introduction, Jessenovik?' Cowboy said. 'She's not too far past her prime. Hear she's still real good at . . .'
> 'Lady present,' Vik reminded them.
> 'Who?' Slim grinned. 'Big Mac? This woman's all cop. Wouldn't want her to dropkick me.' (42)

Slim's comment evokes the racial construction of the ungendered Black Savage, neither male nor female, but an animal expected to display unusual feats of power and strength. The implication that Marti has to compensate for her elevation into the role of detective by performing as a super-hero is rejected though. She also unpacks the macho posturing of the police(man's) role:

> Marti went to the Baxter autopsy Tuesday morning. Vik showed up too. They both watched without gagging or even flinching. She knew she was just proving that she was a tough cop and could handle anything, but Vik was there for the same reason. (138)

It is Marti's street-knowledge that gets the results, her refusal to romanticize the town and crucially her ability to see and read the urban underclass, the throwaway citizens, make visible the invisibles, which drives the investigation. Another progressive aspect of *Dead Time* is the scope of the racially marked characters who aren't structurally employed to enrich and define White identity, but constitute the impression of an independent multi-ethnic professional community.

In the Game, published by The Naiad Press and set in Chicago, is a Black lesbian yuppie novel, featuring investment banker and member of the bourgeoisie Virginia Kelly who

> had spent the whole of my professional life, my formative years if you will, in the 1980s where you are what you owned. (2)

She adds that 'dykes [also] had lately discovered consumption' (18), and money, and the lack of it in a society which confers membership on the basis of having it is a central tenet of her murder investigation.

In the Game is at once a legitimation of Black and lesbian middle-class existence, and an investigation of how precarious that status is.[57] It is quintessentially a 1990s text. Baker's astute social comment comes after twenty years of liberation politics, oscillating between a sense of arrival and an awareness of the intransigence of oppression:

> black women have to be about ten times better looking than your average white dyke in flannel to get noticed at a majority watering hole. And in our own places, where we can find each other expecting nothing short of perfect understanding, there is the serial disappointment of a reflection that is both different and the same. It is staggering how deeply we must know and love ourselves as black women to kiss the mirror with open eyes. (17)

> Reading a gay paper is like pinching yourself and finding you are really there. (21)

In part a critique of the commodification of relationships and the way people use each other for financial and emotional gain, the motivation for murder is revealed to be old-fashioned jealousy. The formal innovation of this novel consists of the revelation that Virginia's best friend, the woman she is trying to acquit, did commit the killing; she confesses and then tries to murder Virginia in an attempted cover-up. *In the Game* is an indictment of the idealist fiction of 1970s counter-culture which proposed a community without conflict. The sober tone of *In the Game* comes from its pulls-no-punches investigation into a sub-culture standing (stressfully) on the edge of Reaganomics. Its assimilation and negotiation of these values exacts a price, but the text refrains from sliding into maudlin pessimism. This 'new realism' leaves Virginia mourning her idealized friend, but ready to pick up the pieces of her less glamorous relationships. In all the texts proferred by Black authors this reintegration is a key moment of closure.

Finally Barbara Neely's *Blanche on the Lam*, also published by St Martin's Press, is a finely crafted murder mystery improbably proposing a Black feminist cleaning woman, on the run in North Carolina from a minor fraud charge, as the central sleuth. In the crime pansophy servants are below consideration as suspects, never mind as investigators. Like Guy's Imamu, Blanche's criminality is petty, born of poverty: she has had to bounce a couple of bad cheques since four of her White employers have gone on holiday without paying her first. As Frankie Bailey has mentioned, female servants in early genre fiction were meek, cringing, and dialect-speaking,[58] faithful to their (White) families, archetypally Mammy figures. However, as (the ironically named) Blanche observes, they are perfectly placed as detectives:

> reading people and signs, and sizing up situations, were as much part of her work as scrubbing floors and making beds. (3)

They are also well placed as figures of social critique: as Nanny tells her granddaughter in Zora Neale Hurston's *Their Eyes Were Watching God* (1937):

> 'De nigger woman is de mule uh de world.' (16)

Through the eyes of Blanche, for it is her gaze which directs the narrative and interprets for the reader, we are temporarily allowed to perceive the complex negotiations necessary for her economic survival. She has to find the murderer to prevent her own indictment:

> she knew of two many innocent black people who'd gone to jail and never got out not to be afraid. 'Criminal justice' was a term she found more apt than it was meant to be. (112)

Like Imamu, she is forced to prove her innocence in a system which occludes Black with Guilty.

Neely thoroughly deconstructs the two most tenacious coded Black figures in American fiction, the Mammy, and the feminized, impotent Uncle Tom, by foregrounding the two characters' self-conscious rendition of the roles:

> An hour after she'd phoned, a sweaty, red-faced boy delivered the four bags of groceries she'd ordered. He gave Blanche the cheeky 'Hey, girl' greeting that teenage white boys working up to being fully fledged rednecks give grown black women in the South. Blanche hissed some broken Swahili and Yoruba phrases she'd picked up at the Freedom Library in Harlem and told the boy it was a curse that would render his penis as slim and sticky as a lizard's tongue. The look on his face and the way he clutched at his crotch lifted her spirits considerably. Nina Simone's version of 'I Put a Spell on You' came rolling out of her mouth in a deep, off-key grumble. She ran a carrot through the food processor until it was a pile of thin orange coins. (31)

> Blanche was unimpressed by the tears, and Grace's Mammy-save-me-eyes . . . She never ceased to be amazed at how many white people longed for Aunt Jemima. (33)

Nate, the family retainer, appears to be every inch a victim of what Blanche calls 'Darkies' Disease' (40), the self-deception that dedicated indentured servants carry, the belief that they are part of the family and not employees. Nate shuffles subserviently around, eyes to the ground, and describes to Blanche his relationship to the family:

> 'I been working for this family since Miz Em was a girl. Come here to work when I was twelve years old. So was Miz Em. We got the same birthday, ya know.' Nate hooked his thumbs in the straps of his overalls. ' I worked for her daddy and her daddy's daddy . . . Outlived both them suckers.' Nate chortled a vicious little laugh and headed for the back door. (47)

He is indebted to Miz Grace, who whilst a girl saved Nate from a lynching from the Ku-Klux-Klan as she needed him to attend to her dog. This is doubly ironic for Nate, who recognizes his ambivalent value as useful only in looking after *animals*. It is Grace who murders him in order to silence him. Apparently servants are not as reliable as they used to be.

Blanche on the Lam, like most of these texts, is a view from the underside of society, a tale of survival expressed in biting humour. It draws on the genre of slave narratives in that Blanche's trajectory is emancipatory: in reflecting upon her 'constitutional distaste for being any whiteman's mammy' (179) she rejects the traditional 'job for life', the live-in domestic work offered in order for her to keep quiet, in favour of, like her forebears, going north for the relative independence of hourly paid day work. Although Boston represents another kind of enemy territory, another form of insecurity, the transition is a symbolic one. A change of consciousness depends on what Black feminist Patrice L. Dickerson has called 'the interdependence of thought and action'.[59] The journey is also an internal one, away from the vestiges of 'race memory'[60] which may cause Blanche to assume her own inferiority, towards the 'free mind' of self-definition. The convention of individualism which informs the actions of the traditional detective is being appropriated here, but it is simultaneously being deconstructed: Blanche's opportunities are made possible precisely because she has a network of other women, friends and family, who support her. Blanche is not a lone private investigator positioned on the edge of society through a romanticized personal choice. Her survival depends on sharing a culture of resistance which Black women have necessarily made a community. Thus the model of the Black extended family, centred around strong women, parallels the White upper-class patriarchal family, permeated by avarice, sickness, and stupidity.

The most striking feature of the novel as far as my enquiry is concerned is the way in which the book is perfectly structured as a mystery. Whereas with a significant number of the more politicized texts studied the form is subsumed, or is discordant to the message, in *Blanche on the Lam* the function of detection is highly harmonious with the heroine's whole technique of survival. Her analytical gaze has been knowingly, self-consciously deployed for generations, its power as a weapon recognized by those who have been imprinted by its violence:

> Was it just that old race thing that had thrown her off when her eyes met Grace's? Her neighbour Wilma's father said he'd never in his adult life looked a white person in the eye. He'd grown up in the days when such an act very often ended in a black person's charred body swinging from a tree. (92)

It is the sideways glance which informs an investigation, the ability to see what others cannot see. Perceiving a situation correctly is so much more necessary if one is at risk. This ability to watch and observe is made possible precisely because of the vocational demand that Black female domestics remain invisible, their labour performed imperceptibly, without infringing upon ruling White reality. Extending W. E. B. Du Bois's formulation of the 'veil',[61] which, of course, also deflects and refracts the gaze of domination from knowing 'the truth' of the submitted, Black women are able operate a vision which Patricia Hill Collins has identified as the 'outsider-within' perspective:

> a unique Black women's standpoint on self and society. As outsiders within, Black women have a distinct view of the contradictions between the dominant group's actions and ideologies.[62]

She quotes Black feminist poet Audre Lorde as saying:

> In order to survive, those of whom oppression is as American as apple pie have always had to be watchers. [63]

It is this movement away from objectification, to self-definition, to subjectification, which empowers this text as a social critique.

In this chapter I have tried to show the movement within the crime fiction genre from images of denigration, which construct Black

Woman as a sight, towards a new generation of investigatory visions, controlled by the shifting gaze of Black women themselves. The sample is admittedly small; it does not reflect a sea-change, but at least it is a suspicion of progress. Although there must be many more crime novels by Black women which don't even get published, which also reflects the 'Whiteness' of the genre as it is institutionalized in censorship, it is undoubtably the case that in terms of literary activity, the number of Black women writing formulaic crime is minimal. I see the intransigence of the form as a reason for this. There are aspects of the form which facilitate a self-conscious entry into the genre for Black authors, but ostensibly the crime novel does not meet the needs of Black women authors at the moment. In some ways looking for evidence of a generic shift is asking the wrong kind of question. A progressive race politics allows a limited restructuring in these texts, although it is mostly only foregrounded as a theme. Orientalist discourse has conspired with the crime novel's structure of the threat as Other to constrain a more radical break in the form. Using Lord Cromer's formulation, the Oriental does not see 'the truth', but s/he may reveal a set of fictions.

The literary tradition of the Black Diaspora has had a race against time[64] in making visible the dehumanizing racism of post-colonialism and the displaced hatred present in its structures of racial Othering. Crime fiction does not readily accommodate this agenda *but* if we look to other areas of Black literary activity for comparable activity we can find how certain transferable aspects of the form have been appropriated and reinscribed. Central to the Black literary tradition has been the investigation of crimes against Black people. The search for Black history, similarly, has been enacted by a process of discovery which has depended upon the skills of detection. The enquiry has involved sifting through evidence – documentary, archival, written material and oral, through interviewing and story-telling – using classic investigatory techniques. The strong moral impetus for this endeavour, the desire to right wrongs, the search for 'truth' and 'identity', evokes key themes from the detective novel. Many narratives by Black women have a mystery at their heart; one thinks, for example, of Alice Walker looking for Zora Neale Hurston's grave in *In Search of Our Mother's Gardens* (1983) – the title itself is indicative – or in *The Color Purple* (1982) – where have Nettie and the children gone? In Toni Morrison's *Beloved* (1987) what has happened to the dead child, and in *Song of Solomon* (1977) what is the significance of the opening suicide? So in conclusion, rather than bemoaning the way in which Black authors have failed to enhance the White form of crime fiction, therefore replicating the Orientalist stance of assimilating difference, I think a more useful critical approach is to explore the new synthesis of forms being created within a separable tradition of Black fiction. Unfortunately, a more thorough treatment of this is required than I can cover here.

5

The inverstigators[1]
Lesbian crime fiction

A new type of fiction appeared during the 1980s, lesbian crime, in which sexy superdykes strode the city streets in their steel-capped DMs, swinging their double-headed axe, slayed patriarchs in their wake. Almost all the novels present the figure of a woman on the cover, foregrounding the lone heroine against a darkened building, a synecdochal city. Can the mythically misogynistic monological male hard-boiled detective be transformed by a lesbian-feminist reading? Two archetypal traits lend the potential. First, he is a crusader, traditionally representing and reasserting with moral certitude the *status quo*, a redemptive figure, single-handedly stemming the tide of chaos. His morality of unequivocal self-assertion reflects the cult of individualism reified by Thatcherism and Reaganism. Aspects of feminism too were characterized by these same tendencies of evangelistic salvation ('I was an unhappy heterosexual until I found Women'), tempered, in the late 1980s, with a re-emphasis on discovery of 'self' and subjectivity. Second, the detective hero is an outlaw, and here the parallel with lesbianism is clear. He is alone, isolated, on the edge, an observer, not a participator. This motif of lesbian identity has been imposed and internalized ever since *The Well of Loneliness* (1928), occasionally transformed by an inversion which endows lesbians with a superior vantage point from which to analyse the vagaries of institutionalized heterosexuality. So, the detective hero exhibits a paradox: he is at once a representative of society and a critique of it.

Popular lesbian-feminist crime novels have tended to produce a particular version of this antithesis. Manifestly they are opposed to patriarchy; implicitly, however, they depend on many aspects of the mainstream genre, such as an overriding Manichean morality of good versus evil, notions of unified subjectivity, innateness, natural justice, and tidy textual closures. These can be addressed as masculine forms.

In this section I plan to look closely at several of these novels to discern how far they conform to these historic types, potentially inhibiting a radical reading. These novels, however, have evolved primarily out of lesbian, rather than crime, fiction. This literary practice has inevitably been preoccupied with issues of sexuality and identity. For many women it serves as a way of rendering explicit their repressed/suppressed desires. Thus I would like to explore how subversive, given their conflated (and conflictual?) generic positioning, these texts can be. To this end I have employed a Foucauldian perspective, assuming that resistance to sexual conventions is significantly constrained by the character of discourse itself.[2] I try to indicate how, because that space has already been defined, articulating new meanings is, to borrow Annette Kolodny's term, a minefield.[3] To illustrate: do the novels, by simply substituting the strong hero with the strong heroine, push the reader into a limiting positive images strategy reminiscent of the Images of Women protagonists of the 1970s? Do these texts, in short, undermine themselves by attacking reductionism and then employing it as a form of resistance (replacing 'all lesbians are bad' with 'all lesbians are good', for example)?

The lesbian crime novel has its origins in the lesbian pulp fiction of the 1950s and early 1960s. Recent critical attention to these texts[4] has drawn attention to their pathologizing psychoanalytic construction of lesbianism, typical of the crude Freudianism prevalent at that time serving to normalize the post-war nuclear family: lesbians were, simply, sick.[5] A paradigm of deviance, drugs, and urban decay located these literary lesbians in lonely antithesis to the security of the suburban American dream. But the sheer popularity of these dime novels suggests a longing for the Other which sales supported – potboilers from the Fawcett Gold Medal series[6] sold thousands. Along with the occasional actual mystery were a plethora of splendidly sordid sensationals such as *Strange Sisters* – 'The Savage Novel of a Lesbian on the Loose' by Robert Turner,[7] or *The Shadowy Sex* by Hilary Hilton, or *Twice As Gay* – 'Lesbos in High Heels and Leather' by Nan Keene, or the lurid and luscious *Lesbians in Black Lace* – 'They were Twilight Girls, Black Nylon Lovers' by Claire Arthur. These books were primarily about sex, supposedly for the prurience of the straight male reader, but there is no doubt that lesbians read these texts too, and probably for the same reasons. The quasi-criminalized underworld of the thriller – an apt term given their erotic content – conferred upon the reader illicit excitement whilst simultaneously returning her to a legitimate 'normalcy' at the end, with the deviants despatched into death or despair. A more radical sub-text survived though. Take, for example, the docu-fiction by Ann Aldrich *We Walk Alone: Through Lesbos' Lonely Groves* (Fawcett Gold Medal (1955)) – the cover declaims 'Of the love that dwells in the twilight – of the love that can never be told', yet the text, written by a self-proclaimed lesbian claims that far from being taxonomized as a deviant, the lesbian 'is any woman', 'Look at her . . .' the introduction demands. Indeed, a sub-genre of lesbian romances by authors such as Ann Binyon, Paula Christian, Randy Salem, and Valerie Taylor, did just that – scrutinize lesbian subjectivity by investigating and examining the legacy of dominant cultural constructions and their effects upon the ghetto. But there is also a strong sense of self-definition, of sub-cultural resistance, and of survival in these novels which makes them the precursors of the lesbian crime novels of the 1980s.

The first lesbian feminist crime novel was M. F. Beal's *Angel Dance*, published by The Crossing Press in 1977. Perversely I believe this first book to be just about the best: it's an angry, complex, visionary indictment of hetero/patriarchal capitalism steaming with the peculiar energy of 1970s protest culture. The Chicana detective and first-person narrator, Kat Guerrera, has already been arrested several times. She is positioned personally and politically as a subversive, offering a cross-referencing critique of the way class, race, gender, and sexuality interface to uphold the hegemonic order. The corrupt power of the state is seen as being so extensive that, as Klein has pointed out, 'justice' as a concept of civil society cannot be invoked:

> The novel suggests that the only action anyone can take is guerrilla warfare against individuals who represent the attitudes of the patriarchal system. Knowing the truth does not lead to justice or action; and radical feminism cannot work within the system.[8]

Kat's friend and dedicated activist Lenore expresses it thus:

> 'Every front has its guerrillas defining perimeters and it's important to understand this activity because the struggle in the center is always the same.' (208)

The figure of the lesbian guerrilla was an icon of 1970s resistance distilled by materialist philosopher Monique Wittig in her novel of

1971 *Les Guérrillères.*[9] This invention of a new, militant category of lesbian inspired by the historical myth of the Amazon invigorated a whole community of women to exact 'war' on the political institution of heterosexuality. In *Angel Dance* the war is a violent one. Explicit images of sexualized torture are represented along with the brutal rape, oral and genital, of the protagonist Kat. Later at a separatist refuge an anonymous rapist is stapled to a tree by his testicles and left to die. Unlike the anaesthetized violence of the conventional novel this is the voice of anger which galvanized the feminist campaigns of the 1970s to make sexual violence against women visible. The vehemence of these revenge fantasies operates to repudiate Woman as passive victim.

Angel Dance differs from all the other novels to be discussed in this chapter in the degree of difficulty and density of the narrative. Hired to protect famous feminist anthropologist Angel Stone by her husband and half-brother Michael Tarleton, Kat uncovers the Stone families' CIA-linked drug-running operation from the Far East. Michael has filmed soldiers trafficking the heroin, and for this he is murdered. Then the government-connected hoods direct their cover-up towards Angel and her associates. The thriller structure also enacts a second level of narration: Angel keeps disappearing into a network of feminist underworlds, and in the hunt-and-chase tradition Kat's task is to track her down.

By appropriating the sign of Woman-as-enigma, *Angel Dance* recalls many textual forebears and forecasts its reiteration as a feminist hermeneutic – 'What is Woman?' One manifestation of this is as a function of lesbian romance; Angel is the ideal woman, the spectacle of desire which drives Kat's investigation. Kat/Angel operates as a doubling structure common to the crime novel. Metafictionally there is even a film called 'Angel Dancing', made by Michael, of Angel as a sexual sight. Significantly he breaks the frame by reaching in front of the camera to caress her breast. Kat is watching Michael watch Angel, but Angel has set this scene up, and Kat thinks:

> I felt, how to say? in the shallow waters of that same neuroticism, straining towards omniscience; why need to know? I was a spy in Angel's life and she for some reason desired to be spied upon. (69)

It is, crucially, a piece of film which constitutes the evidence the enemy will kill for, further reinforcing this problematization of the real and the imaginary, and the spectacle. Finally, though, Kat does sleep with Angel, the 'Girl of My Dreams' (189):

> I researched, I examined, I *investigated* Angel Stone: moles, dimples, both scars. We said maybe a dozen words, among them: Me *What happened, Angel?* She: *I don't remember*. Her body was delicious; long legs, beautiful blond *accoutrements*. In the films she seemed finished, doll-like; but this living flesh arranged itself too briefly for any images to form. (192)

At the moment Angel becomes real to Kat, the erotics of investigation are made plain (as Angel tells her: 'Detectives are genital, clients are cerebral' (258)), and she becomes again the elusive split subject, her body splintered as '*accoutrements*', her image deferred like desire. This structure of displacement/objectification rejects the linear trajectory that the sought can ever be found. Ultimately Kat's investigation brings more, not less danger to Angel, as she exposes both her story and her place of safety. Thus, by impugning the very structure of investigation, the first lesbian crime novel acts as coda to the rest.

One function of the generic convention of the crime novel is the assurance of cohesion, and the containment of threat and danger. This presupposes a level of readerly angst/fear/suspense. In her analysis of gothic novels, Tania Modleski[10] proposes that these provide a release for women's feelings of estrangement, disorientation, and importantly *paranoia*. One suspected cause of paranoia is social isolation, and if this is a problem for heterosexual women, how much more so for lesbians who are alienated from 'society' on two levels. Although I think there are inherent problems of definition here related to *perceived* and *real* social threats (it is too easy to dismiss acts of homophobia as 'imaginary'), I think Modleski's model has some compatibility with certain reading strategies in this instance too. Crime fiction is a site for the expression of anxieties about society, and the appeasement of that fear is structurally inscribed in the narrative. As the paranoid's fears are projected on to a perceived 'enemy', a primary psychoanalytic scene is being replayed. Modleski invokes W. W. Meissner[11] in describing how, within the process of individuation, the child defines itself through opposition. The need for an enemy, therefore, may be a necessary step towards a conception of self as a separate identity. This model may be useful in understanding why early feminism during the 1970s had such a clear construction of men as the enemy, whereas feminism during the 1980s tried to critique a more complex construction of social forces like gender, race, class, and sexuality in which the binary us/them became highly problematized.

Whilst in the crime novel the enemy is named and destroyed, in the lesbian and feminist crime novel the terms are often effectively inverted so that the state becomes the site of (paranoidal?) fears and the sleuth the Other, and usually, the victor. The resolution is achieved in two stages: first through self-determination (the process of individuation essential to the thriller mode), and second through integration and communality, features shared by most lesbian novels. The first phase is often represented by 'coming out', the second by finding a lover (romance), or the lesbian community (politicization). The protagonists deal with fear and paranoia through action, by becoming active agents of their own destiny. The formation of identity happens through the solution of a crime. The central narrative device and locus of readerly pleasure is *discovery*.

Suspense, in the crime novel, derives from adopting the perspective associated primarily with an individual, who is the source and arbiter of readerly pleasure. At a simplistic level, what happens to her happens to the reader, whilst disbelief is 'suspended'. Within the fictional world of the crime novel all appearances are ambiguous, and the protagonist is the sole repository of trust, a lone stable point surrounded by chaos. In four of these novels, *Mrs Porter's Letter* (1982) and *The Burnton Widows* (1984) by Vicki P. McConnell, and *Murder in the Collective* (1984) and *Sisters of the Road* (1986) by Barbara Wilson, which are as much concerned with the process of becoming a lesbian as with the solution of a mystery, the text posits lesbianism as a strategy for dealing with evil and disruption. Lesbianism is depicted as an inner natural state lying dormant and waiting to be discovered; it is a beacon of authenticity in a perverse and fragmented society. This notion of a core of human nature, untouched and unpolluted by society, is in the idealist tradition of Reich and Fromm, and relates to the enduring myth of sex as being the repository of secret and profound truth in the individual's soul, or centre.

The opposition authentic lesbianism/inauthentic heterosexuality has been identified in such early novels as Rita Mae Brown's *Rubyfruit Jungle* (1973),[12] and continues to structure many lesbian novels of 'self-discovery'. The premise that there is a 'self' to discover is problematic. Invoking a concept of a fixed, stable, natural essence forming the truth of identity is politically naive for lesbians, as this argument is always used more efficaciously against them in support of heterosexuality. It can also be employed to differentiate between 'real' (authentic) lesbians and 'political' (inauthentic) lesbians (a redundant division if ever there was one). However, an attempt to invert the terms of the given is still one significant step in the process of resistance, provoking some cultural struggle over definition. It is a Foucauldian reverse discourse in action.[13]

According to Foucault discourses are constituted by power. Legitimate or 'true' discourse, the discourse of heterosexism, for example, can be visualized as an area that is bound by lines of force asserting heterosexuality, in this case, as dominant. True discourse defines two things: first, what is within the 'realm of truth', and second, the difference between truth/untruth. A 'true' answer to the question 'What caused her to be a lesbian?' would be framed in terms of her sin, sickness or failed heterosexuality, but an answer in terms of her childhood obsession with mashed potatoes would be considered 'untrue'. Outside the lines of force is the area of illegitimacy, of alternative – and thus subversive – utterances, lying not within truth/untruth, but 'fiction'. For example, Adrienne Rich's notion of 'compulsory heterosexuality'[14] would fall outside the realm of truth because its very terms are not recognized as legitimate, in other words, it is a fiction. It is also part of a reverse discourse positing a notion of a transhistorical subject ('lesbian') in competition with the legitimate (heterosexual) view of subjectivity.

Nevertheless true discourse is, in a more 'literal' sense, upheld by its own fictions; in mainstream crime fiction, by the end of the novel, the detective hero has reformed the state by imposing order on disruption. If traditional crime fiction is seen as 'true discourse' or even 'true fiction', then we must ask whether lesbian crime fiction is an illegitimate and subversive utterance. According to Foucault, true discourses construct subjectivities. If lesbian crime fiction offers alternative constructions of subjectivity, is it in fact subversive? What are the alternative constructions of subjectivity it posits?[15]

Mrs Porter's Letter (1982) genuflects in the direction of generic homogeneity with its muscle-bound hoods, plotting patriarchs, prostitutes and plane-hopping, but essentially the crime is peripheral; the real purpose of this rootless Denver-based pulp is mystic revelation. The plot consists of Nyla Wade, eight-weeks divorced, a hack journalist with an inner spirit named 'Woman Writer'. Through the acquisition of an antique desk from a gothic junk shop she finds some old love letters and proceeds, by circuitous means, to find and return them to the (secret) sender. The purple prose contained therein renews in Nyla some kind of romantic idealism, a cure for her own steely cynicism. When finally the ardent author, W. Stone, is discovered, 'he' is shockingly a 'she', and the closetry is explained. Except that, given the enthusiastic overuse of the male pronoun every time W. Stone is mentioned, and the subtitle *A Lesbian Mystery*, most readers would guess this at an early stage. The recipient of these lavender lovelines is a Cybil Porter, who stamps her psychic hologram on the subconscious of Ms Wade in the form of a pulsating orchid, which appears at points of (dramatic) climax to indicate her metaphysical presence. These implausible emanations are perhaps the visible extension of that ubiquitous investigative talent: intuition.

Mrs Porter's Letter contains some hilariously clichéd moments, and it is difficult to tell if they are intended as elevated satire, or better still, serious realism. Ms Wade's search for the missing lover, W. Stone, is of course symbolic. She discovers tough prostitute Sara ('her black eyes a maelstrom of mystery' (147)), who functions as the prompter to Ms Wade's proto-lesbianism. There follows the near-obligatory bathroom mirror scene (reminiscent of John Sayles' film *Lianna* (1982)) in which Nyla probes her deepest self, discovers the potential for 'that syncopation of body and mind' only two women could share, and declares 'Yes, I'm probably a lesbian' (162). This personal revelation seems somewhat precipitate. Despite her apparent feminism and, therefore, one would expect, an awareness of the political dimensions involved, after one conversation with the woman she is in love and immediately rejects her previous heterosexuality – dormant though it may be. Nevertheless, this is romance not realism; instantly Nyla is admitted to the secret club of dykedom. A new colleague with a certain 'way of standing' (180) gives Nyla a knowing smile:

> As I put my hand out to shake hers, I wondered what kind of sign I was wearing that I didn't have on before. Something she saw and read and wanted me to understand . . . we were two strong women just a little different from everyone around us . . . I had been recognised only a few hours after I had recognised myself. (181)

As Nyla enters the private mystic communion of lesbianism, the reader is inculcated into the pleasures of recognition, transformation and privilege. In the final homily she describes the social prejudice this will entail, but in some epicentral space 'I have Sara within me, Sheila and Yolanda, Betts Wattle, and now, too, Cybil and Winona' (209).

This could be a radical assertion of the collective subject. But I propose this tentatively since lesbianism is also deemed a 'part of nature', a biological rationale excluding political or cultural influences.

The Burnton Widows capers along in a similar mode, Nyla Wade having moved to Oregon enticed from Denver by a job at the *Burnton Beckoner.* A piece of local lesbian history, a gothic castle overlooking Burnton, a family seat of pioneer matriarch Druscilla Ketcham, and scene of a recent gruesome murder, is under threat from property developers. Largely through the effort of 'bent' connections Nyla Wade re-solves the murders of two lesbian lovers, Joan and Valerie, who were butchered in their beds. The connectedness of the gay community is stressed, and indeed, Nyla's detection is reliant on its independent information and skills. This is a communal investigation initiated by sub-cultural loyalties.

The gays and lesbians in Burnton are self-consciously Other to the town, and in the end it is the town itself which is implicated in the form of the local fraternal demagogy, financial corruption tainting all ranks up to the Mayor. The main social fabric becomes the harbinger of criminality, the gay community the repository of moral outrage. This is a neat inversion of the lesbian/gay stereotype 'sick pervert'. The (undiscovered) murderer handles a copy of *Frankenstein* covetously at the scene of crime, and a year later this voyeuristic sadist is hailed as a 'first rate monster' (239); he is, significantly, a lawyer.[16]

The novel opens and closes with a love story, and continually the references flow as to the parallel nature of the two relationships, the first, the murdered Joan and Valerie, the second their avengers, Nyla and Lucy. *The Burnton Widows* is clearly a lesbian romance, but with a spiritual edge similar to *Mrs Porter's Letter.* The ghosts of Valerie and Joan communicate with similar mystic messages, seeming to murmur from walls or with the movement of the sea. It is as though the imposed categorization Other has become internalized and projected into 'otherworldly', and the desire to legitimate a universal lesbian spirituality, a panacea, maybe, for real lesbian loneliness and isolation. This sense of cosmic communality is pleasantly romantic but glosses over the many political facets of subjectivity and difference. The tendency to label a particular cultural experience as paradigmatic has been severely and rightfully criticized by the many Black/disabled/lesbian/working-class women within the Women's Movement. For example, Black lesbians during the 1970s resisted the call for separatism by pointing out that they had a necessary alliance with Black men in struggling against racism. Because both White and

Black women worked together in the Women's Liberation Movement this did not make their lesbian identity, or their experiences of oppression, the same. Too often an attempt to articulate a group's identity becomes spoken by those with the greatest resources, and most powerful voice, the desire to unite coming at the expense of the differently oppressed.

Both these books make light-duty but pleasurable reading; they are in the best tradition of pulp fiction and should be enjoyed as such. Naiad Press publishes predictable, generic romances which are instantly recognizable to the lesbian consumer. In these two novels the key narrative movement is, as aforementioned, self-discovery followed by integration into *communitas*. They provide a *break* from the unmitigating and worthy 'social realism' of the more overtly feminist fictional texts. However, it is not necessarily the case that even the latter will place the self 'in process', problematizing identity as a healthily unstable state. Rebecca O'Rourke's *Jumping the Cracks* (1987), for example, does not particularly focus on subjectivity, but remains a well-crafted acerbic social criticism of Thatcher's divided Britain, refusing the generic convention of a revelatory narrative and positing an unusually unglamorous working-class heroine. Virtually all of these lesbian detective texts are in fact North American imports, with the exception of this one and Val McDermid's serial sleuth Lindsay Gordon, discussed earlier in Chapter 3.

There are texts which combine both concerns. In *Murder in the Collective*, the first novel by established feminist author and publisher Barbara Wilson, we meet Pam Nilsen, thinly disguised proto-dyke. Her hands sweat and her body is wracked by erotic fevers as she gulps and swallows in the presence of Hadley; they do manage to consummate their lust, the romantic tension yoked to the crime fictional hermeneutic of alternate disclosure and disappointment. Wilson is crafty; romantic closure is superseded by a morass of familiar complexity: Elena loves Fran but Fran loves Hadley, Pam loves Hadley but Hadley loves Fran. Pam's new identity gives her individuality through a sense of difference, a political structure reinforced by the text in its dialectical oppositions lesbian/heterosexual, Black/White, poor/rich. The novel problematizes meaning by constantly undermining textual and social conventions; things are never what they seem. 'Identity' is seen as a transitional process of discovery involving contradictory states of desire. Pam moves through a panoply of revulsion and fear, guarded prejudice, nervous involvement, romantic idealism, crunching self-doubt, and finally perhaps, realism: 'Lesbians were no better than anyone else' (164). The overall movement is towards inclusion into a kind of heterogeneous plurality and tolerance.

In *Sisters of the Road* Wilson plays with several forms and ideas first explored in *Murder in the Collective*. The thriller provides a coathanger on which to explore a ranging political critique structurally akin to *Angel Dance*. Wilson confronts the reader with sexual crime through a narrative process in which the reader becomes more and more embroiled in child prostitution and sexual abuse, so much so that in the final denouement the distancing frame them/us breaks down when the sleuth herself is violently raped by the murderer. *Sisters of the Road* sets out to destroy some of the vicariousness of crime fiction – this is no comfortable fantasy. Initially Pam Nilsen almost sidles off the page in self-depreciation; she is indecisive, doubtful, unfit, afraid of heights, and sits on conscience-stricken ideological fences. Pam Nilsen looks 'with an anthropologist's eye', but this gaze has no power to change: 'There were things here I needed to feel as well as witness' (53). Pam's emotional involvement increases with her growing self-knowledge, as an individual and as a lesbian, both resulting in more power to act. The message is also for the reader; she cannot just observe sexual crime and have pity for the victim as Other. The perpetrators are the actual and symbolic father, brother, the site of struggle is the family, and the injured become all women.

This is a recurring theme in lesbian crime fiction; what is the symbolic and psychoanalytic import of 'murdering our fathers'? To retrieve that ideal and perfect union with our mothers perhaps? At this point I can only gesture towards its significance. Paulina Palmer has developed it in her essay 'The Lesbian Feminist Thriller and Detective Novel'.[17] It is an attempt to recover the pre-oedipal state of self in relation to the mother, a mutually beneficial symbiosis ideally constructed as warm, safe, and loving. It reminds us of our crucial interdependence with (and therefore responsibility to) others, destabilizing patriarchal attitudes such as individualism and competitiveness. Julia Kristeva[18] names the pre-linguistic play of]communication between the mother and the child 'semiotic'. It has the power to disrupt the 'iron grip' of the masculine control of language and therefore meaning production itself. The implication here for the form of the crime novel is that its will to knowledge, its epistemological intent (if I can ascribe it with such), is revealed as a structural imperative, performative rather than evaluative. The destabilizing potential here lies in the way that feminist writers may, through fictional style, be impugning 'truth'.

In the last ten pages Pam becomes human as her voyeuristic posturing is discarded and replaced by real, felt, lived experience. As the reader surmised all along, 'it was [her] own life [she] wanted to change' (158). I would suggest that this has another more literary symbolism: the detective hero, unified and reified, can only offer us limited identification and political utility; his 'objectivity' is a masculinized form imposed upon the feminist sleuth. The book points out the complexities of power resident in shared oppression and multiple subjectivities:

> I felt that whatever had made Pam a person, whatever I knew or had known about myself was being crushed out of me, was spinning into fragments like a planet smashed by meteors. (194)

In a clever reversal of roles it is Trish (the 'victim') who picks her up, dusts her off, and stops her acting like a 'crushed grape' (200). Here, again, we experience the importance of seeing the self in relation to others, us in them, and them in us. This is all a far cry from Arthur Conan Doyle's archetypal Holmes, a 'Nietzschean superior man . . . a man immune from human weakness and passions',[19] a man who is essentially invulnerable. Holmes exalts rationality and intellect, and Doyle intended him to be a model to all young men of his time. Feminist fiction has progressed from the 1970s when providing strong powerful role models was a political necessity. Strategic though this was, and is, as Elizabeth Wilson has pointed out, it has a limited use:

> however good it is to be strong, we feel ambivalent about the strong, powerful woman, since this [too] is an image that allows for no moment of weakness, and cannot reflect the diversity and complexity of our desires . . . This is a form of romanticism.[20]

Sisters of the Road problematizes lesbian identity and romance. A seemingly straightforward flirtation between Pam and Best Printing colleague Carole progresses towards the conventional sexual encounter intrinsic to the thriller. But Pam is misreading the signs, Carole isn't interested, and the reader's romantic fantasy is unseated by a further (too real) irony – Carole's new lover is Pam's immediate ex.: 'Oh . . . she said she knew you slightly' (180). The difficulties of romance are treated with self-reflexive humour, and laughter subverts the reader's misplaced fantasies.

The crime novel is a perfect forum for exploring attitudes towards the representation of sexuality through pornography, linked so discursively as it is to vice. Barbara Wilson's novel *The Dog Collar Murders* (1989) is an intellectual investigation into the feminist pro- and anti-porn positions as much as it is a murder mystery. Prominent anti-porn activist Loie Marsh is found strangled by a dog collar at a Seattle conference on sexuality. Pam Nilsen, serial sleuth of *Murder in the Collective* and *Sisters of the Road*, tries to establish the killer. The formal interest in this text lies in the way it propounds the theoretical, slipping into a non-fictional oratory mode allowing the reader to process, through the consciousness of Pam, different sides of the debate. Historically the detective novel's openness to political questioning, and its association with realism, creates a text closer to feminist dialectic than fictional escapism. References to actual protagonists such as Andrea Dworkin and Ros Coward, and the parallel with the controversial Barnard Conference on Sexuality in 1982,[21] mark *The Dog Collar Murders* as internal to the specific disputations on sexuality intrinsic to mid and late 1980s urban lesbian feminism.[22] In the contention around what kinds of alliances feminists can afford to make, it is significantly the right wing representative from the moral majority, the censorship advocate, who does the dirty deed.

Sarah Dreher's Stoner McTavish mysteries (*Stoner McTavish* (1985), *Something Shady* (1986), *Gray Magic* (1987), *A Captive in Time* (1990)) combine the romance and mystery forms in an endearing anti-hero, Stoner. She humorously incarnates the misfit motif pandemic to lesbian identity, a detective outlaw who can reassuredly exorcize the reader's internalized social unease. Like the classical fool she attracts the laughter of self-recognition: although all three novels are ostensibly thrillers, the crime hermeneutics are secondary to Stoner's dogged devotion to Gwen. Each crime/mystery is mainly the enthralling obstacle to love's fulfilment. Also in common with most of these investigators, Stoner is a soft-hearted butch. The lesbian feminism of the 1970s saw sexual role-play as intrinsically regressive, accusing its practitioners of invoking the view of homosexuality as a failed copy of heterosexuality popular in dominant discourse of the 1950s. During the 1980s the reintegration of butch/femme roles into lesbian feminist culture has been an expression of a range of debates concerning the construction of sexuality, as Joan Nestle has argued:

> Butch-femme relationships, as I experienced them, were complex erotic statements, not phony heterosexual replicas.[23]

Nestle goes on to suggest that

> the term *Lesbian-feminist* is a butch-femme relationship, as it has been judged, not as it was, with *Lesbian* bearing the emotional weight the butch does in modern judgment and *feminist* becoming the emotional equivalent of the stereotyped femme, the image that can stand the light of day.[24]

Thus within feminism itself *butch* becomes the despised and fantasized Other, the location of 'real' lesbian sexuality. Is the fact that so many dyke detectives appear as butch fantasies due to the regrettably intransigent masculine conventions of the genre, or could this constitute a radical parody? The figure of the detective is crucially a fantasy of agency, which is culturally conflated with masculinity from both dominant culture and within feminism itself. Could a femme detective focus our desire so effectively? As a subcultural stereotype the butch detective works at two levels of identification for the reader. Not only does she desire the butch, she also wants to *be* the butch.[25] In her outlaw status she promises a romantic, forbidden fantasy and the incarnation of a felt alienation which is fictionally empowered. The convention of the detective hero is being appropriated and destabilized by the parodic acknowledgement that the complex sign 'butch' encapsulates a field of contradictions.

All the detectives discussed so far have been amateurs, positioned to a greater or smaller degree in opposition to the law. There are also a small number of novels which present a lesbian cop, a fantasy figure earthed in this reintegration of the 1950s bar culture resurgent within 1980s identity politics. *Amateur City* by Katherine V. Forrest (1984), and its sequels *Murder at the Nightwood Bar* (1987), *The Beverly Malibu* (1990), and *Murder by Tradition* (1991) introduce Kate Delafield of the Los Angeles Police Department. Kate is the archetypal soft-centred butch, as a cop 'one of the best' (90), a Vietnam veteran who quit law school at the prospect of defending a 'possible criminal' (62). Her 'strong face, those grim features' (33) are 'tight polished planes' (113), her cold blue eyes impersonal and impervious to tears. Her body is 'firmly muscled ... solid ... flatter, tighter' showing 'steeliness' and 'unmistakable strength' (115). Her hatchet features, tempered by tragedy – the death of her parents and the incineration of her lover in a car crash – are at times a 'waxen mask of suffering' (110). This tragic heroine has an Othelloan flaw:

> The tired knowledge that always she was silhouetted against

> her background.
>
> Always.
>
> Always. Growing up she had been taller and stronger, more aggressive than the other girls; in look and manner, hopelessly unfeminine by their standards. Among similarly uniformed women in the Marine Corps, she had been resented for her unusual physical strengths and command presence. She had been the woman reluctantly singled out . . . And always there had been that one most essential difference: she was a woman who desired only other women. (24)

Terms inferring states of sexual darkness, 'essential difference', are reminiscent of Radclyffe Hall, and Catherine Stimpson's theory of the 'dying fall': 'a narrative of damnation, of the lesbian's suffering as a lonely outcast'.[26] Havelock Ellis'[27] refined definition of 'congenital invert' relies on the visible presence of male physical attributes, and Kate Delafield's appearance is paradigmatically masculinized.

Historically women have been drawn to the police and military as professions promising vocational strength and control, and this alliance with the state also upholds the vision of social integration, the need to belong exacerbated by the very difference which excludes. Kate was born in 1946 and her cultural backdrop is lesbian rather than lesbian-feminist – 'All my upbringing, my influences were from the fifties' (120) – and her ground-level politics are informed by that period of reactionary repression and marginalization.

However, it is too easy to see this background as one of passive victimization.[28] Kate's ambivalent position does liberate an objectivity often highly critical of the Los Angeles Police Department's grosser prejudices. Her sidekick Detective Ed Taylor embodies a morality we suppose to be typical of a redneck dick, and Kate's long-suffering disgust highlights both her incongruity and his unquestioned bigotry. In *Murder at the Nightwood Bar* the structures of alienation are reversed, for the Nightwood Bar is a lesbian bar, and Taylor's intimidatory tactics are derided, his masculinity a magnet to ridicule. This is Kate's territory:

> She felt stripped of her grey gabardine pants and jacket, her conservative cloak of invisibility in the conventional world. In here she was fully exposed against her natural background. She recognised aspects of herself in each of the women staring back at her. (11)

Although lesbianism is described in terms of disclosing a natural centre, this image does suggest a more radical notion of subjectivity. Kate begins to see her identity not in terms of being a single coherent individual but a 'self in relation', in the reflection and diffraction of the other women's eyes. This progresses away from the liberal humanist assumption of personal coherence and agency, the ideology of autonomy which strives to disguise the way discourses impose themselves and construct us.

Identity, then, consists of a collection of inconsistent and even contradictory subject positions which compete for our allegiance. To recognize oneself as being split is not to wallow around in self-pitying pieces; rather, this displacement of selves across a range of diverse discourses is implicitly dialectical: 'in the fact that the subject is a process lies the possibility of transformation'.[29] During the progression of the narrative Kate increasingly interfuses with the life of the bar, a movement of inclusion and self-revelation which testifies to the historical importance of the bar in constructing lesbian and gay social history. In the final few pages she relinquishes her role as romantic outsider and attends the Los Angeles Gay Pride Parade. Through symbolic tears she sees the thousands of lesbians and gays who embody a new (for her) *communitas*. The moment of closure and resolution in *Murder at the Nightwood Bar* is not the arrest of the murderer but the integration of one lonely dyke into her culture.

The novel attempts to tackle a tapestry of issues weaving in and out of the designation sexual politics.The victim, Dory Quillin, is an angel/devil, virgin/whore, child/woman enigma who has been subjected to sexual abuse by her father from the age of 5. This is an issue dear to the hearts of lesbians and gay men, so often identified with child molesters in the paradigm 'deviance'. The Quillins, Flora and Ronald, represent archetypal North American respectability; the inference is clear. Flora Quillin is trapped by deceit and denial, a victim of both her husband and religious fundamentalism: the principle of male authority. The destruction at the centre of the biological family is held in opposition to Dory's 'real family, her own people' (175); the bartender Maggie spells out to Taylor the number of gays and lesbians rejected by their parents and siblings, asserting 'we have the power in us to make our own families' (174). The notion of family is central to the text; there is room for diversity in the lesbian family, an alliance formed by necessity for comfort and political expediency. But can this alternative model offer only a defensive refuge? The final, utopian image of the biological family is a poignant plea for inclusion. On the parade Kate sees a banner:

> PARENTS AND FRIENDS OF LESBIANS AND GAYS. She stood, applauding with all the others, as the large contingent walked by holding their placards. Her eyes fastened on a man and woman . . . each with their arm around a young blonde girl between them; and she saw the sign the entwined hands of the parents were holding aloft: WE LOVE OUR GAY DAUGHTER. (180)

A common humanity which includes homosexuals does not, however, extend to criminals; thus the organizing structure us/them is not significantly changed, merely the criteria of membership:

> 'I think it's worth trying to take from the streets creatures who don't deserve to live among human beings.' (92)

Kate's theory about uncleared homicides being committed by 'anonymous roving monsters', together with references to 'sub-humans', and Quillin's 'scummy worthless life', combine to categorize 'deviance':

> Even under ideal conditions, she thought venomously, his crime would not qualify him for the electric chair. Not in California where the prerequisite for the death penalty was murder of a particularly heinous nature, the always problematic 'special circumstances'. Wishing such punishment on Roland Quillin was irrational and vindictive, she conceded; monster that he was, the death penalty seemed like a basic waste of creatures like him. They should instead suffer the more useful fate of assignment for scientific study and experiment, for whatever could be gleaned from a malign cannibal subspecies which had lost the moral right to be treated as anything other than laboratory fodder. (151)

This model of innate depravity derives from a primitive religious dualism, good/evil. Thus the sex-offender is not sick, but sinful.[30] This allows no notion of culturally and historically constructed subjectivity, but depends on a perception of human conscience as universal and inherent.[31] If Man is depicted as a rational agent imbued with an ethical code which he is free to transgress, then by choosing to do so he cannot cease to be human. The text constructs crime as being against nature, and the offender as unnatural. Criminals become commonsensically Other; labelling deviants as non-human in this way exonerates society.

The terms of biological determinism extend to an analysis of lesbianism, frequently an overt enquiry in these texts. Taylor runs the gamut of its causes, social and psychological, and finally Kate explains to Flora Quillin why Dory would 'do such a thing':

> 'I think your daughter loved other women because it was her nature. A lot of people are just simply that way.' (170)

This essentialist definition of homosexuality as an inherent, and immutable state has historically been used by the Gay Liberation Movement to establish homosexuals as member citizens of the liberal pluralist society which rejects homosexuality when perceived as a political and therefore subversive act. However, the gay activism of the late 1980s and early 1990s in Europe and North America has also proved the necessity for a contingent deployment of essentialism. The colonizing and extemporizing of a gay identity for the purposes of political pragmatism has foregrounded the performative function of 'I am . . .', so that identity itself becomes called into question. Preceding the articulation of 'I am . . .', therefore, is an 'as if . . .'.

Returning to the third full-length Kate Delafield mystery[32] *The Beverly Malibu*, Kate investigates another closed circle murder in a Los Angeles apartment block. Poisoned by strychnine and arsenic, an old-time Hollywood film director Owen Sinclair is killed out of revenge. As a 'friendly witness', he informed on fellow filmmakers before the House of Un-American Activities, the 1950s forum for McCarthyism. Forrest foregrounds the lasting effects of the reactionary politics of that period, comparing the 1950s with contemporary 1980s racial and sexual bigotry. However, the text's radical intent is similarly restrained by the casting out of the murderer as bestial:

> [Her eyes] were wide and glittering . . . her lips were drawn back over her teeth, her broad face was a feral mask. (227)

> she was like an animal standing over its kill. Gloating over its kill. Gorging itself over its kill. (232)

> This woman is a monster. (238)

Despite this, *The Beverly Malibu* does develop further the exploration of lesbian identity initiated in *Amateur City* and *Murder at the Nightwood Bar*. The 1980s, as an historical moment, had much in common with the 1950s; the images, style, fashion, and culture of the 1950s were nostalgically re-visioned for 1980s consumption. In the lesbian community the reappearance of butch/femme role-playing was partly playful parody, and partly perhaps a grasp towards a more safely defined, and sometimes romanticized past. Certainly the commodification of identity during the 1980s created the opportunity to 'dress up' as butch or femme as an erotic spectacle. Whereas Kate Delafield had been strongly signified as butch, in this novel she falls for another butch, which requires a sudden shift in her own self-appraisal, and presumably also in the reader's received wisdom that 'opposites attract'. Not only does Kate re-vision herself as a femme, she also has to change her construction of that role as passive, and allow for a new conception of these roles as fluid, not fixed. Indeed, oral and narrative histories of butches and femmes often relate the complexity of these identities, with women having switched from one to the other within and in between different relationships.[33]

The Beverly Malibu, by focusing on the McCarthyite procedure of naming names – an act which destroyed the lives of countless numbers of people who lost their citizenship, their right to belong – gestures towards the power of language to construct and position the individual subject. Feminists have paid great attention to the process of naming as a forum for the operation of gender politics. Men's monopoly over naming, according to Mary Daly, has meant that

> women have had the power of naming stolen from us. We have not been free to use our own power to name ourselves, the world, or God.[34]

The operation of naming is one which lesbian and gay people are particularly sensitive about and subjected to, a fact further reinforced by Kate's firmly closeted lesbianism in the LAPD:

> 'We have over seven thousand police officers and nobody's out, not a soul. You can't begin to fathom the homophobia. My life would be hell.' (61)

As one victim of McCarthyism in the novel puts it:

> 'All my life I've been a symbol.' (261)

Murder by Tradition takes up that institutionalized homophobia further, by making the murder an act of queer-bashing, and extending the narrative enquiry into the legal system itself. When the jury convicts the perpetrator of such violent hatred in a moment of utopian libertarianism, it feels like the 1960s all over again. *Murder by Tradition* is an optimistic salute to the growing mobilization of the Lesbian and Gay Rights Movement of the 1990s.

The other most established lesbian cop is Australian – Claire McNab's Detective Inspector Carol Ashton of *Lessons in Murder* (1988), *Fatal Reunion* (1989), *Death Down Under* (1990), and *Cop Out* (1992), all published by Naiad Press. The issue of closetry builds up steadily through the series as the tension between public and private becomes more explicit. Although the novels are indubitably formulaic romances, they reject the platitudinous reiteration of clichés in favour of lesbian relationships as fraught with negotiation. The challenges to the relationship of Carol Ashton with her lover Sybil Quade include the dangers of desiring a 'straight' woman; the exorcism of the last lover's emotional hold; interdependence versus autonomy; 'space', withdrawal, and vulnerability. The 'acting out' of these conflicts occurs most manifestly in the sex scenes, and the interest of these novels lies in the way dominance/submission imagery is deployed to convey the tension. Desire becomes the vehicle for exploring the exchange of power, as the butch Carol is brought down by the femme Sybil. The balance of power shifts between them, and the reader is able safely and vicariously to experience the sadomasochism of romance. By the close of the novel the couple are restored to equilibrium.

Some of the many pleasures for the reader in these books are: first, the fantasies of power, control, and the definition/naming process that being a law-enforcer permits; second, revenge – patriarchs get gruesomely murdered in horrifically explicit ways which often border on parody; third, the enigma is resolved and it is always comforting to feel that in that restoration of order the good end happily, the bad unhappily. In fact although the scenarios are different, the mechanisms are the same: threat is expunged by the action of the protagonist. Thus (mythical) security is restored. In this respect the sub-genre is somewhat conventional, and cozily self-reflective. Reading these 'right-on leisure novels' was seen by some as a recapitulation to the reactionary politics of the 1980s. Jenny Turner has accused them of 'bourgeois wish-fulfilment' which conflates living the good life with ethical or political campaigning; their

> smirky little in-jokes can only ever work to exclude everybody for whom they are not designed.[35]

It is precisely these conservative aspects of the fictions which make them so amenable to sub-cultural appropriation in the first place. The temptation of assimilation, or at least of being accorded value, and offered safety, is a strong one. From the position of an underclass, this, and a secure bourgeois lifestyle, can often look the same.

Conversely, in lesbian crime fiction readerly expectations are confounded on two generic levels – romance and crime fiction – which creates an emotional elasticity: one must comply with the ironic distance, and question the investment in formulaic satisfaction. The pleasure relies on intertextual awareness: the construction of romantic desire and its concomitant frustration is a familiar literary form, and similarly the search for a personal archetype. The disruption of meaning brings the instability of the form itself to light; the detective story's insistence on factual truth falls into ambiguity and contradiction. Crime fiction texts constantly assure the reader of their mimetic function through continued reference to actual places, dates, people, and organizations. Part of the pleasure of reading depends on this sense of authenticity, allowing the reader to experience normally inaccessible or forbidden activities. So, she can, for a moment, be Detective Kate Delafield of the Los Angeles Police Department beating the shit out of a potential rapist on a gay-bashing spree (*Murder at the Nightwood Bar* chapter 10). This scenario is highly unlikely (one lone policewoman taking on three stoned and homophobic youths armed with pipes . . . and winning), and is merely an expedient exchange of one type of perceived 'reality' for another. Lesbian crime fiction provides a site of struggle over definitions of justice, social status, and sexual identity, positing the lesbian at the centre of meaning dissemination.

Psychoanalytically oriented reader-response critic Norman Holland holds that 'interpretation is a function of identity',[36] and that the reader finds in a text that which she is predisposed to fear or wish for. Part of the attraction of crime fiction is that it offers the reader security and an affirmation of her values. By placing her in the centre of the narrative she becomes the site of meaning production. Into the fictional realm of fear and chaos steps a figure of order and resolution. That figure allays fears for the moment of reading. But this resolution is temporal; one must read again and again. Once the murderer is known one cannot read the book and fear, so that crucial cathartic release is denied.

Traditional detective fiction is a highly formalized and predictable genre offering pleasure and release of tension through the affirmation of received and uncontested meanings. For the feminist/lesbian reader there is some pleasurable complicity with the text in its representation of familiar (sub-)cultural signs. However, the reader becomes disconcerted if these are undermined by parody. The reader's resultant unease reflects her more realistic social positioning, and allows expression to the constant, unconscious shifting of roles/selves necessary for social interaction. These novels are concerned with lesbian identity and subjectivity, a controversial area which is explored pleasurably by employing a narrative process of 'discovery'. Thus, the reader reads to discover 'herself', but also to reconstruct 'herself' as a woman empowered and centred. The novels offer a fantasy of control, and so potentially radically invert the real relations of her oppression.

One more book was such an uncompromising hit with the lesbian community of the mid-1980s that it almost stands as the referent for lesbian crime fiction, operating as a crossover text to a larger, heterosexual audience: Mary Wings' *She Came Too Late* (1986). The text shies away from didacticism; political issues give the book a moral baseline, but 'story' re-emerges with primary importance. Emma Victor ('I'm a victor') works for Boston Women's Hotline, but is cured of political romanticism – 'it doesn't have any flash at all, just a kind of deadly dullness' (17). Issues raised include women and reproductive technology, high society vice and corruption, union busting, the tentative position of charitable organizations relying on private funding and the questionable alliances that that provokes; but these have relational, peripheral importance to the central fantasies of power and desire. Victor is a strong, independent woman in control of her chosen identity and lifestyle – 'life was streamlined and lonely and I was liking it that way'(13). She defines her own boundaries. When Dr Frances Cohen appears, 'A woman even my best fantasies couldn't touch' (6), the reader gets to enjoy that vicarious identification-pleasure as the romance ensues. Cohen is the mother/whore who will nurse you when sick, towel dry your hair, and turn up on your doorstep in her pyjamas. She is a repository of mystery and, in the true crime tradition, is a suspect to the end. (Fears are allayed, she was merely perfecting lesbian frogs.)

The sexual fantasy is overlaid with ambiguity – *She Came Too Late*, as the title would imply, is strewn with innuendo particular to lesbian sexual practice. This creates in the reader a kind of privileged confederacy, a legitimation of illicit pleasures. This text pushes out more explicitly into sadomasochist structures of desire, a subject obsessing urban lesbian communities in the 1980s. The rationale for their constant battles for the 'upper hand' is strikingly similar to arguments put forward by SAMOIS:[37]

> love [was] made possible because the power devils had been admitted and therefore banished. (77)

Victor 'goes shopping' in lesbian bars, gets turned on by striptease, stomps around in black leather and slips from butch to femme. Frances Cohen has her boss 'on a leash' which she can tighten 'anytime I want' (111), has hips 'like two holsters hanging below her waist' (37), and likes power in bed:

> I felt her exploring my mouth, taking it, drawing me into her. I would have been afraid except that I felt her warm hand on my back . . . She had my hands clasped over my head with one strong arm and her other hand went further and further pursuing the boundaries, taking me so far along in the excitement it was nearly pain . . . I fought with the passivity but it was only fun to fight it. I let her go wherever she wanted. (67)

This passivity is indulged because the reader knows Emma Victor is really a Strong Woman permitting her submission fantasies a limited expression.[38]

Much of the pleasure in *She Came Too Late* springs from its sexual openness. This move away from the idealized prescriptiveness of the 1970s involves dipping a toe into murkier waters, a response to a more disseminated dissatisfaction with the romantic dream.[39] Throughout there is a sense of play, laying bare the artifice of gender and subverting our own lesbian dress-codes. Emma dons sheer black stockings, stilettos and a dress as part of a draggish disguise. The detailed process of preparation and bedizenment is a private familiar feminine ritual complicitly enjoyed by the reader, even to the final twirl in the mirror: 'I saw it was good. I was a girl' (90). Emma Victor embodies and unifies the contradictions of gender – she is strong and soft, butch and femme, offering diversity without fragmentation.

Her ability to change subject position not only foregrounds those positions but also provides the reader with some vicarious resolution of the conflicting discourses around sexuality. When Victor walks into 'The Yellow Door' club on Mass Avenue and drops several whiskies she is emulating the hard-boiled dick; she is approached sexually by a man whom she peremptorily disposes of; she watches a striptease depicted in voyeuristic detail. When the stripper fixes her own eyes on Victor the power shifts: 'I watched her decide what to do with me' (180). As she draws a phallic feather boa through her crotch she stares at Victor, who is sexually stimulated. Victor's thoughts move on to male punters and the politics of biological reproduction. As she sits she has passed through several different states of subjectivity, ultimately clearing her mind for action. It looks so easy.

I have tried to show how the quest narrative in these novels is an epistemological one: to discover, to know, what is a lesbian? Diana Fuss suggests further:

> The very insistence of the epistemological frame of reference in theories of homosexuality may suggest that we *cannot* know – surely or definitively. Sexual identity may be less a function of knowledge than performance, or, in Foucauldian terms, less a matter of final discovery than perpetual invention.[40]

Judith Butler in her book *Gender Trouble*,[41] shifted the debate about gender and sexual identity on to the articulation of performative strategies as insubordination. In a recent essay, drawing attention to 'lesbian' as a shifting sign, she describes gayness as being 'necessary drag',[42] the sense of play and the pleasure so prevalent in the production of homosexuality fundamentally destabilizing the seriousness of heterosexuality. Indeed, Butler goes on to suggest that this parodic repetition displayed in lesbian and gay identities, rather than being derivative of a 'true' heterosexuality (and implicated within that structure the binarism of masculinity and femininity), actually exposes heterosexuality 'as an incessant and *panicked* imitation of its own naturalized idealization'.[43] In this structure, then, there is no origin for sexuality in the self which can be authentically expressed, but there can be a great deal of fun to be had on the surface, with illusion, which these fictions can show.

Barbara Wilson's *Gaudi Afternoon* (1991) pushes the fictional exploration of the relationship between gender and sexuality further, and as a novel of the 1990s it indicates possible directions for the form, coupled with the kind of theoretical work generated by sexual theory in the last couple of years. It concerns Cassandra Reilly, a translator who is hired by Frankie from San Francisco to find her gay husband in Barcelona, in order that he might sign some family papers. But the novel soon degenerates into comic gender picaresque: whilst Cassandra in one diegetic world translates a Venezuelan epic pulp romance which feminists have seen as (she says gloomily) 'a paradigm of the condition of contemporary woman' (94), her second task is to be chasing a circling chaos of subjects clinched in a custody contest where each claims to be the real mother. Frankie, the 'wife', is really a male-female transsexual; Ben, the 'husband', is a radical feminist bulldagger; April, her New Age cultural feminist 'girl'friend, an Earth Mother who dislikes children, is a male-female transsexual but Ben doesn't know it; April's 'friend' is her gay closet cross-dressing stepbrother with whom she shares 'Shame Issues'. Meanwhile Cassandra is asked by her top femme girlfriend:

> 'Please, what are you? Woman or man?'
> 'Neither,' I said, in English, then in Spanish, 'I'm a translator.' (74)

Recourse to the body as final determinator is no use. Wilson defamiliarizes it beautifully, with Ben:

> Up close this woman was even more brawnily daunting. Her biceps bulged, her deltoids distended, her pectorals protruded underneath her sleeveless tee-shirt and vest. (63)

> 'Lies, lies, lies,' Ben broke down completely.
> I hated to see a woman go to pieces like that, especially one who looked like Arnold Schwarzenegger. (158)

Ben it is who accuses Frankie[44] of 'usurping [her] biological role' (64), and in their argument deploys the defence of 'nature' to her own detrimental effect. Frankie starts it:

> 'Sometimes I think that my caring about Delilah throws your whole self-concept of motherhood in doubt. If I can be a mother too, what does your motherhood mean?'
> 'There's always one biological mother,' Ben said. 'That's the way it is. And the biological mother always feels different than the other parent.'
> 'I don't believe that,' said Frankie. 'Motherhood isn't about biology, it's about love.'
> 'Don't talk to me about biology meaning nothing,' Ben snapped, starting to walk away again. 'We are our bodies, our bodies make us who we are. You just can't play fast and loose with biology.'
> 'Says the great bodybuilder,' Frankie said snidely. (130)

Recent cultural theory on the body[45] has drawn attention to its construction and commodification as a consumer fetish. Rather than presenting the 'truth' of the body, as in the traditional split between gender/sex, an opposition which discursively legitimates heterosexuality in a complementary binarism, *Gaudi Afternoon* sets up then deconstructs these polarities in order that the 'real' evades our slippery grasp. Thus there is no 'real' lesbianism, which Nestle's refutation of 'phony heterosexual replicas' would seem to imply, but there is no 'real' heterosexuality either.

Foucault has described how all discourses both constrain and construct us in that once we start naming ourselves, and appropriating identities we begin to fix meaning and prohibit flow.[46] It has become critical common sense to invoke the 'risk' of identity. On the other hand it is politically problematic for lesbians to relinquish these acts of naming and identification as the alternative is to accept the labelling of the dominant, or remain invisible. Analysis of these lesbian crime novels has uncovered a dialectic concerning sexual identity which frames that enquiry within an acknowledgement of power relations. To take *She Came Too Late*, for example, I am not proposing there is an equivalence here between sadomasochism and lesbian sexuality. I am saying that because lesbian sexuality is not fixed, should not be fixed, and does not operate beyond power relations (I do not subscribe to the essentialist notion that in lesbianism is the meeting of two equals), it must not be celebrated uncritically, in word or in deed, but constantly critiqued. Victor is strong but enjoys being made submissive. This paradox potentially undercuts the polarities of masculinity and femininity integral to romance. Conversely, the concomitant dependence on traditional notions of order, closure and reason, which situates many of these novels firmly within the dominant genre, offers solace and security. These contradictions in the text mirror the contradictions in the reader. In these alternative constructions of subjectivity the reader's different desires are explored. Fiction is an important site for this struggle.

Discourses, in their effectiveness, obscure their own mechanisms. As Jonathan Cook[47] has so pithily put it, 'Truth is the unrecognised fiction of a successful discourse'. He continues:

> Instead of seeing the literary work as an ideal aesthetic harmony, or the equally ideal resolution of psychological tensions in the author or reader, discourse theory conceives of the literary work as an instance of the historically variable institution of literature, an institution which mediates relations between writer and reader in different ways at different times, and in so doing, echoes, transforms, or challenges the uneven distribution of power within societies.[48]

Whilst being chary of proposing a reductionist claim that what these novels are *really* about is power, it does seem to me that the crime formula does allow for some investigation into the social relations of gender and sexuality, particularly in how these are located in identity. Some of the later texts, in their metafictional self-reflexivity, invoke a kind of essential constructionism which throws the reader back again and again into a parody of the reading process itself. The feverish desire for final comprehension is revealed as the re-enactment of a performance. In a sense, these fictions embody their own truth, that of the relations of power endemic to reading itself.

6

Murdering the inner man?

Psychoanalysis and feminist crime fiction

The relationship between psychoanalysis and crime fiction is one full of interlocking themes, patterns, devices, and desires. At the heart of both is the investigation of a conflict, with the intention of effecting resolution and closure. The figure of the psychoanalyst doubles with that of the detective, as an agent bent on interpreting clues and symbols, a figure of power who applies ratiocinative skills to a particular text. The psychoanalyst is adept at identifying repetition and return, something which characterizes not just the action of a detective, but as Daniel Gunn has suggested in *Psychoanalysis and Fiction*, using Maurice Blanchot and quoting Peter Brooks:

> Narrative always makes the implicit claim to be in a state of repetition, as a going over again of a ground already covered: a *sjuzet* repeating the *fabula*, as the detective retraces the tracks of the criminal. This claim to be an act of repetition – 'I sing', 'I tell' – appears to be initiatory of narrative.[1]

Genre studies have indeed borne this out, as readers compulsively consume one novel after another, and crime fiction is a paragon of its type. So, we already have two formal levels of repetition, of writing and of reading. Gunn asks the question 'does repetition point towards some original movement of unity or always towards division and loss?'[2] We are reminded of the crime narrative's convention of Eden disturbed by chaos, loss, and conflict, the primary hermeneutic being the reinstatement of that paradisiacal unity. But the reader also knows that that return will never be completed, as evil has entered the garden for good; its presence is perversely eradicable. It is tempting to see her repetitive, habitual recourse to rereading the crime narrative as an attempt to regain the pre-oedipal unity, expunging the father – the author of conflict – from consciousness. But here I am jumping ahead of myself – the links between psychoanalysis/literary criticism/narrative/feminism are interwoven and difficult to present in a logically developmental manner. First though, it may help to focus on one famous case of repetitive reading, that of the appropriately named tale, 'The Purloined Letter'.

This short story was written by Edgar Allan Poe in 1844, being the third in a series featuring French detective C. Auguste Dupin; the collection was popularly acknowledged to form the genre's earliest appearance. Written in the first person, the story concerns the theft, and subsequent retrieval, enacted twice, of an incriminating letter. Initially the letter is stolen by a minister from the Queen, in front of the King, who does not notice. The minister's illicit procurement of the letter ensures his power (of blackmail) over the Queen. The Queen, via the Parisian Prefect of Police, attempts to recover the letter from the minister's house, but all his searches fail. Finally Dupin retrieves it whilst the minister is distracted, and it returns, via the Prefect, to the Queen.

Interest in this story has provoked a proliferating pass-the-parcel in reverse, in which critics have wrapped layer upon layer of readings around the original. This major ongoing debate in the field of psychoanalysis and literary theory was instigated in 1956 by Jacques Lacan in his 'Seminar on "The Purloined Letter"', which became his key intervention with post-structuralism. Principally his piece identified certain 'Parallels' in the Poe story, or repetitions. Upon his act of analysis has been superimposed Jacques Derrida's 1975 extended essay 'The Purveyor of Truth', which accuses Lacan of ignoring the literary context of Poe's story, and idealizing the notion of the letter itself as a signifier. Barbara Johnson's (1977) reading of Derrida's reading of Lacan's reading of Poe, 'The Frame of Reference: Poe, Lacan, Derrida', developed the notion of framing further, deconstructing Derrida's own analysis, and in its turn generating another set of interpretations. Jane Gallop suggested that 'The Purloined Letter' functions as a parable of psychoanalysis, and indeed if one were to read the collection *The Purloined Poe* (edited by John P. Muller and William J. Richardson[3]) containing a dozen essays by these eminent critics and more, including Shoshana Felman and Norman N. Holland, one observes continuous return and repetition, privileging the *act* of interpretation over the original event; thus the mirage of the text's 'core truth' becomes exposed by its endless deferral – one can never return to the same place, only hold a mutable memory of it. Thus, we see that the genre's obsessive return to the crime scene, the instigatory event, is each time to change that moment as it is related by each witness, as its meaning in the narrative changes. Also this continual reliving of the event paradoxically signifies its very distance from the present, in the difficulty of its retrieval. Thus the reader's desire is never satisfied, despite the text's promise.

At a brutally simplistic level of analysis, one may perhaps argue that in feminist crime fiction the father is murdered in order that the mother may return. This oedipal scenario has been seen in such texts as Valerie Miner's *Murder in the English Department*, or Barbara Wilson's *Murder in the Collective*, where the death of the patriarch paves the way for the discovery of a symbolic mothering, in feminist sisterhood. But in actuality the vast majority of murder victims in feminist crime fiction are female. On a mundane level it may be that the reader's interest in an investigation in which she is constructed to connive with the feeling that the murder is justified, will inevitably wane. Perhaps the murder of patriarchs is not a functionable convention. However, the constant repetition of the death of female victims in these novels requires some explanation.

Where victims' deaths are due to operation of patriarchal power – for example directly or indirectly from sexual abuse – in Katherine Forrest's *Murder at the Nightwood Bar*, Marion Foster's *The Monarchs are Flying* or Sue Grafton's *'E' is for Evidence*, the reassurance of that repetition could involve the fantasy that such political injustices could be vindicated by the apprehension of the perpetrator and his concomitant punishment. These novels perform a double operation – a primary, political gesture of making visible abuse in a non-sensationalist way, and a secondary one of reassuring readers and victims of abuse that resolution and recovery is possible. But this gestalt operates on a fantasy level only, its relief is transitory, hence the need to repeat the illusion of safety it represents. Along with this illusion of safety is the reminder of the loss of innocence. In some ways the crime novel functions as an anti-romance, in its constant return to violent death, signifying the ultimate loss. Exorcizing this ghost could be its *raison d'être*.

Leaving aside the area of psychoanalytic *reading*, this chapter is also concerned with the presence of a psychoanalytic culture in feminist crime fiction. Within feminism there has been a mixed reaction to psychoanalysis. Prior to the early 1970s the orthodox opinion was that psychoanalysis was antipathetic to feminism, and vice versa. With the publication of Juliet Mitchell's *Psychoanalysis and Feminism* in 1974,[4] there began a reappraisal of Freud and the psychoanalytic project, which was to result in the creation of a whole new area of theory and practice. *Conscious*ness-raising groups of the 1970s had found out the intractability of the *unconscious* to being transformed by political ideology. The inconsistencies apparent between knowledge about sexism and intellectual strategies for its refusal, and the feelings and behaviour of women towards themselves, each other, and men, threw up paradoxes which an exploration of the psyche promised to relieve. Thus there sprang up projects like The Women's Therapy Centre in London, in 1976, which continues to offer humanistic therapies such as Rogerian counselling, Gestalt psychology, psychodrama, transactional analysis and co-counselling, each inflected with a feminist praxis.[5] Many individual women sought out psychotherapy as a way of resolving the pain of abuse and indeed during this period a culture of women's support and counselling fired such initiatives as Rape Crisis and Women's Aid, together with a plethora of helplines and support groups. Psychotherapy and counselling are now an integral part of the feminist movement, even so far as being seen as the 'vanguard' of political work, by alleviating the ill effects of patriarchal violence.

The key word here is 'individual': critics have drawn attention to the way feminism's original activism has been rechannelled into the self, rather than being directed at the state. Indeed, feminism's relocation into identity politics during the 1980s reflects the larger political picture of the period. The individualism, and the move from interest in external states to internal states had manifested itself ultimately in such cultural phenomena as the New Age by the 1990s, but I think it is too reductionist to dismiss this change of direction as purely indulgent and reactionary. The ambivalence which some feminists have expressed towards psychoanalysis, accusing it of élitist, heterosexist theory, and a privileged, middle-class practice, is a criticism I sometimes share. However, a political theory without a place for the unconscious, and a political movement without ears for people's psychic pain, is inadequately formed, and can only offer limited transformation.

Feminists, on the whole, have been critical consumers of psychoanalysis; concern with exploring subjectivity and sexual identity has dominated work since Freud, and in fact women have taken a huge part in constructing the field. Their opposition to Freud has been because of the way his work has been interpreted biologistically to keep women subordinated.[6] Novels, like Slovo's *Death by Analysis*, which foreground psychoanalytic themes and characters tend to replay a discourse of scepticism, ultimately in order to replace a perceived 'fathering psychoanalysis' with a 'mothering psychoanalysis' – the terms are Janet Sayers'.[7] Although there are several novels which present relatively minor or incidental instances of psychoanalysis in their narratives, I have chosen to discuss only those which seem to me to have particular purposes for foregrounding it.

Having dealt with the materialist approach in *Morbid Symptoms*, Gillian Slovo tackles psychoanalysis in her second novel *Death by Analysis* (1986). Hired by her former therapist Franca to find the killer of fellow psychoanalyst and lover Paul Holland, Kate finds herself uncovering another of the repercussions of 1960s revolutionary politics. Paul Holland has used thinly disguised case studies of terrorism while lecturing at a local police college. One of these policemen recognizes himself, previously an agent and infiltrator, and he is now keen to preserve his secret identity. Like *The Price You Pay*, *Death by Analysis* constructs a nostalgic notion of the 1960s, which is both a validation and an indictment of 1980s 'realism'. Slovo depicts the innocence of that 1960s fervour, its idealism blind to infiltration. The members of the cell group are now capitulated into middle-class comfort. The corrupt cop is the clear villain of *Death by Analysis*, and he is summarily executed at the last by that narrative stand-by natural justice. Structurally the novel contains classic crime elements, its radical character comes more from the thematic content: the attempt to foreground psychoanalytic practice as a feminist site of interrogation.

Franca and Kate reunite on 28 July 1981, the night before the royal wedding of Charles to Diana, in a classic cliché of auspiciousness:

> Franca's eyes were still on me. For a moment the crowd seemed to recede into the distance. I felt an uneasy stillness descend. (2)

The detective hermeneutic is interrupted by several flashbacks from Kate's therapy, forming a separate but related text – a metatext. The techniques of psychoanalysis are analogous to close reading, the analyst an observant interpreter of the client as text. In theory one can suppose that the interplay of literary characters can be read as an interplay between elements of the psyche. The two male psychiatrists in *Death by Analysis* – Holland ('He'd specialised in the psychic construction of masculinity and was regarded as something of an expert' (24)) and Greenleaf – are self-appointed patriarchs, both father figures who abuse their power. One is murdered, the other discredited. Kate is at odds with their approach. She interviews one of Paul's ex-clients, Stephen, a student suffering from an extreme rationalist individualism:

> 'Have you any reason to think Paul was murdered?'
> 'None whatsoever,' he said. 'In fact I don't believe in the concept. People select their own fates. You only have to analyse the minutiae of a person's actions to understand why he lands in certain situations. The individual is responsible for his own environment and his actions determine what happens.'
> 'You obviously don't believe in class politics.' (94)

Stephen's character is so parodical that Kate's anti-individualistic socialism is eminently more personable and credible to the reader. Slovo rejects the anti-materialism of traditional psychiatry by unveiling the limiting self-obsession which a purely individualistic approach can encourage, whether in the form of the cult escapism exhibited by Holland's co-trainee Maya, devoted to Bhagwan, the 'new capitalist(s) of eastern religion' (28), or Laura Maxwell, self-glorified and absorbed wholefood profiteer. The psychic children of Holland and Greenleaf are all unpleasant characters. In contrast, the sessions between Franca and Kate have a familiar momentum and integrity to the feminist reader. Franca, whilst conversant with her professional role, neither postures with nor exploits her client. Gradually the power imbalance shifts so that, in the present, when Franca has asked of Kate a professional favour, they equalize their debts in friendship. 'I feel alone', states Kate, 'You're not alone', replies Franca (155). This is doubly symbolic – at a transactional level the women are now peers, and as a fictional construct the lone detective has been exorcized.

During their sessions there is a dialogue between Kate and Franca which briefly represents the materialist criticism of psychoanalysis. Kate attacks with:

> 'I was talking about the disintegration of the Left in Portugal and you put it down to psyches. There are world forces out there you know.'
> 'I don't think you were talking about them . . . you were talking about a different aspect – about the pain you all carried with you, and how that interfered with the attempt to really change yourselves.' (56–7)

Later Kate continues:

> 'Don't you sometimes think you're spending a lot of energy to teach us to conform?' (102)

After years of sitting in the same seat, Kate assertively strides across the room and sits across from and facing Franca. Franca herself snaps at Kate – both are breaking small but significant rules. This contemporaneous debate around psychoanalysis and feminism is controversially articulated in a recent *Trouble and Strife* article by Julie Bindel entitled 'The State of the Movement':

> The individual solution is now the order of the day. Whereas previously your Consciousness Raising group or even your housemates were closely involved in your problems . . . nowadays the automatic response to a problem is a trip to the Therapist, who will put the stamp of validity on your feelings. We are not generalising about anyone in trauma who might need help and doesn't get it from friends – just a particular type of therapy consumer. This type is the middle-class able-bodied WASP who feels left out, shut up and in need of reassurance that the Therapist, for £15 an hour, is only too willing to give.[8]

Labelling this process the Individual Solution Routine, Bindel's assessment concludes with eight questions, including a relativistic 'How much has three terms of Thatcherism to do with all this?'

Maybe Slovo's attempt to address this dilemma is in implying Franca's personal/political *naïveté*. We learn that she is Greenleaf's ex-wife and Holland's former lover (and hence the equation therapist = parent is even more appealing). Her dependence on Kate for action is parallel to Kate's on her for analysis, and this uneasy co-existence is reflected in their final tentative friendship. Ultimately Slovo rejects the individualistic posturing of traditional masculine psychoanalysis, favouring a model of an exchange of equals, struggling together to change social and internal states.

In *Death Comes Staccato* (1986), Kate is commissioned by a young and highly strung violin player to, as it were, avert the male gaze. Rich, tortured Alicia Weatherby is watched at every performance by a strange man. This enigmatic stranger is subsequently murdered, and a hint of the blame is laid on Alicia. Kate clears her, and in the process unravels a suppressed paternity wrangle (Alicia's), a drugs ring including a ruthless and corrupt policeman and the family solicitor, and Alicia's childhood sexual abuse. Slovo thus tackles the unscrupulous greed of the rich, and their acquisitive, possessive, power-abusing sexuality.

Alicia's violin-playing illustrates a 'too intense pain', a 'dread', 'desperation' (2) , she is a girl 'driven by agony' (173), and it is her enigmatic, dark secret which locks the text, directs the hermeneutic of mystery. Slovo takes the archetypal 'mysterious young virgin', and instead of using her to excite sexual prurience in the reader, she portrays what, exactly, this child-worship can inflict. Alicia, unlike her peers, is sexually frigid:

> 'get her in the bedroom, and she turned into a twelve-year-old' (153)

snipes one unsatisfied young man. By making Alicia's sexuality the central mystery Slovo mimics an ancient literary custom, but when the true history is revealed Slovo clarifies the greater truth, that it is the instigator's sexuality at issue, as Kate says:

> 'That's the irony of Alicia's life. For half of it she bore the guilt for something she never did – something she was involved in but was in fact peripheral to . . . The adults were in trouble and she was the casualty. It was nothing to do with her. They just used her . . . Everything seemed to centre round Alicia when in fact it was nothing much to do with her.' (195)

It was her stepfather, whom Alicia had always understood to be her biological father, who was the abuser; he complains plaintively 'you seemed not to mind' (187). The actual murderer, the family solicitor, kills for money and to protect his reputation: Slovo makes the villains the law *and* the father.

Kitty Fitzgerald's *Marge* (1984) is from a different nest. Despite its hybrid form – mainly psychic thriller blended with myth/fantasy, stream-of-consciousness and confessional modes – *Marge* is also a thriller in the traditional sense. Using an increasingly common feminist fictional structure from the early 1980s, the story is built around a handful of women and their interrelatedness. The protagonist is Marge, a woman whose mental illness is depicted according to the anti-psychiatry school of the 1960s epitomized by R. D. Laing. The medical institution has so far exacerbated the emotional damage exacted by a father who has brutalized and murdered her mother, and raped Marge repeatedly since puberty. She is assigned a male social worker who is sexually stimulated by her past. She is hospitalized through a desire not to cure but to control. Professional competition between two women ensures her confusion. The novel indicts this oppression, and attempts to mystify women's madness as a form of power and revenge.

The text uses filmic structures of watching to enhance the gathering dread. Marge constantly watches Maggie, a woman across the street who is concurrently being exploited by a more mundane manifestation of masculinity – a loutish boyfriend who uses and abuses her loneliness. Marge has delusions; she is addressed by the female goddesses of Gaealand who wish to 'destroy Zeus' in his intention to father a new son. This reappropriation of madness-as-spirituality springs from feminist theology, and more latently, from medieval views of madness as visionary. Marge murders Joe (the name is significantly the same as the earthly father of Jesus) in an act to avenge all patriarchal violence, an act of novelistic closure which leaves the reader vicariously condoning a violent revenge fantasy.

The suspense in *Marge* is created by the watching and waiting endured/enjoyed by the protagonist; the reader is Marge who watches, and Maggie who is watched. Because the point of view is predominantly the murderer's herself, the reader is urged to consider murder as a social illness, an inevitability, and potentially the extreme reciprocation of every woman's oppression. The murderer becomes the victim in a moral reversal comparative with that other Marge – Marjorie Adams in *Murder in the English Department.*[9] *Marge* is a strange novel, set in a cross-generic cacophony of styles bordering on the science-fictional; one goddess comments:

> *That is where you and I are now Marge, outside rationality, abnormal . . . but that does not mean less than normal, merely different. Only by stepping sideways into possibilities like this can we be truly alive.* (54)

Ironically it means death for the male abuser. *Marge* is one of a few feminist crime fiction novels which, like Diana McRae's *All the Muscle You Need* (1988), contrive fictionally to represent the therapist metaphorically or actually as 'the rapist', a singularly antonymous reformulation originally employed by radical feminist philosopher Mary Daly.[10] Whereas most liberal texts fall into the 'positive images' category of representation regarding psychoanalysis, these others see it as psychic patriarchy in action, and very much the enemy of women.

The positive link between psychoanalysis, feminism, and crime fiction is made explicit when the investigator is made a female psychoanalyst. The first notable appearance of such was Gladys Mitchell's idiosyncratic serial sleuth Mrs Lestrange Bradley in *Speedy*

Death (1929). Author of *A Small Handbook of Psychoanalysis* (the diminutive term has to be a phallic joke), this consultant psychiatrist to the Home Office employs occultism along with Freudianism, intuition along with scientific ratiocination. Crime critic T. J. Binyon describes her as a 'witch', in a metaphorical relation to the canon pleasingly apposite.[11] Dr Sarah Chayse of Lynn Meyer's *Paperback Thriller* is a cooler, contemporary version, and the epitome of the feminist professional – cultured, with a conscience. This book was published initially by the mainstream press Random House in 1975, and its feminism is firmly positioned within a contemporaneous liberal dialectic. Her sexual liberation is a somewhat laboured point – she has two (male) lovers, and her struggle for autonomy and independence from their nascent protectiveness fixes the text's overt feminist concerns to this period, primarily expressed within the personal politics of a relatively privileged woman. It is constrained within the positive images school of feminist writing prevalent at the time; nevertheless, the text's preoccupation with the parallels between psychoanalysis and crime fiction endows it with some continuing interest. It was reissued by the Crossing Press as recently as 1989.

'Chayse' is both chased, and a chaser herself. The ambiguity of her name is an indicator of the way she shuffles her role as victim/victor. Alerted to the burglary of her office by the reading of its exact description in a trashy novel picked up at an airport (the text flirting with a metafictional self-consciousness which sustains the twin investigations into (a) the crime, and (b) the self), Chayse tracks down the perpetrator of the deed and eventually the motivation – medical malpractice. Dr James Harney is the 'bad doctor' – a man who manipulates emotionally needy people into embarking on his drug treatment programme, a Get Happy Quick cure which leaves them dependent on high doses of amphetamine and heroin. It is a lucrative practice, and serves in the reader to legitimate Chayse, in opposition, as the 'good mother' who endorses the traditional talking cure of psychoanalysis.

The initial transgression of *Paperback Thriller* is the violation of a woman's space, Dr Chayse's office. This structure is repeated in Barbara Paul's novel *Your Eyelids are Growing Heavy* (1981), in which the protagonist is unknowingly hypnotized (he'd 'raped her mind' (161)) in order that she carry out a manoeuvre which enables a rival drug company to gain on its competitor, Megan's employer.[12] Both texts employ the good doctor/bad doctor opposition which serves to process reader's fears of psychoanalysis. Also both articulate the primary criminal act and very feminist concern of 'rape'. Sexualizing the violation in this way could be suggestive of the power male doctors have over their female patients, making explicitly gendered a taboo which is once more gesturing the desire to disable the father. Both 'bad doctors' – Harney in *Paperback Thriller* and Algren in *Your Eyelids Are Growing Heavy* – are discredited and deregistered by the disclosure of their crimes, in fact they are professionally castrated.

In psychoanalysis the concept of psychic space also contains within it a notion of dis*place*ment, or transference. Whereas individual clients are said to map emotional problems on to the patient/therapist relationship, which are then examined within the session, fiction is also expressed as a form of gestalt, in which the reader's concerns are expressed and relieved by the text itself. The relationship between psychoanalysis and narrative is creatively expressed in Catherine Clément's *The Weary Sons of Freud*:[13]

> having read so many case histories, having seen, in books by psychoanalysts, nice little stories, charming little novels or horrible perverse tales, more and more finely chiselled, I finally realized that patients in analysis were not only powerful creative artists but that they also were receptacles for stories. So many analyses, so many scripts; the most banal story, when told in the interlacings of fantasies and the intertwinings of dreams, can provide material for so many fictions. And since you don't enter the psychoanalytic cure without having a troubled past, troubled enough to weigh on your adult life, the simple historical construction of past events can sometimes be enough to sound like a novel.[14]

The fiction comes from the patient in the form of an oral narrative which draws on the cultural myths, tales, totems, and symbols internalized by the subject. Conversely, the subject can also process psychic meaning through the act of narrative reading or interpretation – work by feminists in areas of popular culture, and film theory has testified to this.[15] In *Paperback Thriller* the trauma of Chayse's violation provokes her investigation, which becomes a forum for playing out her anger and hurt:

> It was a classic connection, and I was able to make it. In fact, I had made it. I remembered thinking on the plane that it had been a rape, but I'd blocked it out. (92)

Chayse's own analyst also connects the feelings of violation from the burglary to Chayse's feelings of violation from her lover, and so the process of investigation becomes a catharsis for Chayse, and through her, the reader.

Recalling that this novel is firmly situated within an early 1970s liberal middle-class feminism, the ideology of the independent (individual) woman is centrally important within the narrative. The way dependence on the male is invoked in order to be banished by the text is mirrored in the way the issue of race is treated. As in the Gillian Slovo novels, the main character has a Black assistant. Stanley Livingstone doesn't work for Mr Charlie, but agrees to work for Chayse because 'you're a woman. You are oppressed.' The Black radical is

> 'touchy and proud . . . But he was also efficient, tough, thoughtful, and generous. He could also type like lightning.' (16)

There are several Black characters in the novel, including Harvard's first Black Dean Adam Swett (the name once again is symbolic of the pressure this First Man was under), who is killed by Dr Harney. Chayse suspends the investigation in order to get on with her own life:

> I was no longer concerned with the crime – if there was a crime – but with my reaction. (99)

Thus the novel falls into the practice of being more concerned with internal *reaction* than the criminal *event*, a pattern common in women's crime writing. But Stanley challenges this, when another death galvanizes Chayse's interest:

> 'There's a black guy, see. And he died. And you were looking into it for a while, were all upset about it. You cared. And then you stopped caring. You let it go . . . And now a white guy dies, and it's important. More important because it was a white guy this time?' (104)

Chayse denies this and gives another reason (that the presence of a Nietzschean quotation in the suicide note aroused her suspicions), and responds with 'so you see, it isn't color. Color has nothing to do with it.' This exchange allows for the metonymic expression of a tension within the contemporaneous USA Women's Liberation Movement, which was being accused by Black feminists at the time of racism by exclusion. Further discussion about interviewing a Black witness, Swett's lover, elicits the comments from Chayse that

> 'It's hard to know in a thing like this whether it's better to be a woman or to be black . . .'
> 'Women's liberation says it feels about the same,' [Stanley] said, the smile back, the wise guy reestablished. (104)

The tension between the external (political) action and the internal (psychic) reaction is maintained by the presence of Stanley in the text, But his status as hired help subsumes his discursive authority to Chayse's in the narrative hierarchy. Thus the model of a centred, middle-class liberal feminism remains definitive despite the attempt to populate the text with difference. On another level, the text raises demons in order to dismiss them and placate the reader. But the ambivalent – perhaps ironic – way in which Stanley's final comment can be read indicates a disturbance which prefigures the forthcoming disruption of this seamless liberalism.

Ultimately, though, *Paperback Thriller* is a reassuring read: Dr Chayse is a fantasy figure who confidently confronts her morally disturbed world and internal dislocation with action and analysis thus releasing the reader from the anxiety of the unknown in the process. The foregrounding of the therapeutic value of investigation through confrontation endorses the feminist therapy movement's approach to problem-solving, through focusing on the individual's desire/need for understanding. Chayse makes this observation to the aptly named Assistant District Attorney, Goodman:

> 'that's our business, yours as well as mine.'
> 'Trouble and its alleviation.' (113)

This alliance between the psychoanalyst and the law completes the circle of this text's ultimate conventionality, but it is not without wit: in the final denouement, when the two doctors face each other in true crime style – good versus evil, psyching it out – Dr Harney accidentally shoots himself in the foot. If only the bad were banished that easily – the implication that this form of authoritarian/dependency therapy will timely self-destruct is a fantasy from early 1970s feminists' confidence that their time had come, that the old models would be superseded by a new, co-operative and non-exploitative therapy.

Another feminist therapist/detective is Dr T. D. Renfro of Antoinette Azolakov's *The Contactees Die Young* (1989). This psychotherapist explores a client's apparent brush with the supernatural, in the suspected form of a childhood encounter with a UFO. Tracing the genesis of this nightmare involves a return to the young woman's home in east Texas, a stereotypical small town community which, it transpires, was the victim of a forest fire, started deliberately to cover a murder which Whitney witnessed and has then since repressed. This text has two principal operations: first to ban the spectre of the supernatural, or uncanny, by the process of psychotherapy, thus the psychoanalysis operates to disarm the mystery, as an oppositional discourse paradigmatically linked to rationality. Second, the client Whitney is having therapy to combat her own internalized homophobia. Taking her back to her home is a journey into the past/childhood identity, to explore a psychic history which has its own 'mystery': the two levels of investigation are coterminous. Finding the answer to the disturbing nightmare involves being kidnapped by the murderer, Ross Barnet. Their escape and consequent return to Whitney's family stimulates a welcome and acceptance which expels the fear of homophobia. Thus the closure of the detecting narrative also resolves an internal narrative too, reassuring the lesbian reader on both counts.

A third structure of this novel, however, is not resolved: the relationship between T. D. Renfro and her lover, June. A constant tension is their imminent estrangement as June pursues her career in forestry which will entail her moving away. *The Contactees Die Young* rejects the conventional romantic cliché, in common with other lesbian crime novels discussed earlier, thus, by implication, also rejecting the quick-fix closures of both popular psychotherapy and crime fiction.

None of these novels, however, goes as far as *I, Anna* by Elsa Lewin, in challenging these cosy conventions. This novel most explicitly engages with Freudian psychoanalytic theory. It was first published in New York by The Mysterious Press in 1984, and republished in Britain by Serpent's Tail in 1990. The author is a psychoanalyst, which may explain the dense texturing of symbols, themes, and signifiers which form the backbone of the story. The principal character, Anna, aged 50, is recently divorced. Her ex-husband, who rejected her for a younger woman of 32, has made sure he received the majority of the money and property from the divorce proceedings. Anna, now responsible for their 19-year-old daughter with whom she shares a pokey one-bedroomed flat, reluctantly scrimps together a few dollars for the singles parties, or 'meet markets', which form the last hope of a woman in her position for conventional domestic security. She goes home with a man who forces her to perform fellatio on him. She bites off his penis and beats him to death with a clarinet.

The novel overturns a number of crime clichés; first, in placing the reader's sympathy and identification with the murderer, which, second, places great tension between the reader and the representative of the law, the investigator, Inspector Bernie Bernstein – there cannot be a simple alliance of interest; third, this then relocates the investigatory suspense into the fear of being found out, moving from fourth, an interest in the *event*, to an interest in the *reason*, or motivation. *I, Anna* is a distillation of that shift by women crime writers into the psychological sphere. What leads a woman into murdering a man?

One of the most disturbing aspects of this novel is the way all the characters are at war with each other. The battlegrounds fall into two types: relations between men and women, and relations between parents and children. The conflicts can be read psychoanalytically – as examples of the oedipus complex, for instance, and from a materialist feminist perspective. The psychic conflict between Anna and her daughter Emily concerns the daughter's fight for independence, and her anger with Anna for being a 'failed' mother. Anna's response is spiralling self-denial and guilt, which makes Emily detest her even more. The rawness of these fights resounds with the gender oppression which situates women as masochistic mothers.

The text is overloaded with psychoanalytic signifiers. Anna herself is a modern remodelling of the case which was the starting point of psychoanalysis as the 'talking cure' – Josef Breuer's 'Anna O.', as published in his and Freud's *Studies on Hysteria*.[16] Anna O.'s real name was Bertha Pappenheim, who was, significantly, a pioneering feminist and socialist. Bertha Pappenheim and the protagonist of *I, Anna* share a number of similarities: both are victims of domestic demands in a monotonous family life which have led to feelings of alienation – a condition not unknown to housewives; both show two stages of being, a relatively normal (conscious) one, and a hallucinatory (unconscious) one in which is displayed violence and abuse towards herself and others; both exhibit *amnesia*, the classic symptom of an hysteric; both enter trance-like states, which Pappenheim described as 'clouds', a condition of self-induced hypnosis evincing somnolence and morbid, suicidal tendencies. There are other, behavioural tendencies such as disturbances of vision or balance, the inability to eat and drink, which underscore this equivalence.

Why should the author, as I have interpreted it, have chosen 'Anna O.' as a model for her own protagonist? The symbolism of that 'O' is profoundly feminine – the Woman, who is nothing, the lack, the hole, permanently opened. Breuer underplayed the sexual transference between Anna O. and himself, a fact which Freud later revealed himself as the 'untoward event' which ended the analysis.[17] Freud himself believed in the sexual origin of hysteria;[18] his theory of repression is the cornerstone on which the whole structure of psychoanalysis rests. 'Anna O.', then, is a densely important sign of a Woman constructed by a masculine discourse. Yet there is a contradiction – Bertha Pappenheim's recanting of her trance-like state of 'clouds', the unburdening of her mind through abreaction, her telling of stories, can be read as an instance of women's speech, the enactment of a potentially self-defined liberation. Hence the title of the novel, *I, Anna*, gestures towards this appropriation of the speaking position. Its assertiveness indicates a resolve, a taking of a stand, an act of self-definition. Conversely, it also signifies the impossibility of the unified subject, the split positioning I/Anna prefigures the character's two identities in the narrative as Allegra/Anna. There are also her interior monologues which, as in chapter 32, are consciously aware of a disjunction between 'Head' and 'feelings', i.e. rationality and emotion. Breuer suggested of Anna O.

> That it is hard to avoid expressing the situation by saying that the patient was split into two personalities of which one was mentally normal and the other insane[19]

which resonates with the contemporary Anna. However, the novel goes further than Breuer in depicting an explanation for this insanity. It is a fictional representation (and reinforcement) of woman as victim, in the crime mould, but intentionally foregrounding the gender mechanisms of that process.

Indeed, the anger of the narrative is directed at the sexual exploitation which provokes (and legitimates) revenge. Its most extreme example is the oral rape. The brutality of the description deromanticizes and de-eroticizes the sex act decidedly. The reader's own repulsion then positions her as righteously outraged, prepared to be morally complicit with Anna's reaction:

> He lifted my head and put it on his thigh, near his penis. The hair around it was sticky. I could smell the stale semen. I could smell old juices that were festering there. The stink was overpowering. I was choking. I opened my mouth to breathe.
> 'I want you to eat me,' he said.
> 'No.' I shuddered.

> 'I like it,' he said petulantly.
>
> I moved to get up. He twisted my head and shoved his penis into my mouth. I struggled, gagging. He held my head, pressing it down hard. The sticky hair filled my nose.
>
> 'Suck, suck . . .' he crooned.
>
> I gagged, trying to breathe, trying to break loose, trying to scream, feeling the penis harden as if to burst, feeling the throb, the stench, the horror. And then a gooey mucus filled my mouth, and still he held my head down in the slime and he breathed,
>
> 'That's good, that's good; you're really eating me . . .'
>
> Desperate, enraged, I clenched my teeth through the filth into the flesh in my mouth and bit. I bit with all my strength. (30)

'Anna O.' has closed her mouth. This moment, a violent revenge fantasy, evokes the *vagina dentata*, the spectre of the castrating woman, the virago. The castration complex, according to Freud,[20] resolves the oedipal complex, forcing children to repress their previously incestuous interest in the parent of the opposite sex, instead identifying with the same-sex parent, as part of the socializing project. The unconscious retains the (repressed) conviction that sexual intercourse amounts to a castrating rape of the woman by the man. In the novel *I, Anna* her victim George is a father, and when they arrive back at George's apartment, his son Stevie has to vacate their shared bed. Although the two men are apparently heterosexual, there are several places in the text where they are positioned as homosexual by other characters. Thus the woman represents both castration and regression; Anna's intervention in their lives actually causes the death of two men, George, and by setting up a series of circumstances, Stevie. Stevie's symbolic castration occurs when he is raped by another man, in the so-called 'passive, feminine' role (I use these terms reluctantly).[21] Thus Anna could be read in two ways: as a potentially strong 'castrator', or in fact, as I would see it, one who is 'castrated' – in terms of phallic (social) power – by this sex act which precludes her own eventual death.

This reading is supported in the text by the use of a symbol which Freud himself suggested stands in for the male organ – an umbrella.[22] The use of this symbol in the text is rather multi-layered: as a phallus it is compromised, its 'shaft' (7) is broken, and it flaccidly wobbles and flops over (8). Its condition is highly reminiscent of one of Freud's footnoted cases in 'Frau Emmy Von N.', which follows

'Anna O.' in *Studies on Hysteria*.[23] Another (unnamed) hysteric whom, significantly, Freud is unable to help, cannot walk without the aid of an umbrella. Her condition results, like Anna's, from the loss of a loved partner (in this case her fiancé). After some auto-suggestion from Freud under hypnosis, she breaks the umbrella. However, Freud cannot cure her, as there is some hidden, dark event which she will (can?) not divulge. Linking the two cases together, this one with 'Anna O.', hints at some kind of sexual abuse, something which Freud was rather quick to deduce as metaphorical, rather than literal, in his patients.[24] Freud is not able to get the cause of the woman's hysteria:

> Accordingly, during her next hypnosis, I told her that . . . something else had happened which she had not mentioned. At this she gave way to the extent of letting fall a single significant phrase; but she had hardly said a word before she stopped, and her old father, who was sitting behind her, began to sob bitterly . . . I never saw the patient again.[25]

Significantly the woman's father interrupts/prevents the expression of her secret, and she is silenced. This intertextuality supports the text's feminist agenda: to lay bare and make manifest the emotional and sexual abuse of women.

So, returning then to the umbrella, Anna carries around a broken phallus – a castrated one. She murders the father (George) – another of the patriarchal victims despatched by feminist avengers. Then she leaves the umbrella behind. There is a brief interlude during which Anna experiences release from her pain; but she eventually remembers the umbrella (now a symbol for the murder itself) which she returns to retrieve. Its symbolism is underlined by the fact that it functions as the main clue which provides the detective with the identity of the killer: its recovery precipitates Anna's downfall.

The unconscious use of rain imagery in the previous sentence underlies the dense complexity of this symbol: the umbrella protects Anna from the falling rain – and intertextually – from the *pain* of 'Anna O's' clouds. In constantly losing umbrellas, *forgetting* umbrellas, Anna's inability to protect herself is shown. The umbrella is a symbol of the repressed trauma, and also a symbol of the way she 'forgets' to protect herself. The structure of the narration, forty chapters, is in the third person. Chapter 1 is framed by two prologues in which Anna speaks for herself, in the first person, culminating in her revenge-killing. From then on, Anna's trajectory descends, as she is resituated as the hunted/villain. She loses her narrative voice as the detached, rational, objective investigative narrative takes over. The novel breaks down into different stories of witnesses, the police investigation, and secondary characters. The foil to Anna is Inspector Bernie Bernstein, who takes a personal interest in the case. He trails her, subjecting her to the investigative gaze which makes explicit male desire. He is a paradoxical figure himself, though a victim of the oppression of masculinity, and of racism. His ethnic identity as Jewish means that to be acceptable in the force he has to be a perfect cop; his own history compounds this pressure – he has idealized his father, and wants to be like him, as another policeman observes:

> 'He don't have a mother. Never did. He only had the Ten Commandments.' (241)

Bernie's psychic incarnation of the Law-of-the-Father harms the women around him despite his best efforts to be consciously kind. His estranged wife, Linda, cries:

> 'St Bernard. Your halo is blinding me.' (54)

The image is employed ironically. In the final scene with Anna, Bernie arrives on her doorstep replete with flowers ready to retrieve her from her morbid withdrawal. The reader's hopes are that the romantic discourse will triumph, but this book emanates a very Freudian family romance: true to his namesake, Bernie's appearance brings her comfort, he holds her and she finally cries. Temporarily, he becomes the Good Mother. But his nurturing and emotional honesty brings together the two worlds of the conscious and the unconscious for Anna, and concomitantly the memory of the murder she has so effectively repressed. This confrontation with reality is too much to take, and she shoots herself. Bernie knows it is his fault ('I destroyed her' (300)), and so the narrative closes with another murder, which eclipses the earlier feminist content.

In terms of crime fictional conventions *I, Anna* disrupts the fundamental one: that the detective works for the good, and that he will restore order. Instead, Inspector Bernie Bernstein *despite his intention* creates more chaos, and causes the death of the novel's (however problematic) primary figure – accorded 'heroine', perhaps, only by her long suffering. That this murderer receives divine justice, taking the honourable way out as it were, is a hollow gesture. The novel suggests that the constraints of gender – that women suffer at the hands of men – are too intractable to change. The convention of closure which insists that the detective will 'get his man' makes no allowance for the grey areas of moral uncertainty, where murder is part of a larger social picture. Ultimately, *I, Anna* is an anti-crime novel, laying bare the fact that 'roles' are stronger than 'selves', disrupting and refusing the tradition of individualism, of liberal humanism, which informs the genre.

Finally, *I, Anna* works intertextually on another level: by recalling the Anna who was Sigmund Freud's daughter (rumoured to be a lesbian, she was said to be called by Freud 'my son'). Indeed, the book was published two years after Anna Freud's death, in 1982. Significantly, this leading psychoanalyst spent her last years reading detective stories. Anna Freud was her father's daughter in that she insisted that psychoanalysis is primarily a talking cure – in this the figure of 'Anna O.' is evoked. Further, her birth on 3 December 1895 occurred in the year Freud dated his discovery of the unconscious, and published jointly with Breuer *Studies on Hysteria*, which included the first account of transference. Anna Freud was Sigmund's psychic inheritor, as Janet Sayers has observed:

> She became his Antigone – Oedipus's faithful daughter – as her father more than once called her. She not only nursed him but also edited and became a major exponent of his work.[26]

It was not until Sigmund Freud's decline and eventual death that Anna Freud's individuation from him was fully substantiated. Whereas her father formulated an adult analytic technique, she concentrated on children, a major innovation which has had a huge influence on subsequent psychoanalytic theory and treatment. Her key work was published in 1936, three years before Freud's death. *The Ego and the Mechanisms of Defence* contained two new significant developments – in ego psychology and in adolescent identity formation. Here we have two repeating themes of *I, Anna*, a novel about the struggle for individuation between the Law-of-the-Father, and the disruptive, feminine unconscious.

I, Anna, in the three adolescents Emmy, Stevie, and Theo, narrates the rage children enact on their parents, manifesting in anti-social behaviour and narcissism. Emmy, Stevie, and Theo swing from being aggressor to victim in an emotional and psychic see-saw which seats their respective parents as equally unstable opposites. Children of any age rarely occupy more than a cameo role in traditional crime fiction, being presented at most as objects of exchange in cases of kidnap, or victims of abuse in the more sensationalist stories. In virtually all cases their (infrequent) appearance is highly stylized and idealized, their function merely as adjuncts to the adults' manoeuvring. *I, Anna*, in company with several other texts such as *Death Comes Staccato*, Janet LaPierre's *Children's Games* and *The Cruel Mother*, Elizabeth Bowers' *Ladies Night*, Rosa Guy's *New Guys Around the Block*, Rosie Scott's *Glory Days*, and Iona McGregor's *Death Wore a Diadem*, presents convincing child characters as more than incidental trimming. But *I, Anna* goes further in representing the tortuous psycho-drama of adolescent individuation. Significantly the *mothers* are the principle focus of this rage. French feminist psychoanalyst Christiane Olivier has taken issue with the centrality of the oedipus myth in her book *Jocasta's Children: The Imprint of the Mother*,[27] in which she suggests that the primacy of female mothering in our culture results in a subsequent deep fear of female domination by men:

> But men have no more responsibility for their Oedipal history than we have for our pre-Oedipal drama: both are products of a patriarchal society in which the sovereignty of the mother during childhood sets off, in men, hatred of everything female, and, in women, respect for everything male.[28]

Psychoanalysis is useful to feminism in the way it makes conscious and explicit the roots of social conflict in psychic scenarios, themselves structured cyclically in cultural conditions. *I, Anna* fictionalizes the bitter struggle between (mainly) mothers and children which can be interpreted as implying the sickness at the heart of the conventional nuclear family, where each member vies for a limited resource of love and nurturance. Further, by representing the mothers in the text as each in their own way inadequate to the task, the novel drives apart any conflation between the ideological Mother, and individual women. There are a number of failed mothers in women's crime fiction, actual and symbolic, and I have yet to come across any female investigator who actually *has* a mother (most die off in the operator's childhood). It is interesting to speculate whether this rejection of the image of the mother is an intentional one, in a strategic feminist textual device, or whether it is an unconscious exorcism of an oppressive phantom.

Returning to Anna Freud, her pioneering work in ego psychology in Vienna extended psychoanalysis in this direction, particularly in the USA. *I, Anna* functions intrapsychically by foregrounding within a fictionalized framework the constant conflict in the main characters' identity between ego, super-ego, and id (Freud's tripartite structure of the mind). Her ego is fragile and weak, torn between law and desire, reason and emotion. Popular ego psychology has dominated North American psychoanalysis, and it is perhaps unsurprising that it is in this form that it has traditionally appeared in crime fiction, principally manifested in personality theory[29]. Recently this trend has resulted in the apotheosis of personality theory in the fascination accorded to serial killers, the folk heroes/devils of the 1990s.[30] The gaze has shifted from the detective to the criminal – indeed, the cover of *I, Anna* too has as its subtitle a reviewer's quotation – 'A brilliant character study' (*Booklist*). In a similar way to the lesbian crime fiction previously discussed, all the novels discussed in this chapter interrogate character, or identity, as the locus of mystery and the key to the investigative hermeneutic. On a crude level, then, these texts use psychoanalysis to enhance the preoccupation with personality – and its (mal)formation – which the mainstream has already endorsed. They point to the particular damaging political and social contexts of that process from homophobia (*The Contactees Die Young*), to child sexual abuse (*Death Comes Staccato*, *Marge*), the faulty, patriarchal fathering (*Death by Analysis*, *Paperback Thriller)*, to the very structure of the family itself (*I, Anna*).

Do the texts replace a 'fathering psychoanalysis' with a 'mothering psychoanalysis', as Janet Sayers[31] has argued, representing the swing that women have caused in the field? Certainly the positive presence of psychoanalytic practice in these novels has been represented as such. Conversely the threat of a discourse privileging emotion has seen to be excised symbolically from the most masculinized versions of the genre, as seen in Mickey Spillane's *I, The Jury*, whence the closure depends on the execution of the (sexualized) female psychiatrist who has murdered Hammer's friend and disrupted the homo-social bond. But fictions such as *I, Anna* support Sayers' objection to this idealized mother, and whilst feminist crime novels do – predictably – engage in murdering the Father, surprisingly they can engage with murdering the Mother too. The kind of self-conscious psychoanalytic discourse which appears in these novels is not unified or particularly coherent – I am aware that I have fabricated a sub-genre somewhat prematurely. However, there are connections here which signify a set of interests – between feminism, psychoanalysis, and crime fiction – which were conceivably addressing a readerly need or anxiety of the 1980s. The relationship between the three is somewhat circumferential; nevertheless it articulates a preoccupation with deconstruction/deciphering/destroying the sexism of a powerful cultural discourse concerned primarily with the construction of the individual. Crime fiction offers avenues of transference open to fantasies of destruction and resolution not available in 'the real'. This fledgling sub-genre, then, with its fantasized feminist gestalts, is firmly positioned within the decade of identity politics, which turned inward to 'the self'.

7

'What does it mean to sing "somewhere over the rainbow" and release balloons?'

Postmodernism and the crime fiction of Sarah Schulman[1]

> What does it mean to sing 'somewhere over the rainbow' and release balloons? It made her feel something very human; a kind of nostalgia with public sadness and the sharing of emotions. But then what?
>
> (Sarah Schulman *People in Trouble* (1990, p. 144))

'What is all this post-modernist shit, anyhow?' has been the Left's *cri de coeur* (kneejerk?) response, ever since it became necessary to launch this latest French theory into the political arena. Partly because there is no 'grand narrative' which is post-modernism, a great deal of conceptual confusion and consumer scepticism has characterized its reception. At a recent conference at the University of Sussex, one of its British protagonists was accused of 'word magic' – a heartfelt complaint from one of the many punters who thought they had come to a conference about *politics*. The sometimes bitter contestations over post-modernism's 'radical versus reactionary' status have been played out in fields such as social theory and philosophy. Feminists in particular have expressed antagonism towards its distancing, parodic stance, seeing its abandonment of generalizations, and its rejection of coherent identities (such as Woman), as a luxury only men can afford, given their historical precedence as definers. To argue that all big theory is out, and small theories are in, would seem to encourage the view that difference will endlessly proliferate into a relativist, selfish individualism; Linda Nicholson dubs it 'the view from everywhere'.[2] She goes on to say that

> postmodernism must avoid any simple celebration of difference or of particularity for its own sake[3]

stressing the crucial importance of situating diversity within political contexts.

Lesbian culture, in some ways, is the ideal forum for playing out post-modernist fantasies. Lesbians as a group tend to be highly self-conscious, being impressed by the perpetual need to make visible differences, from each other and dominant heterosexuality – this 'performativity' has been acknowledged as a key lesbian/gay aesthetic.[4] Even on the most intimate 'private' level, lesbian sexual desire requires the inventive reconstruction of roles[5] expressed historically in camp, or butch/femme. Urban sexual identities during the 1980s became inflected with a self-conscious irony expressed in the new fascination with parody which a post-modern aesthetic has generated. A new generation of activists rejected the categories which Lesbian and Gay Liberation proposed for the 1970s, the assimilationist cry of 'Glad to be gay' thought to be insufficiently radical for new times motivated by the rawness of AIDS, and the complexities of 'fucking with gender'.[6] 'Queer' politics

> provide[d] a way of asserting desires that shatter gender identities and sexualities[7]

so that the parameters of discourse once more crash together and recombine. The late 1980s and 1990s has seen an enthusiasm for sexual play which transgresses coherent labels in such transvestic amalgamations as the 'lesbian boy', the 'lesbian Daddy', or the 'dyke queen'. The ground, or essence, of sexual identity is repudiated in this performative sensibility, which perceives of the fictionality in fantasy and desire.

By effecting a close textual analysis of the fiction of Sarah Schulman, I will explore how identities are liberated, multiplied and shifted through her works, examining how these texts manage to extract the best from post-modernism, in its playful unfixing, yet concomitantly how their generation through time reflects a developing discomfort with its alleged depoliticizing tendencies.[8] Schulman's fiction can help us sift out the compatibility of crime fiction and feminism with post-modernism, and hopefully make sense of our own political trajectories from within this potentially confusing combination.

Jim Collins, in *Uncommon Cultures: Popular Culture and Post-*

Modernism, argues how post-modern fictions present new forms of textuality. They are

> responses to the complexities of contemporary cultural arenas . . . The tensions and conflicts within the semiotic environments that are the focus of so many Post-Modernist texts result, in large part, from the struggle of individual discourses to 'clear a space' within a field of competing discourses and fragmented audiences.[9]

In a sense, lesbian and feminist fictions are likewise competing in this space, within an ideological terrain which is populated with historical shifts in definition, and conceptual uncertainty. Geographically speaking the readers are also fragmented and dispersed, their act of reading their only collective, unifying gesture. This interconnecting textuality is problematic, if we take Chris Weedon on lesbian fiction, for example:

> If we are searching for positive lesbian role models or for a recognizable lesbian aesthetic, then a fixed concept of lesbianism is important.[10]

In a previous version of Chapter 5 I wrote about lesbian crime fiction[11] attending to the tension between generic conventions and the emancipatory agendas of the lesbian feminist texts. I argued that the best of these novels play with identity and succeed in offering a vision of community to the lesbian reader. Sarah Schulman's books are part of this sub-genre, distanced from the political realism, positive images school of lesbian crime writing, by the employment of a post-modernist perspective. By writing against this Schulman could be said to be constructing lesbian identity around the landscape of a modern urban condition – changing, fluid, complex and fragmented, fighting for a space juxtaposed with and superimposed on other cultural identities such as Jewish, Black, and working-class, but difficult to fix in any pragmatic way.

These 'ethnocentricities' have been described as Other within an oppositional structure most commonly arranged with the state as the dominant term. Jim Collins is keen to argue that crime fiction offers a critique of the state. According to him, crime fiction affirms an alternative sense of justice, going so far as to suggest that its proliferation in the nineteenth century represented a widespread disillusion with the state, and that 'the class of the detective in considered morally superior'.[12] Thus we may see why disempowered, struggling sub-cultures may be drawn to the genre, living on the margins necessarily creating a specifically distrustful attitude to the dominant doxa. Collins goes on:

> collisions between quite different forms of discourse become basic structuring principles of those texts. These collisions share a common purpose – to demonstrate that our cultures are so thoroughly discourse-based that we cannot even hope to encounter 'real life' unless we investigate the ways discourses fundamentally shape our experience.[13]

Crucially, there is that word again – 'investigate' – invoking the crime narrative, that investigatory hermeneutic which seeks to reveal, disclose, to *know*, and thence, so the myth goes, to empower.

Returning to Collins' formulation of the discursive collision as creating in the crime novel a structure of self-reflexivity, this would appear to have two effects: first, to deconstruct the myth of the homogeneous, self-actualizing, imposed, and monologically intent dominant culture, and second, to provide the potential, in this rupturing, for the subject to answer and synthesize multiple 'calls',[14] thereby stimulating conflict or crisis, and possibilities for new cultural forms. The intertextuality of detective fiction is thematized to the extent that 'texts become virtual microcosms'[15] of the overall field of culture, thus embodying a critique of the epistemological 'will to truth' which at a superficial level crime fiction appears to endorse. It seems to me that the operations of pastiche are implicit within this formulation. In order to illustrate this intertextuality Collins executes a short close reading of P. D. James's *The Skull Beneath the Skin*, which is a novel, as I have argued previously, marked as parody in fluorescence.

The few feminist crime novels appropriating a post-modern aesthetic express their sense of play and experimentation through parody. Barbara Wilson's *Gaudi Afternoon* is a prime example, being a fictional evocation of the queer imperative to 'fuck with gender'. Maud Farrell's *Skid* (1990) is another, one of a couple of crime novels, along with Carole Spearin McCauley's *Cold Steal* (1991), to risk a bisexual heroine. In *Skid* Violet avenges the death of her iconic private investigator father 'Victor', assassinated on St Valentine's Day, in an oedipal narrative investigation of family origins. She is a femme parody of the ghost of her father. But whilst there are traces of parody in virtually all the feminist crime novels I have so far interrogated, none employ the device so self-consciously as those of Sarah Schulman.

Focusing specifically on the first of these novels then, *The Sophie Horowitz Story* was published in 1984 by the lesbian Naiad Press of Florida. Schulman's first novel, set in Lower East Side New York, reveals a cornucopia of literary and political conventions skewered on a sharp satiric wit. The eponymous hera is a writer on a low-budget women's monthly *Feminist News*, started collectively three years previously. With a circulation of seven thousand (plus one thousand distributed free to women in prison), the publication is a parochial forum for feminist exposition and expostulation. Sophie's column is called 'On the Right and Left'. She is stimulated into this stint of investigative reporting by the arrest of a notorious terrorist and her teenage exemplar Germaine Covington, symbol of American disaffected youth. Party to a bungled bank raid, first Germaine is captured and then a faked death frees her. The plot is further enriched by another fabled feminist, Laura Wolfe, who escapes from the scene of this crime, and is pursued by the worshipful sleuthing of Sophie Horowitz. As another remarks, 'looking for Laura Wolfe is a personal journey' (81).

The book has certain thematic similarities with *Killing Wonder* by Dorothy Bryant.[16] In presenting two icons of feminist intervention, elevated to mythical status by an idealizing sub-culture, Schulman addresses the same awed construction of heras. By constantly satirizing the process of sanctification that such self-made martyrs condone, Schulman parodies the resultant disempowerment of the more humble feminist hack. Laura Wolfe was part of a group called Women Against Bad Things, who had 'some kind of politics which none of us understood. Whatever we did, they didn't like it . . .' (5). She addresses the moral prescriptiveness which can emanate from such censorious campaigns, and there is some resonance with the then contemporary movements in feminism which were perceived by some lesbians as anti-pornography and seemingly anti-sex. Laura uses sex as ideological recruitment: 'Laura made me do a whole song and dance just to get a little feel' (7). The novel is, in part, a reaction against this feminist prescriptivity, exposing political hypocrisy.

Germaine Covington turns out to be implicated in framing Laura Wolfe, together with a coterie of accomplices with inverted identities: the District Attorney is a fence, a respected journalist, a sadomasochist clone, a doctor who overdoses an immigrant, an academic who deals cocaine, along with winos who are FBI agents and a radical lawyer who is an avaricious status-seeker. Laura Wolfe, terrorist, appears in the guise of a nun. *The Sophie Horowitz Story* is a parody of 'types', whose ascribed meanings are constantly shifting. The stereotypes derive from both the dominant and the alternative cultural arena, and the only stable point in this satirical onslaught – this literary *carnival* – is Sophie. In her ironic humour she distances herself (and the reader) from the semantic cacophony.

Identity is foregrounded in the novel: Sophie is looking for Laura, and for 'herself'. The reader's pleasure derives from the recognition not of selfhood, but of roles. Schulman deploys metafictional frames to obfuscate these binaries of self/roles, authentic/inauthentic, truth/fiction. Traditional detective fiction is a predictable, highly formalized genre offering pleasure and release of tension through the affirmation of received and uncontested meanings. For the Jewish/feminist/lesbian reader of *The Sophie Horowitz Story* there is some pleasurable complicity with the text in its representation of familiar (sub-)cultural signs. However, the reader becomes disconcerted as these are undermined by parody. The reader's resultant unease reflects realistically her social positioning, allowing expression to the constant, unconscious shifting of roles/selves necessary for social interaction.

Sophie's narration, in the first person, creates the illusion of a central, stable, reliable disseminator of information. Relying on the convention of the detective as confidant and arbiter of truth, the text seduces the reader into a fantasy world, a semiotic *jouissance*, a carnivalized urban crime novel. Even Sophie, however, fails to stay in character at times, missing vital clues, and relying on an intertextual construction of fictional frames within frames to keep her investigation going. One such operates through the character of King James (a literary pun on the Authorized Version), a prolific mystery writer whose heroes are 'real professionals', 'smooth and daring' (unlike Sophie); they 'always know just what to do' (44). The author, who in key crime-writing tradition, is a woman writing under a male pseudonym, takes another apartment in Sophie's building, which overlooks hers in the manner of Hitchcock's *Rear Window*.

Mrs Noseworthy first permeates Sophie's consciousness through the incessant noise of her typing, a metonymic reference perhaps to the pervasiveness of fiction. She is a parody of the spinster sleuth, an impeccably polite, bespectacled pastiche of the patriarchally defined Miss Marple/ Pym/Silver:

> She was, what else can I say, a little old lady . . . Her hair was grey, her face was wrinkled, her dress went down below her knee. (78)

However, she extrapolates their subversive strengths:

> don't underestimate me because I have grey hair. We needn't be macho to be powerful, my dear. (99)

Sitting in her rocking chair, stroking her cat, Mrs Noseworthy proceeds to dissect the process of the investigation and advise her juvenile disciple in a reversal of the classic Holmes/Watson dialogue. She rejects the persona of the detecting super-hero, faultless in every deduction, claiming even 'Henrietta Bell, my greatest detective, makes mistakes' (81). In giving Sophie a copy of one of her adventures, *Murder in the Missionary Position*, Schulman enacts another jibe at convention. When Mrs Noseworthy pulls up at the scene of the final denouement, whisking Sophie away in her lavender BMW, it transpires that her tip-off to the police (in her best Italian accent) ensured the judicious capture of the murderer, the mercenary Mukul Garg. Another recapitulation ensues, suffused with a fictional self-reflexivity comically contrived.

Writing, intertextuality, literary self-consciousness: *The Sophie Horowitz Story* is unrelentingly metafictional. Sophie's investigative trajectory is driven by her nose for a journalistic scoop, and this story is continually remaking itself as one level of interpretation is supplanted by another. Towards the end, Sophie stumbles home and muses on the interrelatedness of the primary characters; they have 'become each other's art' (143).

> The story was almost over. Soon I'd have to sit down and write it. There's a certain relief when that moment comes. I'd lived with these people and this information and now that time was almost up. I could say goodbye to them. (143)

Sophie writes as the author, creating a box-like world into which the reader is inculcated too. The impression is that once the book/box is closed, the characters cease to exist. Indeed, they all seem to disappear within the narrative – Germaine Covington (in a classic thriller cliché) goes into a toilet stall, climbs out through the window and is seen no more; Vivian and Laura Wolfe drive off into deepest New York; Sophie herself, in the final line, is swallowed into the city skyline. Her manuscripts, 'written off' by *Feminist News* as male-identified, are consequently binned. Even the text will disappear.

Writing is seen as a commodity, demystifying the bourgeois romance of expression-as-art. Sophie's motivation for the story is at least partly based in the status and career enhancement such a scoop would bring. Writing sex, though, is a more commercial prospect; Sophie needs to make money quickly so she attacks the typewriter as The Lesbian Pornographer. Private enterprise is cramped by the intention to make it 'real', none of the words are right, and Sophie is stymied at first base. This text thus connives with other lesbian fictions to articulate the gap between the experience and expression of lesbian sex. Whilst the passage could be read as prioritizing experience and 'the body' over writing and language (as an inauthentic construct), I feel the point being made here is that of 'man-made language', which alienates women from similar processes of construction. Women are socialized, however, into reading and writing male subject positions – Sophie swops from lesbian to gay porn, typing a short 'stroke' story of two motorcycle men and a sailor, sellable for fifty dollars. When Evan, her Boy America misfit lodger, tries, however, his 'What makes a Woman Good in Bed' makes 3,000 dollars. His ability to exchange subject positions is an expression of his own gender identity, which defines the available options.

The commodification of identity can also be seen in the way Schulman chooses to depict ethnicity, in particular Jewishness, expressed metonymically through food. Caught in Pizza Hut playing Pac-Man with her brother, Sophie observes:

> Suddenly Ms Pac-Man appears on the electric screen. She's in a maze. She has to gobble up as many little blue dots as she can before the monsters catch her. It's social realism about women and over-eating. (67)

It is a pertinent remark – the prevalence of food in the novel metonymically asserts its Jewishness, but also provides a cultural reference point for all women preoccupied with the inevitable appropriation, treatment, distribution, and fetishism of food. Sophie's investigations are punctuated not by bourbon or Black Label, but blintzes, borscht, and bagels.[17]

Even her Jewish identity is foregrounded as a kind of fiction. In chapter 37, Sophie takes the day off from investigating. In an attempt to reassure herself she visits the Jewish museum. Her understanding of the Holocaust and other systematic pogroms is mediated through exhibits, films, shows, newspapers, and books, the fictionality underscored by describing leading Nazis as an 'infamous cast of characters' (145).[18] Sophie sits down in front of a television which presents a short piece called 'Grandma', unintelligible to the gentile reader:

> What are you doing wearing that *shmata*? You're a *shanda* for the *goyim* . You should only get a good job and earn a living so you shouldn't be a *schnorrer*. (147)

Blending a mass media technology with such a symbol of authentic Jewishness together in a framework labelled art, for common consumption, is indeed post-modern, and for the gentile reader its use of strange nouns renders it almost science-fictional. The novel also concentrates on various aspects of sexual identities, and the vagaries of lesbian culture, 'a certain cynicism developed collectively' (112). As one Black character puts it: 'Well Sophie, we all seem to have our ethnocentricities' (89).

Thus *The Sophie Horowitz Story* can certainly be categorized as parody and excess. The society depicted is indeed caught in a consumerist spectacle which renders political opposition difficult if not purely representational. Affiliated to different, intersecting subcultures, the subject is constantly being reconstructed by consumption, but the mechanism being employed here is not one of meaningless oppression but pleasure. *The Sophie Horowitz Story* is not a depressing book – Schulman's satire is sharp, and the more salient aspects of investigation are tempered, like many mystery novels, by romance. The relationship between Sophie and her lover Lillian is not mythical perfection. Together they are funny, kind, irritable, loving, and sexy – an 'ordinary' couple. Humanity is ultimately left with the personal, rather than the political, and in this way too the text can be described as post-modern. It finishes on such an insular note:

> Sometimes I worry about what's going to happen to me. Sometimes I fantasize about the easy life, but really I don't expect it. I just want to enjoy things, have friends and keep my life interesting. If I stick to my instincts, the world will follow. (158)

Schulman's second novel *Girls, Visions, and Everything* was published in 1986 by the feminist publishing company The Seal Press of Seattle, with the help of the National Endowment for the Arts. It is not a crime novel, but I wish to discuss it briefly as an adjunct to *The Sophie Horowitz Story*, and the third novel *After Delores*. *Girls, Visions, and Everything* lacks the ontological direction of a thriller; its movement is less compulsive and more perambulatory. Set in the same Lower East Side, the protagonist walks the streets, marking out the geography of an urban landscape punctuated by a city mapped out with emotional happenings. Locations are symbols of connection, and constant references to criss-crossing streets remind the reader of the systematic patterns of neighbourhood and community, an antithesis to the alienation of ascending Reaganism. *Girls, Visions, and Everything* is about Lila Futuransky's New York, 'the most beautiful woman she had ever known' (177).

The social realism of the hard-boiled thriller embodies the perspective of the underworld – the streets have to be mean, and filled with crime and corruption. The detective himself is an outlaw, a man in search of a hidden truth – as Raymond Chandler has described him 'a complete man and a common man, yet an unusual man . . . a man of honor'.[19] Lila Futuransky is that man. Her position as a poor Jewish lesbian, pitted against the burgeoning bourgeoisification and consequential breakdown of her urban community, places her in honourable antipathy to the Protestant middle-class conventionalists instigating gentrification and upward mobility. Modelling herself as *On The Road* with Jack Kerouac, Lila Futuransky's adventure is similarly self-exploratory, but based on the *female* experiences a city offers. Her comparison with Jack is the dream of being an outlaw, reconstructed by a feminist consciousness captured within her separate sub-culture; Lila's trip is her constant circling between lovers, friends, and compatriots.

Girls, Visions, and Everything owes an explicit debt to Kerouac, whose writing exposed the Beat Generation of the 1950s to mass consumption. He recorded the life of the American hero/traveller. In *On the Road* (1957) Sal Paradise begins his journey with the words:

> Somewhere along the line I knew there'd be girls, visions, everything; some where along the line the pearl would be handed to me.[20]

The pearl, read as a symbol of female sexuality, is something the active masculine narrator seeks to own. The maleness of this role is also located historically in the figure of the *flâneur*, the nineteenth-century explorer of the modern urban environment. Janet Wolff has described him, and George Simmel's 'metropolitan personality', the *stranger*, in her discussion of the gendering of modernity:

> The *flâneur* – the stroller – is a central figure in [Walter] Benjamin's essays on Baudelaire and nineteenth-century Paris. The streets and arcades of the city are the home of the *flâneur*, who, in Benjamin's phrase, 'goes botanizing on the asphalt'.[21] The anonymity of the crowd provides an asylum for the person

> on the margins of society; here Benjamin includes both Baudelaire himself as a *flâneur*, and the victims and murderers of Poe's detective stories . . . The *flâneur* is a modern hero; his experience . . . is that of a freedom to move about in the city, observing and being observed, but never interacting with others.[22]

He is the knowing, seeing detective, the man whose fragmentary and transient observations allow him to comment on the 'modern condition'. In his freedom to colonize public space he is clearly male – as Wolff says 'Women could not stroll alone in the city'.[23] Conversely, Wolff points out that for Parisian poet Baudelaire the lesbian was the heroine of modernism, although his 'mixed admiration for the lesbian has much to do with her (supposed) "mannishness"',[24] according to Benjamin, confusing gender with erotic orientation. This configuration of textual images endows *Girls, Visions, and Everything* with complex literary echoes evoking the romantic investigator who privileges experience, and the journey, over the arrival.

A similar sort of sardonic wit to *The Sophie Horowitz Story* suffuses *Girls, Visions, and Everything*, but there is also sadness – a sense of decaying nostalgia for streets filled with sisters and brothers sitting languid on the stoop, swopping stories and cementing *communitas*. This is the feminization of the street, the underworld with a human face, with its own moral and family code. It is rich kids who beat the gays and harass the poor, the prostitutes, and the pushers. The lesbians are on the streets, working the burger bar, cruising the ice-cream parlour, and clubbing it at the Kitsch-Inn, currently showing a lesbian version of *A Streetcar Named Desire*. Lila meets Emily here, performing as Stella Kowalski. The shows change every weekend, they are more for the cast than any audience, the art consumed by its own production. The romance between Lila and Emily is ostensibly the main development in the novel, structuring its five parts, one to three depicting its ascension, and four and five the conflicts within itself. The final chapter sees Lila torn between the 'masculine' trajectory of *On The Road* individualism, the expression of the urban street-poem, and the 'feminine' stability of emotion and relationship commitment, which is depicted as static. The dream of adventure has been symbolically transferred to her friend Isabel, to whom she has given her copy of the book, and who now urges Lila that

> 'you can't stop walking the streets and trying to get under the

> city's skin because if you settle in your own little hole, she'll change so fast that by the time you wake up, she won't be yours anymore . . . Don't do it buddy.' (178)

This constant engagement/disengagement with change and transformation is signified by the urban landscape, which is out of their control. Even the protective zones are folding, and yet there are pockets of resistance which pierce the city's metaphoric paralysis with parody: Gay Pride is one such representation, 50,000 homosexuals parading through the city streets, of every type, presenting the Other of heterosexuality, from Gay Bankers to the Gay Men's Chorus singing 'It's Raining Men'.

The Schulman novels each contain secondary hypodiegetic[25] worlds of performance which further fictionalize the primary level of narration. The highly parodic Worst Performance Festival in *Girls, Visions, and Everything* is a two-fingered salute to the liberal avant-garde, earlier depicted in the description of an off-Broadway show which Isabel and Lila see and identify as 'fake social realism':

> All were pretending that they were dramatically interpreting the reality of New York street life. The actors strutted around, jiving like bad imitations of Eddie Murphy imitating a Black teenager imitating what he saw Eddie Murphy doing on TV the night before. The lesbian characters kissed each other and hit each other. The gay male characters made jokes about the sizes of each others penises. The Black characters ran around with afro-picks in their pockets and occasionally stopped combing their hair long enough to play three-card monte while saying 'motha-fucka' a lot and grabbing their own crotches. All of this provided an appropriately colorful background for the white heterosexual characters to expose their deeply complex emotional lives. (18)

Lila, dressed in a tight black t-shirt that says 'Soon To Be A Major Homosexual', comperes the Worst Performance Festival to an audience she derides, opening with the words:

> 'I want to remind you that all of us here together tonight, well, we are a community, a community of enemies. And we have to stay close to each other so we can watch out and protect ourselves . . . Tonight we are proud to introduce our panel of minority celebrity judges from competing cliques to vote down each other's friends.' (149)

It is this level of ironic distance which structures the reader into a fidgety self-consciousness; there are passages of apparently direct emotional verisimilitude between Lila and Emily which suture them into a kind of kitchen-sink realism; then the reader's identification is undercut by an unrelentingly parodic perspective which reappears in the guise of metafictional performance. The text tries to juxtapose a jumble of readerly responses, almost jerking the reader into some consciousness of her activity of creating imaginative space. She reinvents New York from her position of other as a heterotopia of cultural intertextuality; she *is* Jack Kerouac, the character not the author, claiming, even as a Jewish lesbian, that:

> 'the road is the only image of freedom that an American can understand.' (164)

Thus Schulman uses the idea of a perceiving subject caught in some spacial construct which is organized around her/his consciousness; but she inhibits the sense-making process (or narrative hermeneutic) by constantly invoking and corrupting the conventional literary topology. For example, by the use of an imaginary and metaphorical 'Zone of the Interior',[26] Schulman creates a civilized zone of others which is being encroached upon by the moral wilderness of capitalistic aggrandizement.

The street is an image of freedom and paradoxically of violence – she walks unmolested until the final part of the book whence she is sexually harassed by Hispanics, and saved from serious injury from potential queer-bashers by the Black and sick drug dealer Ray. Lila's zone is breaking down:

> People's minds were splitting open right there on the sidewalk. (14)

The fictional worlds start clashing together: Blanche DuBois appears to Emily aged 85 and begging for a dollar. Lila resorts to Emily with a resignation that can only be anti-romance, knowing it is the wrong decision, and nostalgically lamenting the end of the road of self-hood:

> 'I don't know who I am right now', she thought. 'I want to go back to the old way.' (178)

This whimsical nostalgia also highlights some disillusionment with the post-modernist models of space – wherein the public and private are collapsed on to the street, and the same space is being used by different people in different ways. Hierarchies still exist. Being part of a bigger spectacle, being visible as one sub-culture among many, may not necessarily create empowerment, only more competition over a diminishing resource.

After Delores, first published by E. P. Dutton in 1988, and by Sheba Feminist Press in Britain in 1990, is another urban crime novel set in the Lower East Side. A treatment of *After Delores* was broadcast on the British lesbian and gay magazine programme *Out On Tuesday* in March 1990.[27] Introduced by another New York writer Storme Webber as a 'Manhattan microcosm' portraying the 'good dreams and the bad dreams of our neighbourhood', the introductory cameo consisted of Webber's prose poem, listing the many marginalized people resident in Lower East Side, multi-cultural refugees rejected from all parts of the country, and the world.

Schulman, interviewed on the programme, commented on how this battle between disenfranchised sub-cultures, and the bourgeoisification of the Lower East Side, form the backdrop to each of her novels. Describing artists stepping over the homeless on the way to the gallery, she observes:

> society is so stratified that people can occupy the same physical space and never see each other, and also have completely different experiences of that space.

This would seem to be a geographical manifestation of the literary Chinese-box structure, Schulman arguing for an actual separation of cultural locations within the same material site. As Brian McHale[28] has pointed out, post-modernist fiction makes literal the Bakhtinian metaphor of 'worlds' of discourse, and within the novel this polyphonic synchronization of difference produces the effect of *heteroglossia* . Historically, more cosmopolitan cultures with competing sub-cultures have been heterogeneous, the languages or discourses struggling ideologically for precedence,[29] or mutual co-existence. They are paradoxically exclusive and interrelated, zones of experience within a heterotopian space. New York is perhaps the paradigmatic example of a modern heterotopia, and hence *After Delores* enacts these spatio-semiological 'combat zones'. Identity becomes fraught with definition; in one minor example the protagonist and her Hispanic friend Coco Flores see a friend's son Daniel:

> 'That's no Daniel,' Coco said . . . 'That's Juan Colon. Last year he was Juan Colon at any rate. This year he changed his name to Johnny. He's from PR [Puerto Rico].' 'That's no Juan Colon,

> I'm telling you . . . his name is Daniel Piazzola. He's from Argentina.' . . . Johnny Colon, what a liar. (108)

Aside from the ethnic and cultural heteroglossia, there are also continual instances of dramatic, fictional worlds inside the supposedly real, primary level of narration dictated in the first person, the mode historically associated with expressive realism. Schulman self-consciously obscures any unitary monological referent to 'reality' by interlacing the text with framing devices which foreground its instability. Coco Flores is always telling stories; two major characters, Beatriz and Charlotte, are theatrical actors perpetually locked into their own psycho-drama; the *murdered* friend Punkette is the character described as 'the most real' (30). The narrator is, according to Schulman speaking on *Out On Tuesday*, occupying her own

> place of sadness that pushes people into a hallucinatory relationship to the world.

The narrator's space is separate, and interpretive, subjected to being 'on the edge' emotionally and discursively. Her life as an alcoholic working-class waitress is suffused with neglect; she is nailed by despair, a breaking, boundaryless despondency which is the result of Delores leaving for another lover. The narrator has no name; in another effort to problematize the demarcation of zones and spaces, Schulman deprives the text of a clearly determinated speaker, intending that the extremity of her pain will inculcate the reader into

> an unclear space between them and her.[30]

The reader's identification, then, becomes another site of contestation for autonomy. Within the post-modernist text these constituent elements of interconnecting space seldom cohere at the psychological or cultural level, as Peter Currie has argued:

> discontinuities of narrative and disjunctions of personality cannot be overcome – by an appeal to the logic of a unifying metalanguage, a dominant stable discourse, settled hierarchy, or the constituency of the core self.[31]

Hence perhaps that by the conclusion of the novel the central emotional predicament of lost love is unresolved and unchanged, the last lines expressing:

> None of it means anything to me. There was only one thing I really missed. I missed Delores. (158)

The novel, characterized by a nihilistic resignation, resists the convention of closure and re-established normalcy which is an essential prerequisite of classic crime fiction. Nevertheless the narrative trajectory of investigation, tinged with jealousy and revenge, motivates the reader's need for revelation. The protagonist's motivation to find Punkette's killer is confused by her private outrage at being spurned, and instead of being a self-appointed neutral arbiter of social justice, her moral imperative is shown up to be flawed (perhaps an implicit message to the more masculine murder mysteries). The book is punctuated by many verbal interactions and internal musings on murder. She will kill Delores, or the rival, or herself, or Charlotte, or Daniel. The clear categories of detective fiction, or 'functions', to use Propp,[32] are obfuscated by being resident in the same person, hinting towards their interdependence perhaps. Finally she does kill Punkette's murderer, who is a taxi-driver, and she comments:

> The thing about a cab is that you sit back in the leather like a movie star and instead of being part of the street and the life of the city, you only watch it, you don't come into contact. (150–1)

She annihilates the person who is not part of the city.

Textually, the reader's desire for revenge is satisfied, and the mechanism of moral come-uppance is employed. However, the narrator's triumph is curtailed:

> 'I got the guy who killed Punkette. I made everything right. I suffered but I never gave up and now I have a victory, do you hear me? I have a goddamn victory. I won.'
> 'What are you talking about?' Beatriz said. 'You weren't going through all of this to find some man. You are just a lonely person who had absolutely nothing better to do. Don't fool yourself.' (152)

After Delores punctures the transcendent moral prerogative of the hard-boiled dick with this pastiche of proud victory. An injection of the self-absorbed mundanity of human emotion and motivation is a symbolic stripping-down for the likes of Mickey Spillane and his *I, the Jury* ilk. As the protagonist plaintively laments, 'Who's going to get justice for me?' (125) – she is a loser, an anti-hero, denuded even of the romance of outlaw status.

Whereas *The Sophie Horowitz Story* seemed to represent a reasonably positive view of lesbian love, *Girls, Visions, and Everything* contained ambivalences which have become articulated as anti-romance by *After Delores*. The lesbian novel has been restrained by the need and expectation of its readership to represent lesbianism as an affirming lifestyle. *After Delores* resists this romantic enhancement and reproduces an urban realism evoking the hard-boiled tradition. This protagonist does not transcend her environment, however, and remains removed from any emotional or sexual reward. Even the displaced romance between her and Delores does not satisfy the reader, as Coco Flores says:

> 'It doesn't matter who Delores was, why you loved her then and why you hate her now. Delores is a hallucination . . .' (103)

The protagonist has a few sexual encounters which are notably unromantic: she constructs her own fantasy of Charlotte who actually fucks her brutally leaving her with welts and bruises. Looking for her later she peers through the peephole of Charlotte's apartment to see her making love passionately with Beatriz, a scene calculated to underscore her own exclusion. Sexually excited, she rushes round to see a lesbian drag-queen Priscilla Presley:

> She put on rhumba records and we danced around laughing and drinking from the bottle in between sloppy, drunken kisses. Then Elvis sang, 'Wise men say, even fools fall in love'.
> That's when I murmured 'Don't be cruel', and fell on my knees at Priscilla's feet, burying my face in her polyester. (128–9)

The sex is non-threatening by being displaced and enacted at a distance within a parodic eroticization of difference. By synthesizing a 1950s bar culture of butch and femme roles with the mythical incarnation of its two most totemic heterosexuals, Schulman blends the post-modernist revival of romantic irony with lesbian kitsch. Romance is impacted with fantasy with a literary vehemence, determinedly made raw by the erstwhile Delores, as she so bitterly insists:

> You always fall for someone thinking they're someone they're not. Sometimes I think that fashion was made for Delores, because it's so dependent on illusion. (11)

After Delores, by finishing as it began with the same emotional pain which the narrator has not managed to transcend or learn from in the classical realist epistemological manner, rejects the 'grand narrative' of self-improvement. She does not interpret her experience, she has lost the ability to locate herself. Whilst briefly striking a feminist note by the obliteration of a perpetrator of male violence ('It was a man. A man did it' (136)), the narrator still remains positioned as victim. The more extreme feminist ideologies of the universal removal of men are not going to effect change for women. By also so strongly rejecting romance, by rejecting truth in favour of performance, by refusing the representation of an emancipatory parable, Schulman can be said to be expressing suspicion of such universalizing metanarratives. The paralysing sense of loss which suffuses *After Delores* is doubly painful – not only is romance revealed as yet one more fiction, but there is also the grief experienced by the loss of the utopian dream of the 1970s: that you *can* have a relationship with women, and that they are better.

The sadness resulting from this loss of the specificity of gay pride, of lesbian community, of a strong, unified identity, is the flip side of post-modernism, registering with progressively more impetus in these texts. Perhaps this mirrors a wider view. In this chapter I am not wishing to argue that feminism and post-modernism are one and the same, but there are important points of juncture: first, in the desire to denaturalize dominant ideology, and second, in the injection of cultural difference as a field of operation. However, feminism, as Linda Hutcheon points out,[33] is a political force which desires material change; post-modernism is only a critique, with no real theory of agency or political resistance. There is a sense in which a post-modernist analysis does not do justice to Schulman's work – it must be seen as an intersection, along with Schulman's feminism; to read her work in this way must be to open up possibilities, not close them down. The three areas of post-modernism/feminism/authorship inform each other in the texts, but there are inevitably spaces, other strands which are not chased. For example, using the interpretive perspectives I have chosen makes it difficult to communicate the strong political spirit present in all the books: is this caused by a textual disjuncture, or, more likely, the limits of critical method? Or is it, perhaps, that the political impetus of these novels actually *clashes* with a post-modernist aesthetic? Fragmentation and diversity can also cause alienation and apathy, and anaesthetize activism.

In Schulman's fourth novel, *People in Trouble* (Sheba Feminist Press 1990), post-modernist styles and themes continue to be represented, but self-critically. In form the book comes closer to realism than previous works, hinting perhaps at a creeping disillusionment with parody and popular genre. Three central characters work out their relationship to each other, sexuality, and gender: Kate, an artist, is married to Peter; she is also lovers with Molly. Kate's political awakening takes place through her relationship with Molly, who is 'watch[ing] her friends die of AIDS' (back cover). One such friend, Scott, causes Kate to observe that

> 'Sometimes a person has to stop talking about art for a moment and take a look around.' (166)

This novel has the effect of mirroring post-modernism back on itself, as though stepping back, encouraging the reader, Janus-like, both to employ and destroy its own cultural practice. For example, *People in Trouble* expands the apocalyptic tone typical of writers such as Baudrillard, taking this as an opening moment:

> It was the beginning of the end of the world but not everyone noticed right away. Some people were dying. (1)

Then, through a narrative of political enlightenment, it proceeds to reject ironic, depressed disengagement in favour of a compulsion to act, an imperative to change, which is after all dependent on some hope of material revolution. 'Resistance', ultimately, replaces ironic reflection as the key theme. Kate sets fire to her own artwork (metafictionally entitled 'People in Trouble'), killing the billionaire developer who was also its commissioner. Ronald Horne's emporia are incarnations of the post-modernist spirit; his luxury hotel The Castle is modelled on Early Modern Colonialism, his Downtown City, consisting of sky-rise condominiums grouped together as 'Freedom Place', or 'Liberty Avenue', has 'all the elements of a made-to-order American shrine' (28). By incinerating Horne, the text disposes of post-modernism's emptiest excesses. The representation 'People in Trouble' is replaced by a concrete array of 'real' people in trouble, in a distinctly didactic parting shot:

> On the way to his apartment [Molly] was thinking about how sometimes the city gets so beautiful that it's impossible to walk even one block without getting an idea. The idea she got was to try to remember the truth and not just the stories . . .
>
> 'Suffering can be stopped', James said. 'But it can never be avenged, so survivors watch television. Men die, their lovers wait to get sick. People eat garbage or worry about their careers. Some lives are more important than others. Some deaths are shocking, some invisible. We are a people in trouble. We do not act.' (227–8)

Schulman's fourth novel is a warning not to confuse style with political transformations. She manages to express the doubts of those of us suspicious of post-modernism's ironic detachment, which threatens to anaesthetize political subjects. I feel some sympathy for the reader staggering through 'word magic' in order to construct a political praxis; post-modernism can indeed seem like a spell cast to mystify and immobilize. What draws Schulman's work together, however, is a playful exploration of the precarious state of identity, which also manages to implicate political responsibility for action.

Schulman's view of identity as unstable, as fiction, does not *dispose* of identity as a useful category for political change. Her fiction lays bare 'the fear . . . that once we have deconstructed identity, we will have nothing (nothing, that is, which is stable and secure) upon which to base a politics'.[34] Jane Gallop addresses this dialectic in *The Daughter's Seduction*:

> I do not believe in some new 'identity' which would be adequate and authentic. But I do not seek some sort of liberation from identity. That would lead only to another form of paralysis – the oceanic passivity of undifferentiation. *Identity must be continually assumed and immediately called into question.*[35] [My italics]

Although she apparently presumes, in saying this, that there is a simple, stable position from which we can choose or discard an identity; that we can occupy a neutral identity-free space to begin with; and that there are no imposed identities generated by society, rejecting the liberal fallacy of stability should not prevent a positive assumption of identity and action being taken. One can also, by an expedient extension, exchange the term 'identity' for 'politics': knowing that 'politics' too is a fiction fraught with contradiction should not deprive the individual subject of a desire and responsibility for change. In this struggle

> we need both to theorize essentialist spaces from which to speak and, simultaneously, to deconstruct those spaces to keep them from solidifying.[36]

It is this doubling movement which Schulman's fiction narrativizes so lucidly. Perhaps it is not yet the time to turn post-modernism into post-mortemism.

The structure of the classic detective story: the presentation of an enigma and the resolution of that enigma through sequence, causality, and the application of a positivistic rationality expressed through self-determined consciousness, is unseated in these post-modern '*anti* detective' novels, as Jeanne C. Ewert has called them.[37] The linear/teleological structure of the traditional form is disrupted precisely because

> The detective novel is eminently suited to postmodern manipulation because its tacit dependence on the hermeneutic code offers the possibility of disabling that code. Moreover, its protagonist is a conventionally marginalized figure, one on the fringes of society, with no family, no interests other than work, and sometimes without even a name – an apt metaphor for a decentred self and a fragmented consciousness.

This detective spends much of the time walking around in circles, the movement echoing the so-called trajectory of the feminine sentence,[38] enclosed in a labyrinthian, hopeless search for identity and authority. Even the development through time, the logic of the unravelling investigation proceeding sequentially to closure, is disrupted. The post-modern puzzle is not meant to be solved. However, this labyrinth of culture is 'a tension-filled environment' in which 'competitive interpellation is inevitable',[39] hence the potential for new subjectivities to be enunciated and released. Sarah Schulman's fiction offers us a radical deconstruction of the mythic crime narrative, which, like all successful deconstructions, signals the instability of the original form.

8

An unsuitable genre for a woman?

Kathleen Gregory Klein makes this assertion in *The Woman Detective: Gender and Genre* (1988):

> In a general way, all novels featuring women private eyes could be described as parodies.

By adopting the formula but changing this one significant element, authors

> undercut their protagonists to reinforce a social standard of female inequality and, in so doing, undermine the genre.

She calls it 'imitation without reconsideration'.[1] Klein rightly criticizes the implementation of shallow, excessively feminine stereotypes by many male authors, appealing instead for realism, pleading for 'plausible women . . . portraying authentic, lived experience'.[2] She suggests ways for the writer to evade the supposed masculinist norms and values of the conventional crime novel, and so disrupt the textual structure. Klein criticizes unenlightened male authors for 'undermining' the genre, whilst inciting others (feminists) to 'rethink it, reformulate it, re-vision it'.[3] This paradox illustrates the parameters of this book: despite commonsensical attempts to gender the detective novel as masculine, it could also be argued that whilst the form undoubtably can foreground masculine and misogynistic structures, there is also an argument for the form being fundamentally friendly to feminists. Whether this compatibility constitutes breaking the form depends on one's initial starting point as to what constitutes the genre in the first place. Whereas Klein advocates realism as the preferred mode for feminist crime fiction, consigning parody to being an inane repetition of a male form, I think the formal characteristics of the genre are more ambiguous, needing further exploration. In this concluding chapter, therefore, I shall attempt to draw out some of the structural implications for the detective genre, coming out of the preceding chapters' close textual analysis, by now considering the form itself.

In attempting to assert a line of contiguity from the earliest women writers such as Ka (*Mrs Julia Sherlock Holmes*), Mary Hatch (*The Strange Disappearance of Eugene Comstocks* (1895), which featured a transvestite 'anti-female anti-hero'),[4] through the Golden Age writers, the 1940s, 1950s and 1960s, the Second Wave writers, the liberal feminists, socialist feminists, Black and lesbian feminist authors, satire provides one sympathetic strain. Rick Eden, in his article 'Detective Fiction as Satire',[5] argues convincingly for recognizing that *all* varieties of detective fiction are in fact satirical. To concur with his critical evaluation should provoke an examination of feminist crime fiction for the ways in which its *apparent* rebellion actually represents an example of the purest classical form. Starting with George Grella's view of detective fiction as comedy,[6] Eden uses Grella's identification of the detective hero as the comic hero of the sort Northrop Frye has called an *eiron*.[7] According to Grella, detective fiction is a two-tiered form, a comedy of love followed by a comedy of manners. The first is optional, the second essential, and often a satire:

> specifically, a relatively restrained form of the genre Frye calls Menippean satire.[8]

Menippean satire, in its simplest form, consists of a dialogue between stylized characters who merely mouth ideas. The two speakers are an eiron and an *alazon*, someone usually revealed to be 'a self-deluded fool and pompous ass'.[9] Eden continues:

> Detective fiction, not only of the formal school, but of all varieties – begins with the fundamental satiric situation: an eiron enters a society of alazons or impostors and begins to expose them. Eirons are a distinctive type of hero . . . They are almost always outsiders in some sense; often they are actually from another region or country or social class. Morally, intellectually and even rhetorically, they are superior to the alazonic society and consequently aloof. They are not participants so much as unbiased observers.[10]

The second novel by Mary Wings, *She Came in a Flash* (1988), illustrates this theme well. Bostonian Emma Victor, Wings' serial heroine, is regionally displaced to California, 'a fantasy place in everyone's mind'. As a critique of New Age religion (and all cults by extension), Emma investigates the Divine Vishnu Inspiration Commune, a quasi-Hindu quagmire of miscegenated sophistry which has seduced the sister of Emma's best friend, Lana Flax. Lana is murdered principally because of her naive belief in the virtue of Vishnu:

> 'She wasn't just blindly devoted to Vishnu, she was just blind.' (198)

Vishnu himself is a caricature of the benevolent patriarch. Within the period of narration he exists principally as a corpse behind a climatically controlled plexiglass coffin, kept cool to ensure the complete finalization of a financial fraud before the commune discovers his death and disintegrates. This image of benign patriarchy conceals the reality of the religion's corruption, in the form of crooked custodian Sadhima, international drugs dealer, despot, and Don Juan. Thus the benign *symbol* of patriarchy legitimates a covert but active aggressor.

Emma Victor the individual is continually contrasted with the undifferentiated mass of the Divine Vishnus; all dressed in yellow they are an anonymous, homogeneous 'buttercup crowd'. As sheep they have unanimity, and Emma as 'the new kid in school' (48) is an ingénue, and a paragon eiron:

> eirons know their limits. Even though superior, they have no exaggerated self-conceptions. Presumption is the single criterion for alazony, and eirons differ from alazons by not presuming to know what they don't or be what they aren't . . .
>
> Because eirons do not presume to know, they are full of queries; the alazons, by contrast, are full of answers, even if these are lies or half-truths.[11]

Emma is cautious and commonsensical. Her first discussion with an unnamed yellow woman yields little information, merely establishing the woman's eminent alazony:

> 'So how's the food here anyway?' I asked a woman at the rear of the moving flank. She was the only person not hugging or holding someone.
>
> 'You've never eaten here before?' she asked suspiciously . . . She glanced back at the yellow group continuing on without her. I was forcing her to slow down, separating one of the sheep from the flock.

> 'The food is good.' She looked at me carefully. I wasn't yellow and I wasn't eager enough.
> 'I guess I'm really lucky to experience this whole thing for fifteen dollars.' I tried. That was the ticket.
> 'Vishnu says you have to put effort and investment to get into anything,' she burbled.
> 'I guess I haven't tried hard enough.'
> 'But that's the secret,' she raised two pencil-thin eyebrows, 'You have to learn not to try.' (45–6)

The alazons' self-delusion is continually confirmed in an inverse relation to the eiron's discernment. Emma's dramatic function is to expose alazons using her ratiocinative powers, thus leading them into self-betrayal. These mythic functions are fulfilled to the letter as the bower of bliss is proved to be punctured by the phallic serpent. The feminist ideological project appropriates this structure to present patriarchy as synonymous with alazony, thus 'false consciousness' is revealed by an investigation into gender relations. It is a persuasive structure artfully interpellating the proto-feminist reader.

According to Eden, in understanding detective fiction as satire one can see the change from formal to hard-boiled as an evolution from Horatian to Juvenalian satire. In the hard-boiled school the alazonic society is more corrupt and dangerous, crime is no longer localized or potentially controllable. In the formal school the eiron attacks the alazon using *wit* (for example Gladys Mitchell's Mrs Bradley, or Miles Franklin's Zarl Osterley, more latterly Amanda Cross and Val McDermid employ this device), in the essential style of satire described by Frye:

> Verbal rather than physical dexterity is the eiron's primary weapon.[12]

This model evokes the Medusan laugh of feminism, which exposes through ridicule. The defining act of the detective is to reveal the real and sordid nature of the world, but this is achieved obliquely, through the sideways glance of satire. On a pragmatic level verbal rather than physical violence is a safer bet for women. In the hard-boiled school the narration is usually

> flat cold and understated, as though the narrator has absolutely no interest in or sympathy for the alazonic society, or exaggerated and obsessively detailed, as though the narrator finds the alazonic society's histrionic behaviour fascinating.[13]

Wing's first novel *She Came Too Late* , discussed in Chapter 5, is described as 'a contentious whodunnit in the Chandler tradition' (back cover), signifying hard-boiled detection. Chandler's typical linguistic style is continued in *She Came in a Flash*. Lana Flax is described as being 'like a collector doll, perfectly dressed in updated guru chic' (40), Sadhima:

> his full length tumble curls falling to the collar of his designer sportshirt . . . bent down to say something and gave me a shot of his parted hair and clean scalp. A baby shampoo commercial grown up and gone testosterone. (42)

Rick Eden suggests that this style should be read as satiric hyperbole: the alazonic society is indulging in self-parody, 'the impostors are overacting'.[14] The protagonist or eiron is also able to scrutinize the hysterical excesses of masculinity with a deflationary gaze. Masculinity conveniently ends up shooting itself in the foot.[15]

Within this intensely self-enclosed satire can the hero retain any of the reader's serious respect or identification? Does s/he need to? Eden concludes his own essay with Robert Parker's serial hero Spenser, asserting that his knightly perfection is a parody of the romance hero:

> Spenser exemplifies the sort of creation Aristotle warns against – the implausible possibility.[16]

Spenser's romantic and heroic aspirations are satirized from within the text by his lover Susan Silverman (and in *Looking for Rachel Wallace* by his lesbian client). The real target is the *idea(l) of heroism itself*. Eden observes several typical characteristics of the detective hero: he is just a little bit ridiculous; he fails to win a partner; he has not necessarily got superior strength, agility or stamina; in extreme cases he can even be revealed as an alazon himself – a fool or a scoundrel. He maintains that:

> satire features rather oblique and adulterated brands of heroism. Frye points out that 'one of the central themes of the *mythos* [of satire] is the disappearance of the heroic' . . . he is not a full-fledged hero.[17]

Eden takes his model of alazony even further to include not just the detective (who may overestimate his/her skills) but also the reader, who is duped by elaborate false clues, and faked pathways, into revealing her own gullibility. Thus she aspires to be an eiron (through identification with the hero), but fails and falls into the role of alazon. The reader, as a Watson, is at the mercy of structural, rather than avowedly political agendas. Watson is 'the one who advances the wrong solutions', says Franco Moretti.[18] Just like a woman, (s)he 'accumulates useless details';[19] (s)he is a spectator with a sideways glance:

> 'You see,' Holmes continually repeats, 'but you do not observe.'[20]

In surveying feminist crime fiction a differentiation must be made between two types: (a) those novels which are consciously satiric, employing a heroine who undermines her own transcendence (diverse writers include Barbara Wilson, Sarah Dreher, Mary Wings, Sarah Schulman, and Gillian Slovo), and (b) those novels which operate primarily within the romance mode, such as in the sub-genre of lesbian pulp, which deploy a mystery element primarily to frustrate the love interest (writers include Vicki P. McConnell, Claire McNab, Zenobia N. Vole, Marion Foster[21]). There is some overlap, but in principle within the romance framework everyone is promised happiness ever after, and within the satire nothing is really seen to change. The utopian urge is supplanted by the realism that crime can never be excised. Crime scenarios always return us to the beginning, to recover an original story. The only proper sequel is another satire and, as Eden points out, crime readers love a serial. To return to *She Came in a Flash*: although Emma has dutifully dicked her way through to the final denouement and victoriously vanquished the duplicitous Vishnus (verbally and without violence), there is no visible reparation, romantically anyway. After being shot in the leg she is picked up by partially paralysed techno-dyke and alfalfa farmer Roseanna:

> 'I'm not sexually attracted to you, Emma Victor,' Roseanna warned me with a possible wink. We undressed, removing clothes from our limp limbs with the ones that still moved and functioned. We got on the bed and put our assorted legs under the covers.
> 'I know,' I said, lying. (200–1)

True to other scenes in the narrative there is no sexual closure,[22] only an ambiguity which seems to mock the reader's romantic expectations. On the final page we find out that Emma's fantasy partner Frances from *She Came Too Late* has found herself another woman.

Emma, like Rochester, has been physically flawed, but Roseanna is no Jane Eyre, and Emma is left alone with only a hint of companionship. Certainly not enough to invoke a new kind of future.

I have concurred with the common convention that satire, as protest art, suits feminism's desire to parody patriarchal norms and forms. Conversely it is possible to suppose that usurpation could be limited by its very imitation of 'masculine' classical Menippean satire. If we concur with this notion of detective fiction as satire, this overriding classification tends to circumscribe the best efforts of feminists fundamentally to rewrite the form, and we may therefore agree with Jerry Palmer that

> the basic apparatus of the thriller can accommodate more or less any set of political beliefs, precisely because they constitute only a superficial layer.[23]

Perhaps it is more efficacious to examine those specific clichés imbuing crime fiction which, possibly *within an overall conformity*, can be appropriated by feminists for political ends. For example, many a misogynist has filled the need for that staple convention, an 'eminently murderable man'. The simple expansion of the moralistic dualism good/evil can incorporate a further specification female/male, or femininity/masculinity.[24] The desire for a comforting closure defies the pessimism of many earlier lesbian novels which culminated (and often fulminated) in murder or suicide. As the feminist author expresses her own fantasies of justice, her reader temporarily and figuratively gains membership to the law-making élite. By synthesizing the construction 'hero' with 'Woman', writers have been able to project fantasy images of independence and strength to counteract the prevailing fictional construct of woman-as-adjunct-to-man (Watson again).

In establishing the formal compatibilities between the detective novel form and feminism the description of the eiron seems to epitomize the feminist sleuth's battle with the patriarchy. She is a moral watchdog from the Other who paces the streets in order to expose sex/gender oppression. It is a standard device in lesbian pulp; previously noted examples include Kate Delafield and Carol Ashton, and there are more: Gail Murray in Zenobia N. Vole's *Osten's Bay* (1988),[25] Stephanie Nowland in *The Crystal Curtain* (1988) by Sandy Bayer,[26] Helen Keremnos in Canadian Eve Zaremba's series *A Reason to Kill* (1978), *Work for a Million* (1987), and *Beyond Hope* (1987).[27] All posit an independent agent of justice pronouncing guilt not just on a murderer, but also on masculinity as a social ill, by a process of investigatory revelation. Traditional crime fiction exonerates society by apportioning blame on to an individual. Feminist crime fiction makes guilt collective and social, and the need for change structural.

The conspiracy theory, also so necessary to the thriller structure, fits in perfectly with many feminists' suspicion of institutional power, seen as circumscribing female autonomy through diverse and devious means. The act of reading is a skilled deciphering of 'plots', so that the crime can be publicized. The thriller hero is a liberal fantasy antipathetic to state bureaucracy and authoritarianism, and can thus be adapted by the feminist to incriminate its agents and representatives; some examples include crooked police officers[28] such as Crant in Slovo's *Death Comes Staccato* and Pepteen in Joy Magezis' *Vanishing Act* (1988),[29] diplomats in Nancy Milton's *The China Option* (1984),[30] CIA agents in Wilson's *Murder in the Collective* and Wakefield's *The Price You Pay*, and social workers in Fitzgerald's *Marge* (1984). In the publication of feminist crime fiction the foregrounding of all types of crimes of exploitation against women has enabled them to be spoken in a public sphere, the expression not being obviously mediated by those potential perpetrators – men. Whereas crimes of sexual violence such as rape are often trivialized in popular thrillers, in feminist crime fiction the victims are validated by the reader's moral outrage as she is inculcated within a feminist hermeneutic. One could argue that sexual violence operates as a taboo fantasy in mainstream crime, but the context of feminist ideological signifiers would make a similar reading in this sub-genre very difficult. This result is gained in part by the position of the gaze, which shifts from being held by the perpetrator to the victim. The politics of the gaze is openly explored in feminist crime fiction, showing how it is not just sexed and gendered, but also implicated within racial paradigms. Because this genre is so crucially concerned with perception, this allows for a degree of reflective interrogation as to the mechanisms of scrutiny. At a crude level, instead of being titillated by the abused female body, we are inscribed within it, and allowed revenge.

The use of the heroic in the detective novel has been adopted successfully by the lesbian reader to explore notions of selfhood, set against a corrupt and hostile society. The central narrative device 'discovery' can be viewed in relation to her desire to make sense of the malignancy at work in the novel, and by extension placate the pain of the pervading force of homophobia in her world. The process of narrativity, of story-making itself, is thematized and problematized by the form. The lesbian feminist heroine is allowed to invert the meanings ascribed to her by the process of reverse discourse and use narrative structures self-consciously to ram the message home: dominant (patriarchal) society is hence the evil world of crime, and the lesbian feminist perversely the perfect citizen, the repository of morals and all goodness and truth. Her personal narrative of conversion and agency has roots in the early lesbian feminist novel, her politicization is common to all protest literature.

But, whilst there remains a tradition of the unified heroine in feminist fiction, the exploration of fractured selves, frustrated pleasures, and the importance of *communitas* conspire to usurp complacent representations of an uncomplicated individual self, with particular insight when psychoanalytic themes come into play. Also, within both the mainstream and the sub-genre questions of identity are explored which focus around the missing woman, a category which eludes even the best detectives, as she continuously recedes from view. The narrative hermeneutic of discovery also extends to investigating feminism itself. Feminist fictions are read by a community of readers who actively interrogate the texts they see as 'theirs' for an affirmation of sub-cultural belief, and an exploration and dissemination of ideals. The consumption of these texts often constitutes an active reconstruction of political identities.

The central hero, the single viewpoint, the linear sequential narrative neatly closed by a natural conclusion – these are the standard devices of the detective form, and according to some feminist criticism, the standard *masculine* devices.[31] Klein's assessment of feminist detective novels, that 'the imperatives of the genre overwhelm the political implications of the novel',[32] is rather impeded by her limited selection of titles. In concluding she advocates a feminocentric novel which

> does not need a feminist detective but it cannot evade questions of gender – intertwined with those of class, race, sexual preference, and social attitudes . . . Foregrounding gender leads to questioning patriarchist assumptions through creating an interrogative text which urges readers to solve not only the problem of crime but also the problems of the social system.[33]

It has been my purpose in this book to explore more closely the diversity of feminist crime novels which offer some challenge to the view of crime fiction as an intrinsically masculine – and by implication innately conservative – literary form. The issues of gender, sexual politics, race, and class are conscientiously strewn through many, if not most, of the texts I have discussed. Apart from the early radical feminist novel by M. F. Beal *Angel Dance* (1977), Klein's chosen texts are specifically mainstream. She describes feminist texts as a sub-genre of the 1980s, consisting mainly of amateur sleuths who are outside the scope of her book. But conversely it is exactly these texts which gesture most towards her vision of a feminocentric crime novel. It may well be the case that a novel which manages to interrogate the substance of gender, such as Wings' *She Came Too Late*, or both Antoinette Azolakov's *Cass and the Stone Butch* (1987) and *Skiptrace* (1988),[34] can supersede the scenario of the short-sighted chauvinist pro.[35] Fantasy figures such as V. I. Warshawski fulfil a significant feminist function, but the genre's implied critique of heroism is more explicitly exposed when the feminism is consciously marked by class, race, or sexuality. The Othering of the detective hero is always already in the text; feminist writers can exploit this.

In order to prevent the cosy certainty of a re-established *status quo*, Klein advocates an open-ended conclusion to texts, looking to the Brechtian model of epic theatre, which provokes the newly politicized reader into a 'felt need for action'.[36] I would argue that this is most successful when romantic themes do not force the text into a self-satisfied closure. *Murder in the Collective* is a concrete example of this: on the last page the heroine's romantic aspirations are intercepted by crunching realism as her fallen idol Hadley drives away, back to Fran and deaf to Pam. The subsequent page contains an appendix of further information, books, periodicals, and resources:

> ON THE PHILIPPINES, ON FILIPINOS IN AMERICA, AND ON THE ROLE OF WOMEN IN DEVELOPING COUNTRIES. (181–2)

The encoded reader is clearly to be consciousness-raised, chivied and coaxed by the fictional injustices of the text and frustrated romance, into a direction endorsed by a list of reputable campaigns. The subtlety of this engagement is in the manipulation of the emotions. Fiction is used to convince, to persuade, to recruit the raw reader. As an early example (1984), *Murder in the Collective* remains prototypical – barefaced even – in its ideological agenda. This colludes with the feminist literary imperative to 'tell it like it is' – to be authentic, confessional, and realistic. The earnest honesty of some feminist narrators inculcates the reader into the 'truth' of a political experience, and it is by her own credibility that the narrative 'convicts'. The feminist intention connives with the generic convention to produce a plausible world which is ironically *totally illusory*.

If we accept Rick Eden's view, implying that all the best efforts of feminist authors are circumscribed by a hegemonic satiric form, does this leave any woman wishing to write 'otherwise' bound eternally within its masculine arms? This reductive argument is not very useful, assuming, as it does, that a genre is irretrievably fixed. A genre is a dynamic paradigm, dependent on definitions which change over time, a cultural code in which meanings are consistently contested. Volosinov's term 'multi-accentuality'[37] has currency here in its attempt to tie the production of meanings to social relations and struggle, thus:

> The sign itself may, in times of social upheaval, again become fluid with respect to its meaning, and emerge with a completely different evaluative accent that is a mark not of 'intrinsic meaning' but of the social dominance of the group which has appropriated or won (along with other powers) the power to define.[38]

The first thing to remark in relation to the mutability of the sign is the rather obvious assertion that the sub-genre is changing along with the political milieu. The heyday for feminist crime novels was the 1980s. They are an expression of the decade of Thatcherism and Reaganism which reified an individualist, urban culture. The popularity of the sub-genre, by the beginning of the 1990s, began to decline.[39] The historical moment is an important aspect in understanding the appearance of a literary form which has managed to be both comforting and challenging to readers. By offering women a fantasy of individualized power and control, ensconced within a consumer culture, readerly pleasures packaged within a 'right-on' aesthetic became a passport to the more radical effects of these novels in producing an actual (if temporary) change of consciousness.

It would be ridiculous to make a claim that such transpositions effected substantial material change for western women during the 1980s, but each cultural shift is a ripple in the sea of representations which construct our reality. Similarly, a decade obsessed by the police procedural – be it in book, film, or television form – was expressing historically specific and identifiable social fears and desires which can be read as reactionary or progressive. For example, was the hugely popular *Hill Street Blues* providing hunky boys for gay male spectators, sexy and stroppy sergeants for the dykes, formidable female public defenders for the career women, nurturing fathers (in the form of Frank Furillo) for all of us, or a fascist fantasy soap of law and order for those fallible enough to need a final solution to social insecurity? Probably all of this and more, because interpretation is such an inexact science.

Most of the novels discussed in this book, though, are located as subcultural according to production criteria, meaning they are published in a feminist imprint or by a feminist press. Whilst the number of these had declined by the early 1990s, mainstream fictions with feminist messages are at the moment increasing. Aside from the growing popularity of made-for-TV series foregrounding female investigators and adapting the work of female authors (Ruth Rendell is one prime example), there is a fascination with the traditionally perceived 'feminine' forms of the crime novel. Along with the heroicization of the serial killer comes a growing fixation upon the criminal mind, and violent insanity, echoing the psychological thrillers of earlier women writers such as Highsmith. The traditional detective of the whodunit who sifts his evidence, applying rational deduction to a few disparate clues, will become increasingly redundant. Forensic science has put paid to intuitive leaps of deduction – genetic fingerprinting is far more reliable. However, the second scientific route for the detective novel, into psychology, opens up further possibilities for women, as Clarice Starling, FBI agent in the Department of Behavioural Science in *The Silence of the Lambs*, has recently shown.[40]

The popularization of science, gendered in the mass imagery of the medical gaze which specularizes the diseased and broken female body, has appeared in texts such as Patricia Cornwell's *Postmortem* (1990), *Body of Evidence* (1991), and *All That Remains* (1992), and Lynda La Plante's television screenplays *Prime Suspect* (1991, 1992 and 1993), all of which recall an earlier P. D. James novel set in an East Anglian forensic laboratory *Death of an Expert Witness* (1977).[41] These new narratives offer powerful female protagonists operating the gaze – in the case of Cornwell's fiction this is literally executed as the Chief Medical Examiner (pathologist) on the investigation is female. All three books are saturated with the scientific discourse which legitimates the systematic state-sanctified dismemberment of the female body with the kind of empirical detail which borders on the fetishistic. The constituent parts of Woman-as-victim are being dissected and investigated by Woman-as-hero, the implications of which suggest that the search for Woman knows no (bodily) end, and even that there is a serial killer in all of us. The explicit visual presence of death in literature, expressed in such lingering detail through images of decaying, suppurating corpses, can be attributed to both *fin de siècle* fears of degeneration, and to the role that AIDS has taken on as a symbol of this disintegration. Parody, though, is never far behind . . . the presence of gothic clichés (remember the iron mask in *The Silence of the Lambs*?[42]) shifts these grotesque representations from reality into the absurd, removing the horror to a safe distance.

Returning finally to the mainstream novel, I want to end with a text which has mapped the feminist crime novel on to a superlative revenge fantasy – Helen Zahavi's *A Dirty Weekend* (1991). The book is the logical development of the feminist crime novel, it takes the psychological thriller, the polemic, the black comedy and the modern urban novel and inventively synthesizes a hybrid satire in which the hero is a serial killer. Bella is an angel of deliverance, she enacts the rage of the sexually abused:

> In the character of Bella, the humiliation and anger of Everywoman has been condensed, compressed and let explode against the oppressive weight of Everyman.[43]

This modern morality tale of 'stylized thuggery'[44] takes place over a winter weekend when Bella, single occupant of a basement flat, an archetypal victim to the voyeuristic intimidation of a nasty neighbour, finally fights back, creeps up the fire escape, and hammers him to pulp in his own bed. Then follows a sequence of episodic caricatures[45] of male harassment familiar to any female reader employed, presumably, for their universal resonance. Each perpetrator meets a sticky end. The plot is wickedly simple, and unimaginable without contemporary feminist discourse. What keeps the reader engaged is the pull of parody, which reveals the seed of truth contained within the absurd. *A Dirty Weekend*, according to my own small straw poll of readers,[46] expresses the desire of many women to pulverize their oppressors. In a way the emotional power of the book is reminiscent of the anger which galvanized early Women's Liberation. The ending is symbolic too, in a perfect piece of parody Bella meets Jack, the Geordie Ripper, under the pier. Serial killer meets serial killer in the final play-off, at sunrise. She dispatches him with a classic phallic gesture, when the roles of sexual murder are reversed, to the tune of 'The Okey-Kokey':

> The stabbing, she discovered, was something strangely intimate. It took a tender touch to place the knife so neatly. To stab him, she discovered, was to know him . . . You jab-jab here, you stab-stab there. You put it in. You take it out. You put it in again. He felt the knife go in and out. He felt her knife inside him. He didn't know a knife could hurt so much. He would have wept, if he'd had the strength . . . She really got stuck in. (183)

The implication is a warning – the new day dawning contains a Bella, whose revenge is the only form of justice available ('Ask not for whom the Bella tolls. She just might toll for you' (76)). How do we square the return of this vengeful virago with Cassandric portents of New Age gender stereotypes, and fears of the feminist backlash? Fiction articulates social change as a *struggle* over meaning in which former signs return to be reinflected, recombined, and rejuvenated for new phases of resistance.

In this book I began by briefly setting up the historical paradigm of crime fiction and masculinity, referring to the rationalistic, epistemological male gaze of the detective which has been directed at women, or more precisely, Woman. I introduced the figure of the Great Detective as an icon of Man, describing how a line of influence and patronage passed through masculine texts to perpetrate a gendered form. Then I introduced the early female authors as transgressing this form through parody. Texts by these women tended to disrupt male authority myths and deployed stereotyped female characters satirically, against themselves. From the Golden Age onwards female authors have been making the social situation of women a primary theme in crime fiction, exposing the harmful effects of masculinity and femininity. The figure of the hero has been feminized through parody, and the crime form itself became increasingly concerned with the internal effects of the criminal event. The psychological thriller is the mainstream legacy of the changes wrought by women writers on the genre.

Taking two models of feminism popular in the 1970s, influenced by liberalism and socialism, the next two chapters dealt with the relationship between the formal structures of the genre and the respective agendas of these political philosophies. In Chapter 2 I drew attention to the contradictory positioning of liberal feminism, straddling ideological allegiances between the bourgeois centre and the oppositional impetus of feminism. The liberal concept of reason makes crime fiction an ideal form for exploring a humanist identity, but certain people's rights tend to be saved at the expense of others. I showed how within liberal feminist crime fiction there is a surface text, which offers progressive, positive images of empowered women, and a depth text, which conservatively expunges radicalism, 'extremism', and even an acknowledgement of difference from the sphere of liberation. Nevertheless, these novels tend to 'work' better as narratives than the socialist feminist crime novels which often sacrifice pleasure for political correctness. Trying to say something useful about a complex range of oppressions leads some of these novels into formal incoherency. Their lack of self-conscious parody becomes a weakness – sometimes these texts are just too serious, failing to deliver suspense or resolution satisfactorily, degenerating into pedantic political primers. However, where these novels appropriate the negative, or anti-thriller forms, the myth of individualism intrinsic to crime fiction is successfully challenged. Further, they can show how women's experience of alienation can be transformed by self-knowledge, collectivity, and social alliance. This reconstructed hero then provides a fantasized re-entry for the marginalized into society.

In Chapter 4 I discussed whether it is possible, given the narrative constraints of the genre, to avoid being racist. Within Orientalist discourse truth and rationality, two generic essentials, are paradigmatically White constructions. I showed how in feminist crime fiction exotic or criminal racial others – images of denigration – are employed to shore up White identity. I then discussed a small and recent number of crime novels by African-American writers who could constitute a growing trend in feminist crime fiction. Their deployment of the gaze, moving it from White sightings of Blackness to the sideways glance of the 'outsider within' perspective, is ideally suited to a new view of the detective. Investigating a history of oppression, and remembering the past injustices of slavery and colonialism, is a mystery to be brought to light, a crime to be uncovered, and Black writers are synthesizing new literary forms, including the crime novel, to explore this.

The lesbian crime novel offers another outsider or outlaw figure, first appearing in *Angel Dance* as the lesbian guerrilla detective. The quest narrative of the detective novel is thrown into relief as it is first proved dangerous to women, and second revealed as a hopeless endeavour anyway. By problematizing the 'truth' of experience the crime form is thrown into ambiguity and contradiction. The epistemological project of crime fiction – to find and to know – is revealed as a performative rather than evaluative function. The interest and pleasure is generated within the *process* of discovering identity (and reconstructing it), not in finding an essential state of being. The lesbian crime novel relies heavily on parody to denaturalize gender and sexual roles, and highlights the structure of desire integral to the crime novel hermeneutic itself.

The psychoanalyst is a kind of detective, bent on interpreting clues and symbols in order retrospectively to construct a narrative, using techniques aligned to a close reading of texts. Returning to the event is a form of repetition familiar to psychoanalytic scenarios and crime fiction. But psychoanalysis and feminist crime fiction are more concerned with understanding internal effects than external events. Crime fiction offers avenues of transference not available in 'the real', giving an outlet for women's pain and rage experienced as a result of male violence. Hence feminist crime fiction concentrates on the reactions resulting from this psychic and sexual abuse, and the female violence then expressed is seen less as criminal than as taking justified revenge. Psychoanalytic feminist crime novels appeared in the 1980s, a decade concerned with the self, thus fictions which explore character and identity as the locus of mystery and the key to the investigative hermeneutic can be seen as combining concerns from dominant culture and counter-culture (feminism), concretized in the crime form most sympathetic to women writers, the psychological thriller.

In discussing the post-modernist crime fiction of Sarah Schulman I have shown how different aspects of this book's concerns can be combined in one writer's work. Schulman takes the explorations into identity articulated in previous chapters by using the metafictional framing devices and parodic forms of post-modernism to problematize further modern urban sexual, racial, and gender identities, deconstructing the binaries such as self/other, and truth/fiction. She replaces the linear teleological form of the detective story, rejects the male narrative of transcendence, and regenders/resexualizes the hard-boiled novel as female and lesbian – the female *flâneuse* gazes upon the feminine streets of New York. Schulman also manages to inject an imperative of political responsibility into this cacophonic stylistic experimentation and play.

Finally, in this concluding chapter, I have tried to relate these feminist trajectories in crime fiction to some formal implications for the genre. Parody has played an important part in destabilizing dominant myths of gender and sexuality in feminist culture, and we also find that it is integral to the crime form itself. The cross-dressed feminist heroine lays bare the artifice of gender via an investigation into patriarchal effects. By exacting this kind of literary transvestism the feminist text signals one driving mystery of crime novels to be a search for identity – not just the murderer's, but by extension the reader's too. Many other conventions of the crime novel sympathetic to feminism have been capitalized on, but where these have been perceived to be antithetical, the writers studied here have conscientiously broken them. Despite its well-known apparent 'unsuitability' for women, crime fiction clearly can manifest feminine novelistic forms, and feminist political agendas. Its mutability as a genre rests with its ability to combine elements of other forms such as realism and satire which have their roots in a radical sensibility. The peculiar attraction of a crime novel is its ability to appease sometimes contradictory desires, which presumably can placate the feminine and provoke the feminist in all of us.

Notes

1 MASCULINITY AND MASQUERADE *OR* 'IS THAT A GUN IN YOUR POCKET?'

1 Skinner, Robert E. *The Hard-Boiled Explicator: A Guide to the Study of Dashiell Hammett, Raymond Chandler and Ross Macdonald*, The Scarecrow Press, London, 1985, p. 2.
2 Quoted in Symons, Julian *Bloody Murder*, Viking, London, [1972] 1985, p. 33.
3 Ibid., pp. 34–5.
4 Ibid., p. 70.
5 Ibid., p. 66.
6 Reproduced in Winks, Robin W. (ed.) *Detective Fiction: A Collection of Critical Essays*, Spectrum Books, Prentice-Hall, New Jersey, 1980.
7 Quoted in Symons, op. cit., p. 131.
8 Quoted in Grella, George 'The Hard-Boiled Detective Novel', in Winks, op. cit., p. 108.
9 Ibid., p. 117.
10 Ibid., p. 117.
11 See Bloom, Harold *The Anxiety of Influence: A Theory of Poetry*, Oxford University Press, Oxford, 1973.
12 'Old Sleuth' (Harlan Page Halsey) *Gypsy Rose, the Female Detective*, J. S. Ogilvie Publishing Co., New York, 1898 quoted in Blake, Fay M. 'Lady Sleuths and Women Detectives', *Turn of the Century Women* 3 (1), 1986, p. 29. Blake's bibliography provides an excellent source for the identification of contemporary heroines.
13 Slung, Michelle *Crime on her Mind*, Random House/Parthenon Books, New York, 1975, p. xviii.
14 Williams, Gwen 'Fear's Keen Knife: Suspense and the Female Detective, 1890–1920', in Bloom, Clive (ed.) *Twentieth Century Suspense*, Macmillan Books, London, 1990, p. 39.
15 Blake, op. cit., p. 33.
16 Williams, op. cit., p. 37.
17 Semple, Linda and Coward, Rosalind 'Women at the Scene of Crime', ICA talk, London, 19 January 1988. In a later article the authors also

proffered *East Lynne* by Mrs Henry Wood (1861), and *Lady Audrey's Secret* by Mary Braddon (1862) – see Coward, Rosalind and Semple, Linda 'Tracking Down the Past: Women and Detective Fiction' in Carr, Helen (ed.) *From My Guy to Sci-Fi: Genre and Women's Writing in the Postmodern World*, Pandora Press, London, 1989, pp. 39–57.

18 Craig, Patricia and Cadogan, Mary *The Lady Investigates: Women Detectives and Spies in Fiction*, Oxford University Press, Oxford, 1986, p. 20. This study is a useful historical overview, as is Maio, Kathi 'A Strange and Fierce Delight: The Early Days of Women's Mystery Fiction', *Chrysalis* 10, n.d, 93–105.

19 Ibid.

20 I outline the function of parody in crime fiction more specifically in Chapter 8 which summarizes the structural implications for the genre of feminism's more recent appropriations.

21 See Slung, op. cit., p. 14.

22 Blake, op. cit., p. 39.

23 For example, Miss Butterworth, the prototypical nosy old maid in Anna Katherine Green's *That Affair Next Door* (1897), or the more explicitly feminist Violet Strange, appearing in *The Golden Slipper and Other Problems* (1915). See Cornillon, John 'A Case for Violet Strange', in Cornillon, Susan Koppelman (ed.) *Images of Women in Fiction: Feminist Perspectives*, Bowling Green State University Popular Press, Ohio, 1972, pp. 206–15. For further details of the various heroines of this period see Craig and Cadogan op. cit., pp. 15–37.

24 See Shaw, Marion and Vanacker, Sabine *Reflecting on Miss Marple*, Routledge, London, 1991, p. 27.

25 Ibid., p. 10.

26 Semple and Coward, op. cit.

27 Or, if preferred, the ways in which women writers *broke* the form.

28 The epithet also implies the detective story's own redundancy, its peak being past. One might speculate upon a hidden agenda to repudiate women authors' work as relevant to a purely *historic* moment, an arcane form now superseded by the masculine hard-boiled thriller.

29 See, for example, Knight, Stephen *Form and Ideology in Crime Fiction*, Macmillan, London, 1980, pp. 107–34.

30 Knepper, Marty 'Agatha Christie – Feminist', *Armchair Detective* 16 (4), 1983, pp. 398–406.

31 Shaw and Vanacker, op. cit., p. 31.

32 See also Birns, Nicholas and Birns, Margaret Boe 'Agatha Christie: Modern and Modernist', in Walker, Ronald G. and Frazer, June M. (eds) *The Cunning Craft*, Western Illinois University Press, Macomb, 1990, pp. 120–34.

33 See Light, Alison *Forever England: Femininity, Literature, and Conservatism Between the Wars*, Routledge, London, 1991, pp. 61–112.

34 It is an extraordinary fact, given the centrality of her work to British cultural life, that no self-respecting British critic has ever written at decent length about her, or felt impelled to look more closely at what that work might speak to.

Ibid., p. 64. Light's own work, together with that of Shaw and Vanacker's, op. cit., opens up the area.

35 Ibid., p. 64.
36 Ibid., p. 97.
37 For a fuller evocation of the character of Lord Peter Wimsey see Pitt, Valerie 'Dorothy Sayers: the Masks of Lord Peter', in Bloom, Clive, op. cit., pp. 97–113.
38 See Morris, Virginia B. 'Arsenic and Blue Lace: Sayers' Criminal Women', *Modern Fiction Studies* 29 (3), 1983, pp. 485–95.
39 According to Symons, op. cit., p. 118: '*Gaudy Night* is essentially a "woman's novel" full of the most tedious pseudo-serious chat between the characters that goes on for page after page.' Not all critics are so dismissive, or so blatantly sexist – see, for example, Morris, op. cit., and Campbell, Sue Ellen 'The Detective Heroine and the Death of Her Hero', *Modern Fiction Studies* 29 (3), 1983, pp. 497–510.
40 A pseudonym for C. Day Lewis.
41 Campbell, op. cit.
42 Ibid.
43 Wald, Gayle F. 'Strong Poison: Love and the Novelistic in Dorothy Sayers', in Walker and Frazer, op. cit., pp. 98–108.
44 Ibid., p. 107.
45 Ibid., p. 105.
46 Pitt, op cit., p. 103.
47 See Beauman, Nicola *A Very Great Profession: The Woman's Novel 1914–39*, Virago Press, London, 1983, and Light, op. cit.
48 In Steven, Peter (ed.) *Jump Cut: Hollywood, Politics and Counter Culture*, Praeger Press, New York, 1985; see Becker *et al.* 'Lesbians and Film', pp. 296–314, for a concise exposition of acceptable gender pairing or bonding in film narratives – similar structures also apply in literature:

> female friendship is itself limited in literature. In the multitude of buddy films, pairs of men get to act out their adventure fantasies . . . women friends are shown as either: trying to get 'the man's devotion . . . or accepting the judgment of Paris that splits women into narrowly defined "I'm This/You're That" sets of roles'.

49 Pandora Press edition, London, 1987, back cover.
50 Day, Gary 'Ordeal by Analysis: Agatha Christie's *The Thirteen Problems*', in Bloom, Clive, op. cit., pp. 83–4.
51 Light, op. cit.
52 See Williams, Raymond *The Country and the City*, The Hogarth Press, London, 1985, pp. 153–64.
53 Ibid., p. 159.
54 Ibid., p. 156.
55 See Pick, Daniel *Faces of Degeneration*, Cambridge University Press, Cambridge, 1989.
56 See Craig and Cadogan, op. cit., chapters 5, 7, 8 and 9.
57 See Symons, op. cit., chapter 12.
58 Ibid., pp. 143–4.
59 In common with the gothic novel. Indeed there are many cross-genre

links between crime fiction and gothic fiction, arguably the former springing from the latter in the nineteenth century. Tania Modleski takes up the psychoanalytic import of the claustrophobia structure in *Loving with A Vengeance: Mass Produced Fantasies for Women*, Methuen, London, 1984.

60 In Munt, Sally R. (ed.) *New Lesbian Criticism: Literary and Cultural Readings*, Harvester Wheatsheaf, Hemel Hempstead, and Columbia University Press, New York, 1992, pp. 95–114.

61 See the excellent film documentary *Rosie the Riveter*, which explains how

> New popular images in propaganda, like 'Rosie the Riveter' were used to recruit women to fill wartime defence jobs which suffered from the 'man'power shortage caused by the war. . . . Overnight women were trained to be shipbuilders, welders, riveters and machine workers. When World War II came to an end, new propaganda was produced which encouraged women to leave the workforce so the returning soldiers could resume their old jobs. Although 80 per cent of the women wanted to keep their skilled jobs they were laid off in great numbers, many of the 'Rosies' who stayed in the workforce were forced to return to their traditional unskilled positions.

Helaine *Rosie the Riveter*, Victoria Press, USA. Reprinted by Leeds Postcards as We Can Do It! No. L392, Leeds, LS3 1AX.

62 Symons, op. cit., p. 165.

63 Patricia Highsmith quoted in Philips, Deborah 'Mystery Woman – Patricia Highsmith', *Women's Review*, 6, 1986, pp. 14–15.

64 This is true for the novel. However in the subsequent Hitchcock film the character of Guy is much less ambiguous. Unlike in the book, he does not commit murder. The film does not do justice to the novel's moral complexity – Guy is consistently heroic throughout. Maybe Hitchcock as *auteur* needed, for once, an uncomplicated hero. See Modleski, Tania *The Women Who Knew Too Much*, Routledge, London, 1989 for an illuminating problematization of Hitchcock's 'heroes' and 'heroines'.

65 Klein, Kathleen Gregory 'Patricia Highsmith', in Bakeman, Jane S. (ed.) *And Then There Were Nine . . . More Women of Mystery*, Bowling Green State University Popular Press, Ohio, 1985, pp. 170–97.

66 Philips, op. cit., p. 14.

67 Castration imagery is temptingly metaphoric, no biologism intended.

68 Klein, op. cit., p. 174.

69 Paulin, Tom 'Mortem Virumque Cano', *New Statesman* 25 November 1977, p. 745, quoted in Klein, op, cit., p. 182. I find the terms of Paulin's reading too didactic – implying that there is only one true interpretation, that of authorial intent.

70 Symons, op. cit., p. 179, comments that 'in a Rendell novel a couple is not a happy thing to be'.

71 Particularly of the inside of houses, a traditional female domain.

72 The name itself exudes fruity, high indulgence, and indicates an exoticism not immediately apparent thirty years on, when nectarines are ten for ninety-nine pence.

73 Although not in the case of Ann Aldrich.

74 Recently there has been an attempt to reread these novels as marks of visibility in a period (1950s) which was apparently seamlessly heterosexual as far as cultural representation was concerned, functioning as points of identification for isolated lesbians (see Weir, Angela and Wilson, Elizabeth 'The Greyhound Bus Station in the Evolution of Lesbian Popular Culture', in Munt, op. cit.).

75 Their names are significant: the games mistress is called Caroline *Peters*, and Edwina Klein suggests a 'mannish' German psychoanalyst. The name evokes Melanie Klein, whose work is notorious for concentrating on children's sadistic impulses towards their mothers.

76 Dangerous to men, that is.

77 Speaking in Birch, Helen, 'The Darker Sides of the Mind', *Guardian* 28 April 1987, p. 11.

78 Kaplan, Cora 'An Unsuitable Genre for a Feminist?', *Women's Review* 8, 1986, pp. 18–19.

79 I owe the reference to Clark, Susan L. 'A Fearful Symmetry: An Interview with Ruth Rendell', *The Armchair Detective* 22 (3), 1989, pp. 228–35.

80 See Modleski, 1984, op. cit., for an elucidation of this construction in the gothic.

81 Speaking in Birch, op. cit.

82 Clark, op. cit., p. 230.

83 Birch, op. cit.

84 Siebenheller, Norma *P. D. James*, Frederick Ungar, New York, 1981, p. 128.

85 These are elaborated upon in ibid., pp. 89–104.

86 For analysis of Cordelia Gray as a pioneering professional female detective hero see Bakerman, Jane S. 'Cordelia Gray: Apprentice and Archetype', *Clues: A Journal of Detection* 5, 1984, pp. 101–14.

87 Symons, op. cit., p. 178.

88 James asserts in Birch, Helen 'P. D. James's Stylish Crime', *Women's Review* 10, 1986, pp. 6–7:

> 'I decided in this one that Dalgliesh ought to have a senior woman police officer in his team, because the team wouldn't be complete without one. And she's faced with the same sort of problems that an unmarried senior police officer is faced with, the resentment of some of your colleagues and the feeling that if there are domestic problems, you're expected to deal with them. The job is never taken with the same seriousness as it would be for a man. So it's not that one says I'll deal with female rights in this novel – given a woman character, you are faced with them, it's essential to her situation.'

89 See Campbell, op. cit.; Heilbrun, Carolyn 'James, P. D.', in Reilly, John M. (ed.) *Crime and Mystery Writers*, St Martin's Press, New York, 1980, p. 857; Winks, Robin W. 'The Sordid Truth: Four Cases' in Winks, Robin W. (ed.) *Detective Fiction*, Prentice-Hall, New Jersey, 1980, pp. 215–18; Siebenheller, op.cit.

90 Hubly, Erlene 'The Formula Challenged: The Novels of P. D. James', *Modern Fiction Studies* 29 (3), 1983, pp. 511–21.

91 Porter, Dennis 'Detection and Ethics: The Case of P. D. James', in Rader, Barbara A. and Zettler, Howard G. (eds) *The Sleuth and the Scholar: Origins, Evolution, and Current Trends in Detective Fiction*, Greenwood Press, New York, 1988, p. 12.

92 *A Taste for Death*, for example, ridicules left-wing politics to the point of complete caricature.

93 Cixous, Hélène 'The Laugh of the Medusa', *Signs*, Summer, 1976, reprinted in Marks, E. and Courtivron, I. (eds) *New French Feminisms*, Harvester Press, Brighton, 1981, pp. 245–64.

94 I do not subscribe to the theory/position that biological authors necessarily write appropriately gendered texts, but this oft-presented history of the detective story is overbearingly masculine, not just in its stylistic and structural use of masculinized forms (such as the unitary hero, the unproblematic worldview), but also in the overwhelming *absence* of any female/feminine forms. This is perhaps unsurprising given crime fiction's commonsensical reputation as a reactionary genre – specifically the belief that it tends to reflect the politics of cultural hegemony, imposing the ideology of Law. According to the traditional view of the history of crime writing, women as writers and, concomitantly, female protagonists, only stepped in once the parameters had been set. Literary and Cultural Studies courses have endorsed this approach to popular fiction; typical courses on the crime novel or thriller offer eight weeks spent in critical admiration of a variously selected canon of Poe/Wilkie Collins/Conan Doyle/Dennis Wheatley/Hammett/Chandler/Spillane (with a contemporary police procedural movie screened for those students too lazy, broke, or busy to buy and read the books). Two token weeks on Black *versions* (Chester Himes) or female *appropriations* (Christie/Sayers/Paretsky) are conscientiously thrown in at the end. The model for approaching almost any genre study is a standard one, in which non-White, non-masculine, and non-heterosexual narratives are decentred, and delegitimized.

95 In an after-dinner speech to the Baker Street Irregulars, a Holmesian fan club, in New York. See Slung, op. cit., p. 13.

96 Used at the opening session of the 'Questions of Homosexuality II' conference, Institute of Romance Studies, University of London, Malet Street, 6 June 1992.

2 THE NEW WOMAN – A SHEEP IN WOLVES' CLOTHING?

1 The observation was made by Andrea Nye in *Feminist Theory and the Philosophies of Man*, Routledge, London and New York, 1989, p. 5.

2 Sian Griffiths reported in 'Opportunity Knocks Again', *The Higher*, 8 November 1991, p. 8 that

> In 1987/8, the last year for which comprehensive statistics have been published [in the UK], the proportion of women senior

lecturers dropped to 6 percent, against 8 percent in 1980. Over the same period the proportion of women lecturers fell from 19 percent to 14 percent and the proportion of women professors was only 3 percent – one of the lowest in the world.

3 I chose not to execute a reader's survey for this research, nevertheless innumerable informal conversations with readers of feminist crime fiction over the years caused me to form general impressions concerning what women enjoyed reading most. Crucial to readerly pleasure seemed to be her identification with a powerful, strong, female detective who despatched her enemies with profulgent self-confidence and wit.

4 Bennett, Tony 'The Politics of the Popular', in Bennett, Tony *et al.* (eds) *Popular Culture and Social Relations*, Open University Press, Milton Keynes, 1986, p. 7.

5 I employ this term reluctantly, not to endorse its use but to draw attention to the way female actors are marketed, despite professional capability.

6 *V. I. Warshawski* Dir. Jeff Kanew, Silver Screen Partners, 1991.

7 Duncan, Andrew 'Kathleen Turns Up The Heat', *Radio Times*, BBC Publications, London, 2–8 November 1991, pp. 22–4.

8 As a later contributor to the letters page, N. R. Wolfe of Hove, East Sussex, complained (*Radio Times* 23–9 November 1991, p. 113), 'if the genders were reversed and if it were a man who had said "On a night when I'm really hot, I can walk into a room and if a woman doesn't look at me she's probably a lesbian", there would have been a host of objections to an obvious piece of sexism' (and one would hope, some addressing of the comment's homophobia). Thank you to Marcus Roberts for drawing this to my attention.

9 This view operates to undermine itself; by ignoring the presence of various professional and amateur female detectives in both film and television productions such as *Cagney and Lacey*, *Black Widow*, *Silence of the Lambs*, *Blue Steel*, *Juliet Bravo*, *Prime Suspect*, *South of the Border*, *Miss Marple Investigates* and others, Turner inadvertently affirms the masculine norm.

10 Brooks, Richard 'Trigger Happy', *Radio Times*, BBC Publications, London, 23–9 January 1993, pp. 20–1.

11 Ibid., p. 20.

12 Binyon, T. J. *'Murder Will Out': The Detective in Fiction*, Oxford University Press, Oxford, 1990, p. 50.

13 Ibid., p. 55.

14 Heilbrun, Carolyn *Writing A Woman's Life*, The Women's Press, London, 1989, pp. 109–23.

15 'Amanda Cross'.

16 Todd, Janet *Feminist Literary History*, Polity Press, Oxford, 1988, p. 9.

17 Even in the 1960s and 1970s British feminist criticism was influenced by French deconstruction and psychoanalysis that called into question literary constructs like the subject or the idea of the humanist self (ibid., p. 87).

18 See, for example, Morris, Virginia B. 'Arsenic and Blue Lace: Sayers' Criminal Women', *Modern Fiction Studies* 29 (3), 1983, pp. 485–95

where she points out that the working-class villain is guilty of criminal and anti-social behaviour, clearly 'things no lady would do' (494).

19 Zimmerman, Bonnie 'What Has Never Been: An Overview of Lesbian Feminist Criticism', in Greene, Gayle and Kahn, Coppelia (eds) *Making a Difference: Feminist Literary Criticism*, Methuen, London, 1985, p. 180.

20 Todd, op. cit, pp. 27–8. Heilbrun, Carolyn 'Feminist Criticism: Bringing the Spirit Back to English Studies', *ADE Bulletin* 62, 1979, p. 197, reprinted in Showalter, Elaine (ed.) *The New Feminist Criticism*, Virago Press, London, 1986, pp. 21–8.

21 Tania Modleski has captured the preference for Gender Studies over Feminism succinctly in her analysis of an article on Elaine Showalter ('Literary Feminism Comes of Age' by Elizabeth Kolbert, *New York Times Magazine* 6 November 1987, p. 110), in which she identifies Showalter's move from 'gynocritics' (female-oriented criticism) to Gender Studies as being indicative of a general drift towards removing the political edge of feminism for women. See Modleski, Tania *Feminism Without Women: Culture and Criticism in a 'Postfeminist' Age*, Routledge, London, 1991, pp. 3–22.

22 Heilbrun, in Showalter, op. cit., p. 24. Also, by constructing the idea of the 'threat' to literature (Literature), Heilbrun defends a notional High Culture from the 'taint' of the popular, historically a class-bound criticism.

23 Tong, Rosemarie *Feminist Thought*: *An Introduction*, Unwin Hyman/ Routledge, London, 1989, p. 38.

24 Although neither is it intrinsically more progressive.

25 Recently classical liberalism has resurfaced with a vengeance in a particularly stark form, in North American libertarian philosophy, which has inspired the New Right. See, for example, the work of Robert Nozick *Anarchy, State, and Utopia*, Basic Books, New York, 1974.

26 Willis, Ellen 'The Conservatism of *Ms.*', in Redstockings (eds) *Feminist Revolution*, Random House, New York, 1975, pp. 170–1, quoted in Tong, op. cit., p. 38.

27 See Hamilton, Cynthia S. *Western and Hard-boiled Detective Fiction in America: From High Noon to Midnight*, Macmillan Press, London, 1987.

28 Androgyny has been embraced by liberal feminism, for which it has been critiqued: the appropriation of masculinity by female protagonists operates largely to subsume difference as an 'addition' to the masculine model, no significant restructuring having taken place. Critics have argued that androgyny – whether monoandrogyny or polyandrogyny – is inadequate and inappropriate as a political objective. Janice Raymond has called it 'pseudo-organicism', Adrienne Rich 'fail[ing] in the name of difference'. See Jaggar, Alison M. *Feminist Politics and Human Nature*, Harvester Press, Brighton, 1983, pp. 88 and 97.

29 Evans, Sarah Jane 'Sister of the Shock', *Guardian* 25 August 1987, p. 8.

30 Ibid.

31 Palmer, Jerry *Thrillers: Genesis and Structure of a Popular Genre*, Edward Arnold, London, 1978, p. 64.

32 Ibid., p. 85.

33 Different types of feminisms offer a variety of positions on the family;

whether 'natural', nuclear, collective, adoptive, extended, pretended, or dissolved, the centrality of the family to feminist theory is as the primary locus for sex/gender oppression. What to do about it is where ideologies disagree. A comparative, definitive work is needed.

34 Conversely this social contract is contingent on some commitment by the state to 'serve and protect': Warshawski is dependent on Chicago's finest legal, media and medical institutions for information and assistance. In the penultimate chapter of *Bitter Medicine*, a (very liberal token Black) police detective bursts into the final confrontation, gun blazing in classical filmic style, and saves Warshawski's life.

35 See, for example, Jaggar, op. cit.

36 Ibid., pp. 27–35.

37 Ibid., p. 31.

38 Quoted in ibid., p. 32.

39 Ibid., p. 33.

40 Palmer, op. cit., p. 85.

41 H. W. Feldman identifies this in his 'Ideological Supports for Addiction', quoted in Palmer, op. cit., p. 37. This anthropomorphizing is important – Sergio's feline characteristics locate him as a devious and ruthless criminal according to the paradigm, and render his membership of liberal society (humanity) void.

42 Both Amanda Cross and Sara Paretsky have articulated how their heroines function as alter-egos and fantasy figures of empowerment; for example: 'V. I. has given me a voice, given me the courage to say a lot of things I wouldn't say in my own voice', Sara Paretsky speaking in an interview 'Shooting From the Hip and the Lip' with Liz Thomson, *Books* 6 (3), 1992, p. 4. See also Heilbrun, op. cit., pp. 109–23. She writes of both her heroine, Kate Fansler, *and* her authorial persona of Amanda Cross in these terms.

43 Klein, Kathleen Gregory *The Woman Detective: Gender and Genre*, University of Illinois Press, Urbana and Chicago, 1988, p. 206.

44 Reddy, Maureen T. *Sisters in Crime: Feminism and the Crime Novel*, Continuum Books, New York, 1988, p. 104.

45 Millhone's own immediate family are all dead, their absence signifying their unavailability, and by implication the idea that biological families are never there when you need them.

46 To compare a male writer favourably with a female writer in a literary critical forum is to evoke reverberations from the acrimonious responses to Kristeva's theory of the semiotic, in which male avant-garde writers exemplify the feminine realm of her 'semiotic'. Nevertheless, my tokenistic refute to determinism, and residual traces of liberalism enjoin to provoke the honorary inclusion of Robert B. Parker's *Looking for Rachel Wallace* as an example of how the liberal feminist *text* may conceivably have a male author.

47 Evoking the hard-boiled's historically communist origins in Dashiell Hammett's Continental Op as an employee of the Pinkerton Agency.

48 Dunant, Sarah 'Rewriting the Detectives', *Guardian* 29 June 1993, p. 28.

49 Reddy, op. cit., p. 120.

50 The idea of an independent 'eye' is also crucial to liberal culture, as the

history of the British newspaper the *Independent* shows: as a result of Tory Rupert Murdoch's purchase of *The Times*, defecting journalists who feared for their editorial autonomy set up the competing broadsheet as a publication conceived as being non-aligned to any political party or ideology, i.e. as an independent. This myth of being able to 'step outside', to 'view objectively' a culture over which one had freedom to choose positions or alliances is crucial to the construction of the private eye, who in her/his detection, can 'see' the truth.

51 Du Maurier, Daphne *Rebecca*, Victor Gollancz, London, 1938.

52 Cameron, Deborah and Frazer, Elizabeth *The Lust to Kill*, Polity Press, Cambridge, 1987, back cover.

53 Ibid., p. 176.

54 Smith, Rupert 'Portrait of a Friendship', *Radio Times* 11–17 April 1992, pp. 28–30.

55 O'Reilly, Emma-Louise 'Little Sister Hits the Trail', *Guardian* 26 May 1987, p. 10.

56 Whether or not this is a good or bad thing I'm not sure – is it better to be ridiculed or not even shown?

57 O'Reilly, op. cit.

58 Dollimore, Jonathan *Sexual Dissidence: Augustine to Wilde, Freud to Foucault*, Clarendon Press, Oxford, 1991. He identifies two fields of operation which he labels as the 'paradoxical perverse' and the 'perverse dynamic':

> the most extreme threat to the true form of something comes not so much from its absolute opposite or its direct negation, but in the form of its perversion; somehow the perverse threat is inextricably rooted in the true and authentic, while being, in spite of (or rather because of) that connection also the utter contradiction of the true and authentic. This connects with and partly explains another paradox of perversion: it is very often perceived as at once utterly alien to what it threatens, and yet, mysteriously inherent within it. Such paradoxes of the perverse . . . constitute what I shall call the paradoxical perverse, while the perverse dynamic signifies the potential of those paradoxes to destabilise, to provoke discoherence. Both the paradoxical perverse and the perverse dynamic are categories with obvious deconstructive potential. (121)

59 Professor Stuart Hall, speaking on the programme *I Want Your Sex*, a documentary on the myth of Black hypersexuality shown as part of the *Without Walls* series broadcast on Channel 4, Tuesday 12 November 1991. The fascination is not limited to liberal texts. Erlene Hubly in 'The Formula Challenged: The Novels of P. D. James', *Modern Fiction Studies* 29 (3), 1983, p. 519, makes this comment concerning P. D. James' novel *The Black Tower* (1975), and her fictional world: 'It is a world in which all values are inverted . . . a world in which the most powerful love scene in all the novels takes place between two homosexual men.'

60 Jaggar, op. cit., has drawn attention to the contradictions within liberalism which threaten its own basic suppositions. Not only does liberal theory contain many different strands, but also each subject, and

writer, or text, described above has its own set of contradictions. I use 'liberalism' to denote therefore a general set of ideas, to which these novels *to a greater or lesser extent* aspire. That we are all, as texts, variously contradicted and fragmented, is a theoretical given.

61 Todd, op. cit., p. 87.

62 See Modleski, op. cit.

63 Gerrard, Nicci 'Sleuth Sayings', *Observer* Sunday 27 June 1993, p. 62.

3 A CASE OF 'DEATH BY POLITICAL CORRECTION'?

1 I am using the designation '1980s' in the traditional Cultural Studies sense, i.e. in the concept of a decade which does not necessarily contain strict boundaries but in this case describes a cultural moment loosely contemporaneous with Thatcherism – 1979 until the early 1990s in Britain.

2 Here I am employing Heidi Hartmann's definition of patriarchy as: 'a set of social relations between men which have a material base, and which, though hierarchical, establish or create interdependence and solidarity among men that enable them to dominate women'. Hartmann, Heidi 'The Unhappy Marriage of Marxism and Feminism', in Sargent, Lydia (ed.) *Women and Revolution: A Discussion of the Unhappy Marriage of Marxism and Feminism*, South End Press, Boston, 1981, p. 14.

3 Young, Iris 'Socialist Feminism and the Limits of Dual Systems Theory', *Socialist Review* 10, 1981, pp. 169–88.

4 Mitchell, Juliet *Woman's Estate*, Pantheon Books, New York, 1971.

5 I am making use of Alison Jaggar's discussion of the structure of alienation as the quintessential socialist feminist insight into women's oppression; see Jaggar, Alison M. *Feminist Politics and Human Nature*, Harvester Press, Brighton, 1983, chapter 10.

6 The one political belief that the thriller could not accommodate is anti-individualism, for, as we shall see, individualism is fundamental to the thriller. Palmer, Jerry *Thrillers: Genesis and Structure of a Popular Genre*, Edward Arnold, London 1978, p. 67.

7 Ibid., p. 219–20.

8 As a lecturer in a prestigious British university said to me recently, 'In order to buy students you must have tokens.'

9 *I Shot My Husband and No-One Asked Me Why* produced and directed by Clare Beavan and presented by British feminist journalist Beatrix Campbell, Scarlet Productions, was broadcast on Channel 4, Monday 20 June 1988. According to the programme every year in the USA about one thousand women kill their abusing partners.

10 On the 'feminist backlash' see French, Marilyn *The War Against Women*, Hamish Hamilton, London, 1992, and Faludi, Susan *Backlash*, Chatto & Windus, London, 1992.

11 Cranny-Francis, Anne *Feminist Fiction*, Polity Press, Cambridge 1990, p. 164.

12 Cranny-Francis, Anne 'Gender and Genre: Feminist Rewritings of

Detective Fiction', *Women's Studies International Forum* 11 (1), 1988, p. 71.

13 See Chapter 4.

14 Also published in 1984 was Barbara Wilson's *Murder in the Collective*, which epitomizes socialist feminism's all-encompassing critique of social formations of domination, subordination, and subversion. As an early feminist crime novel it retains the campaigning quality of 1970s counter-literature but equally it could be read as a prototype for many successive texts published during the 1980s, which dropped the complex critique but retained many of the basic forms present in *Murder in the Collective*. I discuss the novel more specifically in Chapter 4.

15 Moretti, Franco *Signs Taken for Wonders*, Verso, London, 1988, p. 139.

16 Palmer, Paulina 'The Lesbian Feminist Thriller and Detective Novel', in Hobby, Elaine and White, Chris (eds) *What Lesbians Do in Books*, The Women's Press, London, 1991, p. 15.

17 D'Acci, Julie 'The Case of Cagney and Lacey', in Baehr, Helen and Dyer, Gillian *Boxed In: Women and Television*, Pandora Press, London 1987, p. 205.

18 Ibid., p. 223.

19 Gamman, Lorraine 'Watching the Detectives', in Gamman, Lorraine and Marshment, Margaret (eds) *The Female Gaze*, The Women's Press, London, 1988, p. 22.

20 Alcock, Beverley and Robson, Jocelyn 'Cagney and Lacey Revisited', *Feminist Review* 35, Summer, 1990, p. 45.

21 Back cover of the novel.

22 See Chapter 4.

23 A mainstream, internationally marketed Hollywood buddy series, *Miami Vice* depends on the traditional frisson between opposites which the Black/White team of detectives Tubbs and Crockett makes more visibly obvious. The dark/fair dynamic is almost a requisite of Buddy teams – cf. *Butch Cassidy and the Sundance Kid* and *Starsky and Hutch*. In the racially mixed *Miami Vice*, the Black cop is a less important Watson figure, a 'shadow', to the more glamorous White star, perpetuating the traditional hierarchy. The feature film series *Lethal Weapon* also plays on the structure of ethnic opposites for narrative tension and momentum.

24 According to the BBC (personal phone call 16 August 1990), although parallels between *Cagney and Lacey* have been drawn, the similarities were not intentional. The average viewing figures for *South of the Border* were between 5.5 and 6 million, reasonable considering the peak transmission time of 21.20. The producer Caroline Alton expressly preferred the use of new writers such as women and ethnic minorities, although there was no explicit policy on script content.

25 From the smallest clues that have been dropped to a knowing audience, actors, screen characters, and audiences have been complicit in cementing sub-textual allegiances since the film industry began.

26 For different reactions to the Spielberg film adaptation see: Bobo, Jacqueline '*The Color Purple*: Black Women as Cultural Readers', in Pribram, Dierdre (ed.) *Female Spectators: Looking at Film and Television*, Verso, London, 1988, pp. 90–109; Stuart, Andrea '*The Color Purple*: In

Defence of Happy Endings', in Gammon, L. and Marshment, M. (eds) *The Female Gaze*, The Women's Press, London, 1988, pp. 60–75; Bourne, Stephen '*The Color Purple*', *Films and Filming*, June, 1986, pp. 26–7; Halprin, Sara '*The Color Purple*: Community of Women', *Jump Cut: A Review of Contemporary Media* 31, 1986, pp. 27–8; Jaehne, Karen 'The Final Word', *Cineaste* 15 (1), 1986, p. 60.

27 Child sexual abuse reoccurs frequently in feminist crime fiction. Since modern society is keen to make this particular crime invisible, and because it is often seen as the cause of 'abnormal' behaviour, child sexual abuse is constructed as a mystery waiting to be unlocked. As such, it provides a logical theme for crime fiction. Whilst applauding the attempt to present child sexual abuse as part of the historical experience of many adult men and women, I am concerned that within its representation there may be narrative expediency. In *South of the Border* the subject is introduced at a very late stage in the narrative, and is not developed. This may be because a sequel is anticipated.

28 Day, Marele *The Life and Crimes of Harry Lavender*, Allen & Unwin, Sydney, 1988, p. 70.

29 Back cover.

30 Barrett, Michèle *Women's Oppression Today: The Marxist/Feminist Encounter*, New Left Books, London, 1980, Verso, London, 1988 (revised edn).

31 Brenner, Johanna and Ramas, Mari 'Rethinking Women's Oppression', in Lovell, Terry *British Feminist Thought*, Basil Blackwell, Oxford, 1990, p. 153.

32 Barrett, op. cit., pp. 222–3, quoted in ibid., p. 153.

33 Babuscio, Jack 'Camp and the Gay Sensibility', in British Film Institute *Gays and Film*, London, 1977, p. 40. Whilst being wary of the essentialist tendencies of such a notion – Andrew Britton has criticized it for containing two false propositions in that: a) There exists some undifferentiated 'mainstream consciousness' from which gays, by the very fact of being gay are absolved, and b) that 'a perception of the world which is defined by the fact of one's gayness' necessarily involves a heightened awareness – one can still argue that oppression creates the potential for critical distance. Britton, Andrew 'For Interpretation: Notes Against Camp', *Gay Left* 7, Winter 1978/9, pp. 11–14.

34 See Tyler, Carole-Ann 'Boys Will Be Girls: The Politics of Gay Drag', in Fuss, Diana (ed.) *Inside/Out: Lesbian Theories, Gay Theories*, Routledge, London, 1991, pp. 32–70 for a critique of the rehabilitation of camp and female impersonation, which can sometimes contain misogynistic messages.

35 Quoted in Symons, Julian *Bloody Murder*, Viking, London, 1975, p. 125.

36 This structure is one of the pervading myths of modern life. For further elucidation see Williams, Raymond *The Country and The City*, The Hogarth Press, London, 1985. The structure particularly suits the crime novel.

37 Hughes, Robert *The Shock of the New*, BBC Publications, London, 1980, p. 351.

38 The inverted commas are employed ironically, at least in part.

39 In particular, but others are included too.
40 Worpole, Ken *Dockers and Detectives*, Verso, London, 1983, p. 23.
41 Whether I do or not is not the point.

4 'A CHANGE IS GONNA COME'?

1 I am grateful in particular to helen (c)harles, and to Reina Lewis, Eva Mackey, and Graham Dawson, for their comments on the ideas behind this chapter.
2 Said, Edward *Orientalism*, Routledge & Kegan Paul, London, 1978, p. 38.
3 See Pick, Daniel *Faces of Degeneration*, Cambridge University Press, Cambridge, 1989, for an analysis of nineteenth-century fears of degeneration and their link to the imperialist project.
4 For reasons of textual expediency I am capitalizing both White and Black as terms taxonomizing ethnic identity, but recognize their separate generation as signifiers.
5 Bloom, Clive 'West is East: Nayland Smith's Sinophobia and Sax Rohmer's Bank Balance', in Bloom, Clive (ed.) *Twentieth Century Suspense*, Macmillan Books, London, 1990, pp. 22–36.
6 Ibid., p. 27.
7 Ibid., p. 33.
8 See further Spivak, Gayatri Chakravorty 'Three Women's Texts and a Critique of Imperialism', in Gates, Henry Louis Jnr (ed.) *'Race', Writing, and Difference*, University of Chicago Press, Chicago and London, 1985, pp. 262–80.
9 There are a few examples – see Bailey, Frankie Y. *Out of the Woodpile: Black Characters in Crime and Detective Fiction*, Greenwood Press, New York, 1991, for a comprehensive description. It is easier for a White woman to fulfil the detective's role as her social construction as intuitive, observant, and attentive to detail provides pathways which are not open in the same way to Black male characters.
10 Dove, George N. 'Dorothy Uhnak', in Bakerman, Jane S. *And Then There Were Nine . . . More Women of Mystery*, Bowling Green State University Popular Press, Ohio, 1985, p. 85.
11 Ibid., p. 91.
12 But Dove's analysis frequently falls into a sentimentalizing humanism which comprises himself as critic along with Uhnak as author.
13 Gilman, Sander L. 'Black Bodies, White Bodies', in Gates, Henry Louis Jnr (ed.) *'Race', Writing, and Difference*, University of Chicago Press, Chicago and London, 1986, pp. 223–61.
14 Ibid., p. 256.
15 Ibid.
16 Said, op. cit., p. 3.
17 Note, for example, how the syntax and register of the final sentence 'there was great joy among the Palestinians' consigns them to and contains them within a mythical, childlike, picture-book, Christian past.
18 Attempts to delineate the range of work constituting Black feminist theory are constrained by space. However, the following texts would

provide an introduction: hooks, bell *Ain't I a Woman: Black Women and Feminism*, Pluto Press, London, 1982; hooks, bell *Yearning: Race, Gender and Cultural Politics*, Turnaround Press, London, 1991; Davis, Angela Y. *Women, Race and Class*, Random House, New York, 1981; Moraga, Cherrie and Anzaldua, Gloria (eds) *This Bridge Called My Back: Writings by Radical Women of Color*, Kitchen Table Press, New York, 1981; Hull, Gloria T. *et al.* (eds) *All the Women are White, All the Blacks are Men, But Some of Us are Brave: Black Women's Studies*, The Feminist Press, Old Westbury, New York, 1981; Wallace, Michele *Black Macho and the Myth of Superwoman*, Verso, London, 1978 and 1990; Collins, Patricia Hill *Black Feminist Thought: Knowledge, Consciousness, and the Politics of Empowerment*, Routledge, London, 1991. Kitchen Table Press in the USA and Sheba Feminist Press in the UK have concentrated on publishing fiction by Black women.

19 In relation to African-American texts see Evans, Mari (ed.) *Black Women Writers*, Doubleday, New York, 1984; Christian, Barbara *Black Feminist Criticism: Perspectives on Black Women Writers*, Pergamon Press, New York, 1986; Wall, Cheryl A. *Changing Our Own Words: Essays on Criticism, Theory and Writing by Black Women*, Routledge, London, 1990. Willis, Susan *Specifying: Black Women Writing the American Experience*, Routledge, London, 1990; Gates, Henry Louis Jnr *Black Literature and Literary Theory*, Methuen, London, 1984.

20 Hannah Wakefield's second novel, *A February Mourning* (1990), is sited at Moleham Peace Camp (an anagram of Molesworth/Greenham, two British Peace Camps established outside US Forces bases), which sets up discursive polarities between pacifism and terrorism, and abortionists and pro-life Catholics, in which liberalism is critiqued. *A February Mourning* is multi-discursive, one potential strength of the pluralistic liberal position. Peace camp mysteries are almost a sub-genre of feminist crime fiction, a result of the political alliances between pacifism and feminism made during the early to mid-1980s. The high profile of Greenham Women's Peace Camp caused many converts to feminism, pacificism and lesbianism. Other literary examples include: Joan Smith's *Why Aren't They Screaming* (1988), and Val McDermid's *Common Murder* (1989).

21 Minette Marrin's novel *The Eye of the Beholder* (1988) is similarly concerned with the intelligence forces as the 'dark' underside of modern society. This novel is anti-bureaucratic and pro-individualism, but the attempt to critique the anti-semitism of the Western Alliance (offering another different construction of Othering) is somewhat undermined by the dated representation of the Eastern Bloc countries as scheming commies (yet another variation on cultural Others – although the two are discursively conflated in right-wing racist ideology). A final scene in which a conveniently placed godfather, the First Sea Lord, bails the protagonist out, takes the text into parody, and much of its radical critique is lost.

22 See Alcock, Beverley and Robson, Jocelyn 'Cagney and Lacey Revisited', *Feminist Review* 35, Summer, 1990, pp. 42–53, for an elucidation of how the two eponymous characters are structured antithetically as Woman/not-Woman.

23 This expression of anxiety is particularly Canadian – Canada contains many multi-ethnic immigrant groups, which culminates in a mainstream multiculturalist liberal discourse almost becoming the norm.

24 Pratt, Mary Louise 'Scratches on the Face of the Country; or What Mr Barrow Saw in the Land of the Bushmen', in Gates, Henry Louis Jnr (ed.) *'Race' Writing, and Difference*, University of Chicago Press, Chicago and London, 1986, pp. 138–62. See also a more extended version in Pratt, Mary Louise *Imperial Eyes: Travel Writing and Transculturation*, Routledge, London, 1992.

25 Ibid. (1986), p. 142.

26 Ibid., p. 143.

27 Ibid., p. 145.

28 Ibid., p. 152. But intervene he did.

29 See Slotkin, Richard 'The Hard-Boiled Detective Story: From the Open Range to the Mean Streets', in Rader, B. A. and Zettler, H. G. (eds) *The Sleuth and the Scholar*, Greenwood Press, New York, 1988, pp. 91–100. An investigation into the televisual representation of the Los Angeles riots of 1992 would make fruitful arguments for the continuing use of this imagery in dominant and popular culture.

30 This presumably unintentional *double entendre* is a testament to my earlier argument that homo-eroticism/homophobia consistently underpins these liberal texts.

31 See Gilman, op. cit.

32 For a further discussion on this structure see Bloom, op. cit. Of course, orientalized prostitutes are stock figures – usually secondary victims – in crime fiction.

33 Slovo comes from a highly politicized family. Her mother, Ruth First, was a writer and anti-apartheid activist assassinated by the South African security forces in Maputo, 1982.

34 As San Franciscan author Armistead Maupin said in his 'ICA Talk' at the Institute of Contemporary Arts, London, Spring 1990 about coming out as gay: 'Until then I'd been a racist and I'd been a terrible little snob and it made a huge *difference* in my life – it democratized me.' [My italics]

35

> 'Beauty is truth, truth beauty' – that is all
> Ye know on earth and all ye need to know.

John Keats, 'Ode on a Grecian Urn' (1820).

36 For example, in the form of popular anthropology programmes, where western Man goes to exotic places to meet 'primitive' people who will teach him something important about himself.

37 An ironic comment on the way we have to adopt the dominant viewing/reading position no matter what our cultural identity, a structure feminist film theorists such as Laura Mulvey and E. Ann Kaplan have suggested.

38 North American Black politics has resisted the idea of diffusely fragmented subjectivities, preferring the model from African-American Studies of how in the split identity specific certain hierarchical relations exist (as between the African heritage and the appropriated European culture). For elucidation see Gates, Henry Louis Jnr 'In Her Own Write', Introduction to *Six Women's Slave Narratives*, Oxford University Press, Oxford, 1988, pp. vii–xxii.

39 Said, op. cit., p. 21.

40 Spivak, op. cit.; see also Lewis, Reina 'Only Women Should Go to Turkey: Henriette Browne and Women's Orientalism', *Third Text* 22, Spring, 1993, pp. 53–64.

41 There is a history in White feminist writing which struggles to construct a non-Orientalist relation between self and Other; see for example, Pratt, Minnie Bruce 'Identity: Skin, Blood, Heart', in Bulkin, E., Pratt, M. B. and Smith, B. (eds) *Yours in Struggle: Perspectives on Anti-Semitism and Racism*, Long Haul Press, New York, 1984, pp. 9–63.

42 Ibid., p. 272.

43 In Harasym, Sarah (ed.) *The Post-Colonial Critic: Interviews, Strategies, Dialogues*, Routledge, New York and London, 1990.

44 Maureen Reddy in *Sisters in Crime: Feminism and the Crime Novel*, Continuum Books, New York, 1988, pp. 33–6, discusses the amateur detective created by Marcia Muller, the Chicana Elena Oliverez. Despite the fact that Reddy has described the three novels *The Tree of Death* (1983), *The Legend of the Slain Soldiers* (1985), and *Beyond the Grave* (1986) as being 'feminist in the deepest sense of the term', and that '[Muller] sets the Oliverez novels almost entirely within the Mexican-American community of Santa Barbara, with Elena's cultural and ethnic heritage a central fact of her character and of the crimes she investigates' (34), I have found them impossible to obtain for the benefit of this study. The implication of this is an indicator of publishing and distributive norms.

45 Brown, Sterling 'Negro Character as Seen by White Authors', *The Journal of Negro Education* 2, 1933, pp. 179–203.

46 See Said, op. cit.

47 Rabinowitz, Peter J. 'Chandler Comes to Harlem: Racial Politics in the Thrillers of Chester Himes', in Rader and Zettler, op. cit., p. 27.

48 Bailey, op. cit., p. 102.

49 As I write this I am hearing on the news of the response by Black youths to the acquittal verdict returned on the Rodney King case, the Black Los Angeles motorist viciously beaten by four White policemen. As an area of one hundred square miles of the city burns, fifty-eight people, mainly Black males, are dead, over 2,000 are injured, and nearly 12,000 have been arrested. A more graphic instance of the relationship between urban African-American youth and the law could not be imagined.

50 The semantic origin of this term is in the pejorative use of the image of the mule.

51 Christian, op.cit., p. 199.

52 Ibid.

53 A scapegoat structure strikingly similar in effect to Sula's rehabilitation of Medallion in Toni Morrison's novel *Sula*, which also centres around a homo-erotic friendship, this time between two women, see Smith, Barbara 'Toward a Black Feminist Criticism', *Conditions Two* 1970, pp. 25–44; Morrison, Toni *Sula*, Grafton Books, London, 1982.

54 Du Bois, W. E. B. *The Souls of Black Folk*, Avon Books, New York, [1903] 1989, p. 3.

55 Some see this as an inevitable signifier of post-colonialism and slavery. In the Caribbean a matrifocal society draws its legacy from the serial

monogamy imposed on slave women and girls. In the Deep South slave fathers were seen as functional in reproductive terms but not needed emotionally to nurture, therefore men were often separated from their families, leaving women to do the parenting.

56 Christian, Barbara 'Shadows Uplifted', in Newton, Judith and Rosenfelt, Deborah (eds) *Feminist Criticism and Social Change*, Methuen, London, 1985, pp. 206–7.

57 As Patricia Hill Collins op. cit., p. 60, has put it:

> On all three dimensions of middle-class power – economic, political, and ideological – the Black middle-class differs from its white counterpart. Persistent racial discrimination means that Black middle-class families are less financially secure than members of the white middle-class.

58 Bailey, op. cit., p. 102.

59 Quoted in Collins, op. cit., p. 28.

60 I am using this term to describe a socially constructed, not innate phenomenon.

61 An image which despite the maleness of its original construction testifies to the persistence of the repressed Other (in this case femininity), and the way in which Black men are feminized by western culture. See, for example, Garber, Marjorie 'Black and White TV: Cross-Dressing the Color Line' in *Vested Interests: Cross-Dressing and Cultural Anxiety*, Routledge, London and New York, 1992, pp. 267–303.

62 Collins, op. cit., p. 11.

63 Lorde, Audre *Sister Outsider*, The Crossing Press, Trumansberg, New York, 1984, p. 114, quoted in Collins, op. cit., p. 91.

64 With the abolition of slavery in 1833 a literary tradition became possible. Previous to this Black literacy was illegal in the USA. The ability to read and write, and therefore to reason, was seen as proof of humanity. Justification for slavery was seen in terms of Black animality, therefore evidence of literary competence threatened the hegemony of slavery itself.

5 THE INVERSTIGATORS

1 An earlier version of this chapter appeared in Radstone, Susannah (ed.) *Sweet Dreams: Sexuality, Gender, and Popular Fiction*, Lawrence & Wishart, London, 1988, pp. 91–120.

2 See especially Foucault, Michel *Power/Knowledge: Selected Interviews and Other Writing 1972–77*, ed. Gordon, Colin, Harvester Press, Brighton, 1980, and Foucault, Michel *The History of Sexuality Vol.1: An Introduction*, Peregrine Books, Harmondsworth, Middlesex,1984.

3 Kolodny, Annette 'Dancing Through the Minefield: Some Observations on the Theory, Practice and Politics of a Feminist Literary Criticism', *Feminist Studies* 6 (1), 1980, pp. 1–25.

4 See Adams, Kate 'Making the World Safe for the Missionary Position', in Jay, Karla and Glasgow, Joanne (eds) *Lesbian Texts and Contexts: Radical Revisions*, New York University Press, New York, 1990 and

Onlywomen Press, London, 1992, pp. 255–74; Hamer, Diane 'I Am a Woman: Ann Bannon and the Writing of Lesbian Identity in the 1950s', in Lilly, Mark (ed.) *Lesbian and Gay Writing*, Macmillan, London, 1990, pp. 47–75; Weir, Angela and Wilson, Elizabeth 'The Greyhound Bus Station in the Evolution of Lesbian Popular Culture', in Munt, Sally (ed.) *New Lesbian Criticism*, Harvester Wheatsheaf, Hemel Hempstead and Columbia University Press, New York, 1992, pp. 95–114.

5 See the popular text by Caprio, Frank S. *Female Homosexuality: A Psychodynamic Study of Lesbianism*, The Citadel Press, New York, 1954, for a disturbing representation of lesbians as immature, neurotic, threatening, sadistic narcissists. The medicalizing discourse does not quite obscure the subtextual titillation rendered reader-friendly in the presentation of 'Case Histories' (chapter 13) and 'Autobiographical Confessions' (chapter 14).

6 Kate Adams describes this house as 'at the bottom' of the publishing pecking order.

7 Turner, Robert *Strange Sisters*, Beacon/Signal Books, n.d.; Hilton, Hilary *The Shadowy Sex*, Beacon Softcover Library, n.d.; Arthur, Claire *Lesbians in Black Lace*, New Chariot Library, Hollywood, 1963; Keene, Nan *Twice as Gay*, After Hours Books, 1964. The lack of bibliographic information printed on the books themselves, and the fact that they are not recorded in the US Library of Congress, reinforces their counter-cultural location. Thank you to Susan Everson of Falmer Library, Brighton Polytechnic, for exhaustively pursuing some record of their publishing history.

8 Klein, Kathleen Gregory *The Woman Detective: Gender and Genre*, University of Illinois Press, Urbana and Chicago, 1988, p. 220.

9 Wittig, Monique *Les Guérillères*, Viking, New York, 1971. Originally published by Editions de Minuit, Paris, 1969.

10 Modleski, Tania *Loving with a Vengeance: Mass Produced Fantasies for Women*, Methuen, London, 1984.

11 Meissner, William W. *The Paranoid Process*, Jason Aronson, New York, 1978, p. 767, quoted in Modleski, op. cit., p. 24.

12 Dollimore, Jonathan 'The Dominant and the Deviant: A Violent Dialectic', *Critical Quarterly* 28 (1 & 2), 1986, pp. 179–92.

13 To quote Sonja Ruehl, 'Inverts and Experts: Radclyffe Hall and the Lesbian Identity', in Brunt, Rosalind and Rowan, Caroline (eds) *Feminism, Culture and Politics*, Lawrence & Wishart, London, 1982, p. 18:

> Once a category like homosexuality has been set up and individuals have started to be defined by it, then the so-named 'homosexuals' may group under it and start to speak for themselves. So, Foucault says, 'homosexuality began to speak on its own behalf . . . often in the same vocabulary, using the same categories, by which it was medically disqualified'. He calls this process the development of a 'reverse discourse'.

It is a debatable point whether Foucault can be interpreted as positing a subject to liberate.

14 Rich, Adrienne 'Compulsory Heterosexuality and Lesbian Existence', in

Snitow, Ann Barr *et al.* (eds) *Desire: The Politics of Sexuality*, Virago Press, London, 1984, pp. 212–41.

15 To stretch the analogy, one can ask the same question of the relationship between lesbian-feminism and the dominant hegemonic discourse. To square the circle, one might also investigate in what ways if any lesbian crime fiction 'upholds' the politics of lesbian feminism(s).

16 In several of these texts the binary heterosexual sickness/homosexual health is common, and relates back to themes in earlier novels such as *Rubyfruit Jungle*, as previously mentioned. For an interesting exposé of the ideological conflation between sex, health and sickness, see Mort, Frank 'The Domain of the Sexual', *Screen Education* 36, Autumn, 1980, pp. 69–84, and Bland, Lucy 'The Domain of the Sexual: A Response', *Screen Education* 39, Summer, 1981, pp. 56–67.

17 Palmer, Paulina 'The Lesbian Feminist Thriller and Detective Novel' in Hobby, Elaine and White, Chris (eds) *What Lesbians Do in Books*, The Women's Press, London, 1991, pp. 9–27.

18 See the essay 'Inscribing Femininity: French Theories of the Feminine' by Jones, Ann Rosalind in Greene, Gayle and Kahn, Coppelia (eds) *Making a Difference: Feminist Literary Criticism*, Methuen, London, 1985, pp. 80–112.

19 Symons, Julian *Bloody Murder*, Viking, London, [1972] 1985, p. 66.

20 Wilson, Elizabeth *Mirror Writing: An Autobiography*, Virago Press, London, 1982, p. 155.

21 See Vance, Carole S. *Pleasure and Danger: Exploring Female Sexuality*, papers from the conference 'Towards a Politics of Female Sexuality', Barnard College, New York, 1982, Routledge & Kegan Paul, Boston, Mass., 1984.

22 See, for example, for the debate in Britain: Simmonds, Felly Nkweto 'SHE'S GOTTA HAVE IT: The Representation of Black Female Sexuality on Film', *Feminist Review* 29, 1988, pp. 10–22; Chester, Gail and Dickey, Julienne (eds) *Feminism and Censorship: The Current Debate*, Prism Press, Bridport, 1988; Ardill, Susan and O'Sullivan, Sue 'Sex in the Summer of '88', *Feminist Review* 31, Spring, 1989, pp. 126–34; Norden, Barbara 'Campaign Against Pornography', *Feminist Review* 35, Summer, 1990, pp. 1–8; Ellis, Kate, O'Dair, Barbara and Tallmer, Abby 'Feminism and Pornography', *Feminist Review* 36, Autumn, 1990, pp. 15–18; Rodgerson, Gillian and Semple, Linda 'Who Watches the Watchwomen?: Feminists Against Censorship', *Feminist Review* 36, Autumn, 1990, pp. 19–24.

23 Nestle, Joan *A Restricted Country*, Sheba Feminist Press, London, 1988, p. 100.

24 Ibid., pp. 106–7.

25 I am appropriating a model here first articulated by Richard Dyer in his paper on 'The Sad Young Man', given at the *Questions of Homosexuality Conference*, Institute of Romance Studies, University of London, 6 June 1992.

26 Stimpson, Catherine 'Zero Degree Deviancy: The Lesbian Novel in English', in Abel, Elizabeth (ed.) *Writing and Sexual Difference*, Harvester Press, Brighton, 1982, p. 244.

27 Ellis, Havelock 'Sexual Inversion' in *Studies in the Psychology of Sex*, 2 vols, New York, [1901] 1986, 1:1, p. 122. Quoted in Stimpson, op. cit., p. 248.

28 As Weir and Wilson, op. cit. have argued, lesbian culture of the 1950s had its own liberatory strategies, including the creation of urban bohemianism, and the central significance of the bar as a resource. The image of the 1950s as seamlessly oppressive does not allow for a view of culture as being a constantly contested field between dominant and subordinate interests.

29 Belsey, Catherine *Critical Practice*, Methuen, London, 1980, p. 65.

30 By depriving him of his human status, and according him an animal status, this excuses any amount of physical experimentation and abuse; this is the very hierarchy the Animal Rights Movement is at pains to critique. Moreover, the implicit conflation of 'animal' with 'evil' reveals a conceptual confusion on the nature of deviancy: an animal cannot be consciously malignant.

31 This universality is implicitly western and Caucasian as the (racist) use of 'cannibal subspecies' suggests, evoking, as it does, an image of the African savage.

32 The character also forms the basis for the short story 'Jessie' in Forrest's science fiction and mystery collection *Dreams and Swords*, Naiad Press, Florida, 1987, pp. 9–42.

33 For further elaboration see Nestle, op. cit.; Nichols, Margaret 'Lesbian Sexuality: Issues and Developing Theory', in The Boston Lesbian Psychologies Collective (eds) *Lesbian Psychologies*, University of Illinois Press, Boston, 1987, pp. 97–125; Jeffreys, Sheila 'Butch and Femme: Now and Then', in The Lesbian History Group (eds) *Not a Passing Phase*, The Women's Press, London, 1989, pp. 158–87.

34 Daly, Mary *Beyond God the Father: Toward a Philosophy of Women's Liberation*, Beacon Press, Boston, 1973, p. 194.

35 Turner, Jenny 'Right-ons', *London Review of Books* 13 (20), 24 October 1991, pp. 22–3.

36 Holland, Norman N. 'UNITY IDENTITY TEXT SELF', *Proceedings of the Modern Language Association* 90, 1975, p. 816. Quoted in Freund, Elizabeth *The Return of the Reader: Reader Response Criticism*, Methuen, London, 1987, p. 124.

37 SAMOIS is a lesbian-feminist sadomasochist organization based in San Francisco.

38 However pleasurable this proves to be, I am reminded of E. Ann Kaplan's cautionary:

> to simply celebrate whatever gives us sexual pleasure seems to me both problematic and too easy: we need to analyse how it is that certain things turn us on, how sexuality has been constructed in patriarchy to produce pleasure in the dominance-submission forms.

Kaplan, E. Ann 'Is the Gaze Male?', in Snitow *et al.*, op. cit., p. 328.

39 See work on romance by feminist critics such as: Taylor, Helen 'Romantic Readers', in Carr, Helen (ed.) *From My Guy to Sci-Fi: Genre and Women's Writing in the Postmodern World*, Pandora Press, London,

1989, pp. 58–77; Griffin, Christine 'Cultures of Femininity: Romance Revisited', CCCS Occasional Papers, University of Birmingham, 1982; Radford, Jean (ed.) *The Progress of Romance: The Politics of Popular Fiction*, Routledge & Kegan Paul, London, 1986; Thurston, Carol *The Romance Revolution: Erotic Novels for Women and the Quest for a New Sexual Identity*, University of Illinois Press, Champaign, 1987.

40 Fuss, Diana (ed.) *Inside/Out: Lesbian Theories, Gay Theories*, Routledge, London and New York, 1991, pp. 6–7.

41 Butler, Judith *Gender Trouble: Feminism and the Subversion of Identity*, Routledge, New York and London, 1990.

42 Butler, Judith 'Imitation and Gender Insubordination', in Fuss, Diana (ed.) *Inside/Out: Lesbian Theories, Gay Theories*, Routledge, London and New York, 1991, p. 18.

43 Ibid., p. 23.

44 The name *has* to be a joke.

45 See, for example, Foucault (1984), op. cit., and *Discipline and Punish: The Birth of the Prison*, translated by Sheridan, A., Peregrine Books, Harmondsworth, 1977; Butler, (1990), op. cit.; Gatens, Moira *Feminism and Philosophy: Perspectives on Difference and Equality*, Polity Press, Cambridge, 1991; Barrett, Michèle *Women's Oppression Today: The Marxist/Feminist Encounter*, Verso, London, 1988 (revised edn), Introduction; Willis, Susan *A Primer for Everyday Life*, Routledge, London and New York, 1991, pp. 62–85; Meyer, Richard 'Rock Hudson's Body', in Fuss, op. cit., pp. 259–88.

46 Foucault (1984), op. cit.

47 Cook, J. 'Discourse', in Fowler, Roger (ed.) *A Dictionary of Modern Critical Terms*, Routledge, London, 1987, p. 64.

48 Ibid., p. 66.

6 MURDERING THE INNER MAN?

1 Brooks, Peter 'Freud's Masterplot' in Felman, Shoshana (ed.) *Literature and Psychoanalysis*, Johns Hopkins University Press, Baltimore, 1977, p. 285. Quoted in Gunn, Daniel *Psychoanalysis and Fiction*, Cambridge University Press, Cambridge (USA), 1988, p. 133.

2 Gunn, op. cit., p. 5.

3 Muller, John P. and Richardson, William J. (eds) *The Purloined Poe: Lacan, Derrida and Psychoanalytic Reading*, Johns Hopkins University Press, Baltimore, 1988.

4 Mitchell, Juliet *Psychoanalysis and Feminism*, Pelican/Penguin Books, Harmondsworth, 1974.

5 See Krzowski, Sue and Land, Pat (eds) *In Our Own Hands*, The Women's Press, London, 1981, and *In Our Experience*, The Women's Press, London, 1988, for a detailed description of the work performed at The Women's Therapy Centre.

6 See Mitchell, op. cit. and Frosh, Stephen *The Politics of Psychoanalysis*, Macmillan, London, 1987, pp. 174–207 for a description of these disputes and further detail on the work feminists have executed within the field of psychoanalysis.

7 See Sayers, Janet *Mothering Psychoanalysis*, Hamish Hamilton, London, 1991 for a description of how leading women psychoanalysts after Freud – Helene Deutsch, Karen Horney, Anna Freud, and Melanie Klein – set up the psychoanalytic focus on mothering in opposition to Freud's more patriarchal emphasis on fathering (in the oedipus complex), which has come to dominate the entire subsequent theory and practice of psychoanalysis. Like Christiane Olivier, Sayers believes that 'forgetting the father' actually does both women and men a disservice, as essentially both figures are necessary. Apart from sharing both critics' concern with the way mothering as a process is constructed in our culture, I would reject their implicit bias in favour of heterosexuality and linking it so firmly with reproduction. Instead I would suggest that parents of either biological sex can supply the role of 'other' necessary for individuation from the biological mother.

8 Bindel, Julie 'The State of the Movement', in *Trouble and Strife*, 1988, pp. 50–2.

9 And even that symbolic murderer, Jessie, in Bryant, Dorothy *Killing Wonder* (1981).

10 See Caputi, Jane and Daly, Mary *Webster's First New Intergalactic Wickedary of the English Language*, The Women's Press, London, 1988.

11 Binyon, T. J. *'Murder Will Out': The Detective in Fiction*, Oxford University Press, Oxford, 1990, p. 27.

12 This cultural concept of a woman's space is located in a middle-class feminism which draws from discourses of property and popular psychology; it is an image which has spurned many political actions in the last twenty years, informing a praxis of separatism and 'women-only' spaces in many areas of feminist culture from Rape Crisis lines, to conferences, to collections of critical essays.

13 Clément, Catherine *The Weary Sons of Freud*, trans. by Nicole Ball, Verso, London, 1978 and 1987.

14 Ibid., p. 38.

15 See, for example, Modleski, Tania *Loving with a Vengeance: Mass Produced Fantasies for Women*, Methuen, London, 1984; De Lauretis, T. *Alice Doesn't: Feminism, Semiotics, Cinema*, Indiana University Press, Bloomington, 1984; Mayne, Judith *Revision: Essays in Feminist Film Criticism*, American Film Institute, Los Angeles, 1984; Doane, Mary Ann *The Desire to Desire*, Indiana University Press, Bloomington, 1987; Mulvey, Laura *Visual and Other Pleasures*, Macmillan, London, 1989; Gledhill, Christine *Home is Where the Heart Is*, BFI/Macmillan, London, 1989.

16 See 'Case I: Fräulein Anna O. (Breuer)', in Freud, Sigmund and Breuer, Josef *Studies on Hysteria* [1895], translated by Strachey, James and Alice, Pelican Freud Library vol. 3, Penguin Books, Harmondsworth, 1974, pp. 73–162.

17 See Freud, Sigmund 'The History of the Psychoanalytic Movement', translated by Brill, A. A. (1917), in Strachey, James (ed.) *Historical and Expository Works on Psychoanalysis*, Pelican Freud Library vol. 15, Penguin Books, Harmondsworth, 1986.

18 See Freud, Sigmund 'The Psychotherapy of Hysteria', in Freud and Breuer, op. cit., pp. 337–93.
19 Freud and Breuer, op. cit., p. 101.
20 See Freud, Sigmund *On Sexuality*, translated by Richards, Angela, Pelican Freud Library vol. 7, Penguin Books, Harmondsworth, 1977.
21 In fact the only 'real' homosexual in the novel is this anonymous rapist who assaults young men and then murders them, thus reinforcing the stereotype of violent pederast. Whether this is offset by the majority of characters' selfishness and abuse of others is a debatable point. I feel that the construction of this episode in the book reinforces psychoanalysis's prejudice in seeing homosexuality as a narcissistic, regressive, underdeveloped sexuality stuck in emanating heterosexual gender identities.
22 See Freud, Sigmund 'Lecture 10: Symbolism in Dreams' [1914], in *Introductory Lectures on Psychoanalysis*, translated by Strachey, James, Pelican Freud Library vol. 1, Penguin Books, Harmondsworth, 1973, p. 188. Elsewhere, in chapter 6 section E of *The Interpretation of Dreams* Freud makes the point that the interpretation of symbols is a complex, subtle matter, rejecting the kind of crude 'pop' symbolism which has come to proliferate in literary analysis (of which the identification of phallic symbols must be the most common). See 'Representation by Symbols in Dreams – Some Further Typical Dreams', in Freud, Sigmund *The Interpretation of Dreams* [1900], translated by Strachey, James, Pelican Freud Library vol. 4, Penguin Books, Harmondsworth, 1976, pp. 466–529. Hence I am aware that this kind of appropriation is open to some problems, and I am grateful to Graham McFee for drawing this to my attention.
23 Freud and Breuer, op. cit., pp. 161–2.
24 See work on 'Dora', particularly, in which feminists have argued that this was an issue Freud could not face, and avoided; Rush, Florence 'The Great Freudian Cover-Up', *Trouble and Strife* 4, Winter, 1984, and 'Hysteria or Resistance – Dora The Great Freudian Cover Up Part II', *Trouble and Strife* 15, Spring, 1989.
25 Freud and Breuer, op.cit., p. 162.
26 Sayers, op.cit., p. 150.
27 Olivier, Christiane *Jocasta's Children: The Imprint of the Mother*, translated by Craig, George, Routledge, London, 1989. The thesis behind this book is a worthwhile attempt to deconstruct the Mother, but I also felt that it did not take the ideological/social conditions sufficiently into account, and that it regretfully fell into a homophobic mode in several places, in common with many psychoanalytic texts which see homosexuality as immature, pathologized, or narcissistic, or even completely unrealizable within a seamlessly heterosexual paradigm.
28 Ibid., p. 117.
29 For an example of the way ego psychology has developed, see Maddi, F. R. *Personality Theories: A Comparative Analysis*, The Dorsey Press, Homewood, Ill., 1980.
30 Among the televised trials of actual serial killers, and their massive representation in the popular media, from news items to 'true crime' magazines, the permeation through Western culture of 'factionalized'

(i.e. based on real people) accounts of serial killers has resulted in a new sub-genre of thrillers, of which the Hollywood blockbuster *Silence of the Lambs* (1991) was a prime example. Contemporaneous with this release was the counter-cinema movie *Henry: Portrait of a Serial Killer* (1991), which rejected the investigative trajectory altogether. Henry's personality was the sole site of textual interrogation, thus manifesting the 'psychological' trend of crime fiction, as instigated by women writers, in its logical (and most disturbing) extreme. Martin Scorsese's (1992) film *Cape Fear* can be read as part of this trend. His authority as *auteur* – perceived by some as the best living North American director – renders his choice of subject intrinsically mainstream.

31 Sayers, op. cit.

7 'WHAT DOES IT MEAN TO SING "SOMEWHERE OVER THE RAINBOW" AND RELEASE BALLOONS?'

1 Thanks to Lois McNay, Janet Harbord, and Linda Rozmovits for reading and commenting upon earlier drafts.

2 Nicholson, Linda J. (ed.) *Feminism/Postmodernism*, Routledge, London, 1990, p. 9.

3 Ibid., p. 10.

4 See Butler, Judith 'Imitation and Gender Insubordination', in Fuss, Diana *Inside/Out: Lesbian Theories, Gay Theories*, Routledge, London and New York, 1991, pp. 13–31.

5 Here I would disagree with theorists such as Sheila Jeffreys who propose a model of the eroticization of sameness and equality as being true homosexual desire – see Jeffreys, Sheila *Anticlimax*, The Women's Press, London, 1990. This self-interrogation, though, is double-edged: to what extent are we implicated in the dominant construction of homosexuality as *the* site of inquiry into identity, which is underwritten by presumptions of what is 'normal' and therefore beyond examination?

6 'Queer means to fuck with gender. There are straight queers, bi-queers, tranny queers, lez queers, fag queers, SM queers, fisting queers in every single street in this apathetic country of ours.' Anonymous leaflet: 'Queer Power Now', London, 1991, quoted in Smyth, Cherry *Lesbians Talk Queer Notions*, Scarlet Press, London, 1992, p. 17.

7 Ibid., p. 60.

8 See, for example, Callinicos, Alex *Against Postmodernism*, Polity Press, Cambridge, 1989.

9 Collins, Jim *Uncommon Cultures: Popular Culture and Post-Modernism*, Routledge, London, 1989, p. 27.

10 Weedon, Chris *Feminist Practice and Poststructuralist Theory*, Basil Blackwell, Oxford, 1987, pp. 160–1.

11 Previously published in Radstone, Susannah (ed.) *Sweet Dreams: Sexuality, Gender and Popular Fiction*, Lawrence & Wishart, London, 1988, pp. 91–120.

12 Collins, op. cit., p. 35.
13 Ibid., p. 60.
14 Ibid., p. 40.
15 Ibid., p. 60.
16 Bryant, Dorothy *Killing Wonder*, The Women's Press, London, 1981.
17 Feminist fiction, like much women's fiction, is full of food – see Russ, Joanna 'Somebody's Trying to Kill Me and I Think It's My Husband: The Modern Gothic', *Journal of Popular Culture* 6, Spring, Bowling Green University Popular Press, Ohio, 1973, pp. 666–91. Often, in lesbian crime fiction, after a scene of narrative suspense, the sleuth cooks a delicious meal which serves to placate the reader's tension, to normalize the fictional realm, and thus to ensure her continuing identification with the protagonist.
18 Presumably this structure is not intended to convince the reader, in the manner of neo-fascist groups and intelligentsia, that the Holocaust was a Jewish conspiracy myth peddled for sympathy and political power. Perhaps it is a comment on a culture's alienation from its own history, and the impossibility of retrieving truth.
19 Chandler, Raymond *The Simple Art of Murder*, Ballantine Books, New York, 1972, pp. 20–1.
20 Kerouac, Jack *On the Road*, Penguin Books, Harmondsworth, [1957] 1972, p. 14.
21 Benjamin, Walter *Charles Baudelaire: A Lyric Poet in the Era of High Capitalism*, New Left Books, London, 1973, p. 36.
22 Wolff, Janet *Feminine Sentences: Essays on Women and Culture*, Polity Press, Cambridge, 1990, p. 39.
23 Ibid., p. 41.
24 Ibid., p. 42.
25 See McHale, Brian *Postmodernist Fiction*, Routledge, London, 1987 for an excellent elucidation of post-modernist literary structures, despite its masculine bias and occasional homophobic remarks.
26 Pynchon, Thomas *Gravity's Rainbow*, Viking Press, New York, 1973, p. 711.
27 Schulman speaking on *Out on Tuesday*, 27 March 1990, Channel Four.
28 McHale, op. cit.
29 For an example of this see Hebdige, Dick *Subculture: The Meaning of Style*, Methuen, London, 1979.
30 Schulman, op. cit.
31 Currie, Peter 'The eccentric self: anti-characterization and the problem of the subject in American postmodernist fiction', in Bradbury, Malcolm and Sigmund, R.O., (eds) *Contemporary American Fiction*, Edward Arnold, London, 1987, p. 54.
32 Propp, Vladimir *Morphology of the Folk-Tale*, University of Texas Press, Austin, 1968, 2nd edn.
33 Hutcheon, Linda *The Politics of Postmodernism*, Routledge, London, 1989.
34 Fuss, Diana *Essentially Speaking: Feminism, Nature and Difference*, Routledge, London, 1990, p. 104. This is a familiar worry which emanates

from what some see as the disintegration of the national Women's Liberation Movement during the early 1980s.

35 Gallop, Jane *The Daughter's Seduction: Feminism and Psychoanalysis*, Cornell University Press, Ithaca, 1982, p. xii, quoted in Fuss, op. cit., p. 104.
36 Fuss, op. cit., p. 118.
37 Ewert, Jeanne C. 'Lost in the Hermeneutic Funhouse: Patrick Modiano's Postmodern Detective', in Walker, Ronald G. and Frazer, June M. *The Cunning Craft*, Western Illinois University Press, Macomb, 1990, p. 167. Ewert discusses the work of Alain Robbe-Grillet, and Patrick Modiano.
38 See the work on *écriture feminine*, by French literary theorists such as Julia Kristeva, Luce Irigaray, and Hélène Cixous.
39 Collins, op. cit., p. 89.

8 AN UNSUITABLE GENRE FOR A WOMAN?

1 Klein, Kathleen Gregory *The Woman Detective: Gender and Genre*, University of Illinois Press, Urbana and Chicago, 1988, pp. 173–4.
2 Ibid., p. 228.
3 Ibid., p. 227.
4 Maio, Kathleen L. 'A Strange and Fierce Delight: The Early Days of Women's Mystery Fiction', *Chrysalis* 10, n.d., pp. 93–105.
5 Eden, Rick A. 'Detective Fiction as Satire', in *Genre* 16, University of Oklahoma, Autumn, 1983, pp. 279–95.
6 Grella, George 'The Hard-Boiled Detective Novel', in Winks, Robin W., (ed.) *Detective Fiction*, Prentice-Hall, New Jersey, 1980, pp. 107–20.
7 Frye, Northrop *Anatomy of Criticism*, Princeton University Press, New Jersey, 1977.
8 Eden op. cit., p. 284.
9 Ibid.
10 Ibid., p. 285.
11 Ibid., pp. 285–6.
12 Ibid., p. 286.
13 Ibid., p. 292.
14 Ibid.
15 This is expressed literally in the ending of *A Paperback Thriller* – see chapter 7.
16 Eden, op. cit., p. 294.
17 Ibid., p. 294.
18 Moretti, Franco *Signs Taken for Wonders*, Verso, London, 1988, p. 148.
19 'While the criminal opens the action and the detective closes it, Watson drags it out.' Ibid., p. 146.
20 From Conan Doyle, A. 'A Scandal in Bohemia', quoted in ibid., p. 147.
21 Foster, Marion *The Monarchs are Flying*, Firebrand Books, Ithaca, 1987.
22 This is also reminiscent of Schulman's *The Sophie Horowitz Story*.
23 Palmer, Jerry *Thrillers: Genesis and Structure of a Popular Genre*, Edward Arnold, London, 1978, p. 67.
24 Or, more likely, female/masculinity; the biological term is wedded to the cultural term intentionally as frequently in feminist fiction the females

are unproblematically blameless, as patriarchy's victims or feminism's victors. Men, however, are sometimes treated as cultural animals and are therefore occasionally redeemable – Ted Perkins in the Sarah Dreher novels, or Sam in the Gillian Slovo novels are examples. Usually masculinity, rather than simply males, is the ideological perpetrator.

25 Vole, Zenobia N. *Osten's Bay*, Naiad Press, Florida, 1988. A perfectly crafted pulp novel, *Osten's Bay* is lesbian Mills and Boon with an ecological conscience.

26 Bayer, Sandy *The Crystal Curtain*, Alyson Publications, Boston, 1988. *The Crystal Curtain*, in common with Camarin Grae's books, links evil with the psychic and supernatural. It contains the most sensationally gruesome scenes in any lesbian literature I have read, presumably in order to communicate the violent extremes that masculinity and madness may cause.

27 Zaremba, Eve *A Reason to Kill*, PaperJacks, Ontario, 1978; *Work for A Million*, Amanita, Toronto, 1987; *Beyond Hope*, Amanita, Toronto, 1987. Klein, op. cit., p. 180, describes *A Reason to Kill*, as 'an inadvertent parody. Eve Zaremba sets up her hard-boiled detective to play Sam Spade but fails to provide a workable script'. Unfortunately Zaremba's three novels all seem to fall slightly short of conscious satire; the attempt to emulate the traditional form successfully is too worthily exacted.

28 Unless they are female.

29 Magezis, Joy *Vanishing Act*, Pandora Press, London, 1988.

30 Milton, Nancy *The China Option*, Pluto Press, London, 1984.

31 As Klein, op. cit., p. 224, points out regarding heroism:

> As the protagonist is not simply a man but the glorification of masculine traits, the substitution of a woman with her own feminine virtues or incompletely assumed masculine ones leaves the novel without its center. But, it is not the decentered genre which is mocked. Rather it is the deficient hero/ine.

This response is conditional on the type of reader. Some may say a novel without a centre is a radical form; Klein is describing a particularly masculine point of view.

32 Ibid., p. 227.

33 Ibid.

34 Antoinette Azolakov combines literary sense with excellent characterization in both novels, which treat the interaction of butch/femme/feminist selves with humorous sensitivity.

35 In a footnote Klein, op. cit., p. 229, mentions briefly the following novels as being feminocentric and as offering a challenge to generic restrictions: Amanda Cross's *Death in a Tenured Position* and *No Word from Winifred*, Barbara Wilson's *Murder in the Collective* and *Sisters of the Road*, Valerie Miner's *Murder in the English Department*, and Barbara Paul's *The Renewable Virgin*. But since her otherwise excellent study does generally consider feminist novels unsuccessfully conventional, this short note which covers very disparate novels sadly does not do justice to her main argument.

36 Ibid., p. 228.

37 Volosinov, V. *Marxism and the Philosophy of Language*, Seminar Press, New York, 1973.
38 Fiske, John *et al.* (eds) *Key Concepts in Communication*, Methuen, London, 1983, p. 144.
39 The Women's Press catalogue of Autumn 1992 has just five crime novels, of which Mary Wings' new novel is the only original publication. *Divine Victim* continues in hard-boiled parodic mode, but returns to Gothic mystery roots; two novels by Deborah Powell are historical classic gumshoe dramas; two more reprints of Marcia Muller's bestseller series starring Sharon McCone are likely to maintain the dominance and popularity of the liberal feminist private investigator.
40 Harris, Thomas *The Silence of the Lambs*, St Martin's Press, New York, 1988.
41 It is also germane to remember that Watson was a doctor.
42 Directed by Jonathan Demme, 1991.
43 Unacknowledged review, *Sunday Tribune*, inside flyleaf of Zahavi, Helen *A Dirty Weekend*, Flamingo Books, London, 1992.
44 Unacknowledged review, *Marie Claire* magazine, back cover.
45 The efficiency of these profiles depends upon the way in which they are communicated as too real – they are painful to read.
46 A handful of Brighton women, Summer, 1992 – not exactly a scientific grouping, but their unanimity was convincing.

Fictional bibliography

Aldrich, Ann *We Walk Alone: Through Lesbos' Lonely Groves*, Fawcett Gold Medal Books, New York, 1955.

Armstrong, Charlotte *Mischief*, Pandora Press, London, [1951] 1988.

Azolakov, Antoinette *Cass and the Stone Butch*, Banned Books, Texas, 1987.

—— *Skiptrace*, Banned Books, Texas, 1988.

—— *The Contactees Die Young*, Banned Books, Texas, 1989.

Bailey, Hilary *Hannie Richards: The Intrepid Adventures of a Restless Wife*, Virago Press, London, 1985.

Baker, Nikki *In the Game*, Naiad Press, Tallahassee, 1991.

Bayer, Sandy *The Crystal Curtain*, Alyson Publications, Boston, 1988.

Beal, M. F. *Angel Dance*, The Crossing Press, Freedom, [1977] 1990.

Bell, Josephine *The Port of London Murders*, Pandora Press, London, [1938] 1987.

—— *Easy Prey*, Pandora Press, London, [1959] 1988.

Bland, Eleanor Taylor *Dead Time*, St Martin's Press, New York, 1992.

Bowers, Elizabeth *Ladies Night*, Virago Press, London, 1990.

Bradford, Kelly *Footprints*, The Crossing Press, Freedom, 1988.

Branch, Pamela *Murder's Little Sister*, Pandora Press, London, 1989.

Brand, Christianna *Green for Danger*, Pandora Press, London, [1945] 1987.

—— *London Particular*, Pandora Press, London, [1952] 1988.

Brown, Rita Mae *Wish You Were Here*, Bantam Books, New York, 1990.

Bryant, Dorothy *Killing Wonder*, The Women's Press, London, [1981] 1982.

Bushell, Agnes *Shadowdance*, The Crossing Press, Freedom, California, 1989.

Christie, Agatha *The Mysterious Affair at Styles*, Triad/Panther Books, St Albans, [1920] 1978.

Cody, Liza *Dupe*, Arrow Books, London, [1980] 1991.

—— *Bad Company*, Arrow Books, London, [1982] 1991.

—— *Stalker*, Arrow Books, London, [1984] 1992.

—— *Head Case*, Collins, London, 1985.

—— *Rift*, Collins, London, 1988.

—— *Backhand*, Chatto & Windus, London, 1991.

Cornwell, Patricia *Postmortem*, Futura Publications, London, 1990.

—— *Body of Evidence*, Macdonald & Co., London, 1991.

—— *All that Remains*, Little, Brown & Co., London, 1992.

—— *Cruel and Unusual*, Little, Brown & Co., London, 1993.
Cross, Amanda *Death in a Tenured Position*, Ballantine Books, New York, 1981.
—— *Sweet Death, Kind Death*, Ballantine Books, New York, 1984.
—— *No Word from Winifred*, Virago Press, London, 1987.
—— *A Trap for Fools*, Virago Press, London, 1990.
Crossley, Barbara *Candyfloss Coast*, Virago Press, London, [1988] 1991.
Day, Marele *The Life and Crimes of Harry Lavender*, Allen & Unwin, Sydney, 1988.
Dreher, Sarah *Stoner McTavish*, Pandora Press, London, [1985] 1987.
—— *Something Shady*, New Victoria Publishers, Vermont, 1986.
—— *Gray Magic*, New Victoria Publishers, Vermont, 1987.
—— *A Captive in Time*, New Victoria Publishers, Vermont, 1990.
Farrell, Maud *Skid*, The Women's Press, London, 1990.
Fisher, Rudolph *The Conjure Man Dies: A Mystery Tale of Dark Harlem*, Ann Arbor Paperbacks/University of Michigan Press, Michigan, [1932] 1992.
Fitzgerald, Kitty *Marge*, Sheba Feminist Publishers, London, 1984.
Forrest, Katherine V. *Amateur City*, Pandora Press, London, [1984] 1987.
—— *Dreams and Swords*, Naiad Press, Tallahassee, 1987.
—— *Murder at the Nightwood Bar*, Pandora Press, London, 1987.
—— *The Beverly Malibu*, Pandora Press, London, 1990.
—— *Murder By Tradition*, Naiad Press, Tallahassee, 1991.
Foster, Marion *The Monarchs are Flying*, Firebrand Books, Ithaca, 1987.
Franklyn, Miles *Bring the Monkey*, Pandora Press, London, [1933] 1987.
Freeman, Gillian *An Easter Egg Hunt*, Hamish Hamilton, London, 1981.
Fremlin, Celia *The Hours Before Dawn*, Pandora Press, London, [1959] 1988.
Gee, Maggie *Dying, In Other Words*, Paladin, London, [1981] 1987.
Gilbert, Anthony *The Spinster's Secret*, Pandora Press, London, [1946] 1987.
Godfrey, Ellen *Murder Behind Locked Doors*, Virago Press, London, 1989.
Grafton, Sue *'A' is for Alibi*, Bantam Books, New York, [1982] 1987.
—— *'B' is for Burglar*, Macmillan, London, [1985] 1988.
—— *'C' is for Corpse*, Macmillan, London, [1986] 1988.
—— *'D' is for Deadbeat*, Macmillan, London, [1987] 1989.
—— *'E' is for Evidence*, Bantam Books, New York, [1988] 1989.
—— *'F' is for Fugitive*, Bantam Books, New York, [1989] 1990.
—— *'G' is for Gumshoe*, Macmillan, London, 1990.
—— *'H' is for Homicide*, Bantam Books, New York, [1991] 1992.
—— *'I' is for Innocent*, Macmillan, London, 1992.
—— *'J' is for Justice*, Macmillan, London, 1993.
Grant-Adamson, Lesley *The Face of Death*, Faber & Faber, London, 1985.
—— *Patterns in the Dust*, Faber & Faber, London, 1985.
—— *Guilty Knowledge*, Faber & Faber, London, 1986.
—— *Wild Justice*, Faber & Faber, London, 1987.
—— *Threatening Eye*, Faber & Faber, London, 1988.
—— *Curse the Darkness*, Faber & Faber, London, 1990.
Guy, Rosa *The Disappearance*, Dell Publishing Co., New York, 1979.
—— *New Guys Around The Block*, Penguin Books, Harmondsworth, [1983] 1989.

Hart, Ellen *Hallowed Murder*, The Seal Press, Seattle, 1989.
Highsmith, Patricia *Strangers in a Train*, Pan, London, [1950] 1968.
—— *Found In the Street*, Penguin Books, Harmondsworth, 1986.
Hurston, Zora Neale *Their Eyes Were Watching God*, Virago, London, [1937] 1986.
James, P. D. *Shroud for A Nightingale*, Faber & Faber, London, 1971.
—— *An Unsuitable Job for a Woman*, Faber & Faber, London, 1972.
—— *Death of an Expert Witness*, Faber & Faber, London, 1977.
—— *The Skull Beneath the Skin*, Sphere Books, London, [1982] 1983.
—— *A Taste for Death*, Faber & Faber, London, 1986.
—— *Devices and Desires*, Faber & Faber, London, 1990.
—— *The Children of Men*, Faber & Faber, London, 1992.
Komo, Dolores *Clio Browne: Private Investigator*, The Crossing Press, Freedom, 1988.
LaPierre, Janet *Children's Games*, Virago Press, London, 1990.
—— *The Cruel Mother*, Virago Press, London, 1990.
Lawrence, Hilda *Death of a Doll*, Pandora Press, London, [1947] 1987.
—— *Blood Upon the Snow*, Pandora Press, London, [1946] 1988.
—— *Duet of Death*, Pandora Press, London, [1949] 1988.
Lewin, Elsa *I, Anna*, Serpent's Tail, London, [1984] 1990.
Lynch, Lee *Sue Slate: Private Eye*, Naiad Press, Tallahassee, 1989.
McCauley, Carole Spearin *Cold Steal*, The Women's Press, London, 1991.
McConnell, Vicki P. *Mrs. Porter's Letter*, Naiad Press, Tallahassee, 1982.
—— *The Burnton Widows*, Naiad Press, Tallahassee, 1984.
—— *Double Daughter*, Naiad Press, Tallahassee, 1988.
McDermid, Val *Report for Murder*, The Women's Press, London, 1987.
—— *Common Murder*, The Women's Press, London, 1989.
—— *Final Edition*, The Women's Press, London, 1991.
—— *Dead Beat*, Victor Gollancz, London, 1992.
—— *Kick Back*, Victor Gollancz, London, 1993.
—— *Union Jack*, The Women's Press, London, 1993.
McGregor, Iona *Death Wore a Diadem*, The Women's Press, London, 1989.
Machin, Barbara *South of the Border*, The Women's Press, London, 1990.
McNab, Claire *Lessons in Murder*, Naiad Press, Tallahasee, 1988.
—— *Fatal Reunion*, Naiad Press, Tallahassee, 1989.
—— *Death Down Under*, Naiad Press, Tallahassee, 1990.
—— *Cop Out*, Naiad Press, Tallahassee, 1992.
Macquet, Claire *Looking for Ammu*, Virago Press, London, [1988] 1992.
McRae, Diana *All the Muscle You Need*, Spinsters/Aunt Lute, San Francisco, 1988.
Magezis, Joy *Vanishing Act*, Pandora Press, London, 1988.
Mainwaring, Marion *Murder in Pastiche: or Nine Detectives All at Sea*, Pandora Press, London, 1987.
Marrin, Minette *The Eye of the Beholder*, Faber & Faber, London, [1988] 1989.
Meyer, Lynn *Paperback Thriller*, The Crossing Press, Freedom, [1975] 1989.
Miner, Valerie *Blood Sisters*, The Women's Press, London, 1981.
—— *Murder in the English Department*, The Women's Press, London, 1982.
Mitchell, Gladys *Speedy Death*, The Hogarth Press, London, [1929] 1988.

—— *The Saltmarsh Murders*, The Hogarth Press, London, [1932] 1984.
—— *When Last I Died*, The Hogarth Press, London, [1941] 1985.
—— *Laurels Are Poison*, The Hogarth Press, London, [1942] 1986.
Moody, Susan *Penny Black*, Futura Publications, London, 1985.
Moore, Maureen *Fieldwork*, Pandora Press, London, 1988.
Morell, Mary *Final Session*, Spinsters Book Co., San Francisco, 1991.
Muller, Marcia *There's Something in a Sunday*, The Women's Press, London, 1992.
—— *The Shape of Dread*, The Women's Press, London, 1992.
Neely, Barbara *Blanche on the Lam*, St. Martin's Press, New York, 1992.
O'Rourke, Rebecca *Jumping the Cracks*, Virago Press, London, 1987.
Paretsky, Sara *Indemnity Only*, Penguin Books, Harmondsworth, [1982] 1987.
—— *Deadlock*, Penguin Books, Harmondsworth, [1984] 1987.
—— *Killing Orders*, Penguin Books, Harmondsworth, [1986] 1987.
—— *Bitter Medicine*, Victor Gollancz, New York, 1987.
—— *Toxic Shock*, Penguin Books, Harmondsworth, 1990.
—— *Burn Marks*, Chatto & Windus, London, 1990.
—— *Guardian Angel*, Delacorte Press, New York, 1992.
Paul, Barbara *Your Eyelids Are Growing Heavy*, The Women's Press, London, [1981] 1989.
—— *The Fourth Wall*, The Women's Press, London, 1988.
Rendell, Ruth *From Doon with Death*, Arrow Books, London, [1964] 1979.
—— *An Unkindness of Ravens*, Arrow Books, London, [1985] 1986.
—— *Live Flesh*, Arrow Books, London, 1986.
—— *Heartstones*, Arrow Books, London, 1988.
Sayers, Dorothy L. *Gaudy Night*, New English Library, London, [1935] 1978.
Schulman, Sarah *The Sophie Horowitz Story*, Naiad Press, Tallahassee, 1984.
—— *Girls, Visions, and Everything*, The Seal Press, Seattle, 1986.
—— *After Delores*, E. P. Dutton, New York, 1988.
—— *People in Trouble*, Sheba Feminist Publishers, London, 1990.
—— *Empathy*, E. P. Dutton, New York, 1993.
Scott, Rosie *Glory Days*, The Women's Press, London, 1989.
Shea, Shirley *Victims*, Pandora Press, London, 1989.
Slovo, Gillian *Morbid Symptoms*, Pluto Press, London, 1984.
—— *Death By Analysis*, The Women's Press, London, 1986.
—— *Death Comes Staccato*, The Women's Press, London, 1987.
Smith, Joan *A Masculine Ending*, Faber & Faber, London, 1987.
—— *Why Aren't They Screaming?*, Faber & Faber, London, [1988] 1989.
—— *Don't Leave Me This Way*, Faber & Faber, London, 1990.
Stein, Gertrude *Blood on the Dining Room Floor*, Virago Press, London, [1948] 1985.
Stone, Marie *A Little Murder*, The Olive Press, London, 1985.
Tell, Dorothy *Murder at Red Rook Ranch*, Naiad Press, Tallahassee, 1990.
Tennant, Emma *The Last of the Country House Murders*, Faber & Faber, London, [1974] 1986.
—— *The Bad Sister*, Faber & Faber, London, [1978] 1989.
—— *Two Women of London*, Faber & Faber, London, 1990.

Tey, Josephine *Miss Pym Disposes*, Penguin Books, Harmondsworth, [1946] 1983.

Thomson, Lesley *Seven Miles from Sydney*, Pandora Press, London, 1987.

Uhnak, Dorothy *False Witness*, Ballantine Books, New York, 1981.

—— *Victims*, Arrow Books, London, 1987.

Vine, Barbara *A Dark-Adapted Eye*, Penguin Books, Harmondsworth, 1986.

—— *A Fatal Inversion*, Penguin Books, Harmondsworth, 1987.

—— *The House of Stairs*, Penguin Books, Harmondsworth, 1989.

—— *King Solomon's Carpet*, Penguin Books, Harmondsworth, 1992.

Vole, Zenobia N. *Osten's Bay*, Naiad Press, Tallahassee, 1988.

Wakefield, Hannah *The Price You Pay*, The Women's Press, London, 1987.

—— *A February Mourning*, The Women's Press, London, 1990.

Warmbold, Jean *Dead Man Running*, Virago Press, London, [1986] 1991.

—— *The White Hand*, Virago Press, London, 1990.

Williams, Amanda Kyle *The Providence File*, Naiad Press, Tallahassee, 1991.

Wilson, Barbara *Murder in the Collective*, The Women's Press, London, 1984.

—— *Sisters of the Road*, The Women's Press, London, 1987.

—— *The Dog Collar Murders*, The Women's Press, London, 1989.

—— *Gaudi Afternoon*, Virago Press, London, 1991.

Wings, Mary *She Came Too Late*, The Women's Press, London, 1986.

—— *She Came in a Flash*, The Women's Press, London, 1988.

Wittig, Monique *Les Guérillères*, Editions de Minuit, Paris, 1969, and Viking, New York, 1971.

Wright-Douglas, Lauren *The Always Anonymous Beast*, Naiad Press, Tallahassee, 1987.

Zahava, Irene (ed.) *The Womansleuth Anthology*, The Crossing Press, California, 1988.

Zahavi, Helen *Dirty Weekend*, Flamingo Press/HarperCollins, London, 1992.

Zaremba, Eve *A Reason to Kill*, PaperJacks, Markham, Ontario, 1978.

—— *Work for a Million*, Amanita Books, Toronto, 1986.

—— *Beyond Hope*, Amanita Books, Toronto, 1987.

Critical bibliography

Abel, Elizabeth (ed.) *Writing and Sexual Difference*, Harvester Press, Brighton, 1982.

Adams, Kate 'Making the World Safe for the Missionary Position', in Jay, Karla and Glasgow, Joanne (eds) *Lesbian Texts and Contexts: Radical Revisions*, New York University Press, New York, 1990 and Onlywomen Press, London, 1992: 255–74.

Alcock, Beverley and Robson, Jocelyn 'Cagney and Lacey Revisited', *Feminist Review* 35, Summer, 1990: 42–53.

Ardill, Susan and O'Sullivan, Sue 'Sex in the Summer of '88', *Feminist Review* 31, Spring, 1989: 126–34.

Babuscio, Jack, 'Camp and the Gay Sensibility', in British Film Institute (ed.) *Gays and Film*, London, 1977.

Bailey, Frankie Y. *Out of the Woodpile: Black Characters in Crime and Detective Fiction*, Greenwood Press, New York, 1991.

Bakerman, Jane S. 'Cordelia Gray: Apprentice and Archetype', *Clues: A Journal of Detection* 5, 1984: 101–14.

Barrett, Michèle *Women's Oppression Today: The Marxist/Feminist Encounter*, New Left Books, London, 1980, Verso, London, 1988 (revised edn).

Beauman, Nicola *A Very Great Profession: The Woman's Novel 1914–39*, Virago Press, London, 1983.

Belsey, Catherine *Critical Practice*, Methuen, London, 1980.

Benjamin, Walter *Charles Baudelaire: A Lyric Poet in the Era of High Capitalism*, New Left Books, London, 1973.

Bennett, Tony, Mercer, Colin and Woollacott, Janet (eds) *Popular Culture and Social Relations*, Open University Press, Milton Keynes, 1986.

Bindel, Julie 'The State of the Movement', *Trouble and Strife*, 1988: 50–2.

Binyon, T. J. *'Murder Will Out': The Detective in Fiction*, Oxford University Press, Oxford, 1990.

Birch, Helen 'P. D. James' Stylish Crime', *Women's Review* 10, 1986: 6–7.

—— 'The Darker Sides of the Mind', *Guardian*, 28 April 1987: 11.

Birns, Nicholas and Birns, Margaret Boe 'Agatha Christie: Modern and Modernist', in Walker, Ronald G. and Frazer, June M. *The Cunning Craft*, Western Illinois University Press, Macomb, 1990: 120–34.

Blake, Fay M. 'Lady Sleuths and Women Detectives', *Turn of the Century Women* 3 (1), Summer 1986: 29–42.

Bland, Lucy 'The Domain of the Sexual: A Response', *Screen Education* 39, Summer 1981: 56–67.

Bloom, Clive 'West is East: Nayland Smith's Sinophobia and Sax Rohmer's Bank Balance', in Bloom, Clive (ed.) *Twentieth Century Suspense*, Macmillan Books, London, 1990: 22–36.

Bloom, Harold *The Anxiety of Influence: A Theory of Poetry*, Oxford University Press, Oxford, 1973.

Bobo, Jacqueline '*The Color Purple*: Black Women as Cultural Readers', in Pribram, Dierdre (ed.) *Female Spectators: Looking at Film and Television*, Verso, London, 1988: 90–109.

Boston Lesbian Psychologies Collective (eds) *Lesbian Psychologies*, University of Illinois Press, Boston, 1987.

Bourne, Stephen '*The Color Purple*', *Films and Filming*, June, 1986: 26–7.

Brenner, Johanna and Ramas, Mari 'Rethinking Women's Oppression', in Lovell, Terry *British Feminist Thought*, Basil Blackwell, Oxford, 1990: 151–69.

Britton, Andrew 'For Interpretation: Notes Against Camp', *Gay Left* 7, Winter 1978/9: 11–14.

Brooks, Peter 'Freud's Masterplot', in Felman, Shoshana (ed.) *Literature and Psychoanalysis*, Johns Hopkins University Press, Baltimore, 1982: 280–300.

Brown, Sterling 'Negro Character as Seen by White Authors', *The Journal of Negro Education* 2, 1933: 179–203.

Brunt, Rosalind and Rowan, Caroline (eds) *Feminism, Culture and Politics*, Lawrence & Wishart, London, 1982.

Butler, Judith *Gender Trouble: Feminism and the Subversion of Identity*, Routledge, New York and London, 1990.

—— 'Imitation and Gender Insubordination', in Fuss, Diana (ed.) *Inside/Out: Lesbian Theories, Gay Theories*, Routledge, London and New York, 1991: 13–31.

Callinicos, Alex *Against Postmodernism*, Polity Press, Cambridge, 1989.

Cameron, Deborah and Frazer, Elizabeth *The Lust to Kill*, Polity Press, Cambridge, 1987.

Campbell, Sue Ellen 'The Detective Heroine and the Death of Her Hero', *Modern Fiction Studies* 29 (3) 1983: 497–510.

Caprio, Frank S. *Female Homosexuality: A Psychodynamic Study of Lesbianism*, The Citadel Press, New York, 1954.

Caputi, Jane *The Age of Sex Crime*, The Women's Press, London, 1987.

—— and Daly, Mary *Webster's First New Intergalactic Wickedary of the English Language*, The Women's Press, London, 1988.

Cawelti, John G. *Adventure, Mystery, and Romance*, University of Chicago Press, Chicago and London, 1976.

Chandler, Raymond *The Simple Art of Murder*, Ballantine Books, New York, 1972.

Chester, Gail and Dickey, Julienne (eds) *Feminism and Censorship: The Current Debate*, Prism Press, Bridport, 1988.

Christian, Barbara 'Shadows Uplifted', in Newton, Judith and Rosenfelt,

Deborah (eds) *Feminist Criticism and Social Change*, Methuen, London, 1985.

—— *Black Feminist Criticism: Perspectives on Black Women Writers*, Pergamon Press, New York, 1986.

Cixous, Hélène 'The Laugh of the Medusa', in Marks, E. and Courtivron, I. (eds) *New French Feminisms*, Harvester Press, Brighton, 1981.

Clark, Susan L. 'A Fearful Symmetry: An Interview with Ruth Rendell', *The Armchair Detective*, 22 (3) Summer 1989: 228–35.

Clément, Catherine *The Weary Sons of Freud*, translated by Ball, Nicole, Verso, London, [1978] 1987.

Collins, Jim *Uncommon Cultures: Popular Cultures and Post-Modernism*, Routledge, London, 1989.

Collins, Patricia Hill *Black Feminist Thought: Knowledge, Consciousness, and the Politics of Empowerment*, Routledge, London, 1991.

Cornillon, John 'A Case for Violet Strange', in Cornillon, Susan Koppelman (ed.) *Images of Women in Fiction: Feminist Perspectives*, Bowling Green State University Popular Press, Ohio, 1972: 206–15.

Coward, Rosalind and Semple, Linda 'Tracking Down the Past: Women and Detective Fiction' in Carr, Helen (ed.) *From My Guy to Sci-Fi: Genre and Women's Writing in the Postmodern World*, Pandora Press, London, 1989: 39–57.

Craig, Patricia and Cadogan, Mary *The Lady Investigates: Women Detectives and Spies in Fiction*, Oxford University Press, Oxford, 1986.

Cranny-Francis, Anne 'Gender and Genre: Feminist Rewritings of Detective Fiction', *Women's Studies International Forum* 11 (1), 1988: 69–84.

—— *Feminist Fiction*, Polity Press, Cambridge, 1990.

Currie, Peter 'The Eccentric Self: Anti-Characterization and the Problem of the Subject in American Postmodernist Fiction', in Bradbury, Malcolm and Ro, Sigmund (eds) *Contemporary American Fiction*, Edward Arnold, London, 1987: 53–71.

D'Acci, Julie 'The Case of Cagney and Lacey' in Baehr, Helen and Dyer, Gillian *Boxed In: Women and Television*, Pandora Press, London, 1987.

Daly, Mary *Beyond God the Father: Toward a Philosophy of Women's Liberation*, Beacon Press, Boston, 1973.

Davis, Angela Y. *Women, Race and Class*, Random House, New York,1981.

Day, Gary 'Ordeal by Analysis: Agatha Christie's *The Thirteen Problems*', in Bloom, Clive (ed.) *Twentieth Century Suspense*, Macmillan Books, London, 1990: 80–96.

De Lauretis, Teresa *Alice Doesn't: Feminism, Semiotics, Cinema*, Indiana University Press, Bloomington, 1984.

Doane, Mary Ann *The Desire to Desire*, Indiana University Press, Bloomington, 1987.

Dollimore, Jonathan 'The Dominant and the Deviant: A Violent Dialectic', *Critical Quarterly* 28 (1 & 2), 1986: 179–92.

—— *Sexual Dissidence: Augustine to Wilde, Freud to Foucault*, Clarendon Press, Oxford, 1991.

Dove, George N. 'Dorothy Uhnak', in Bakerman, Jane S. *And Then There Were Nine . . . More Women of Mystery*, Bowling Green State University Popular Press, Ohio, 1985.

Du Bois, W. E. B. *The Souls of Black Folk*, Avon Books, New York, [1903] 1989: 3.

Dunant, Sarah 'Rewriting the Detectives', *Guardian*, 29 June 1993: 28.

Duncan, Andrew 'Kathleen Turns Up the Heat', *Radio Times*, BBC Publications, London, 2–8 November 1991: 22–4.

Dyer, Richard 'The Sad Young Man'; paper delivered at the *Questions of Homosexuality Conference*, Institute of Romance Studies, University of London, 6 June 1992.

Eden, Rick A. 'Detective Fiction as Satire', *Genre* 16, Autumn, University of Oklahoma, 1983: 279–95.

Ellis, Havelock 'Sexual Inversion' in *Studies in the Psychology of Sex*, 2 vols, New York, [1901] 1986.

Ellis, Kate, O'Dair, Barbara, and Tallmer, Abby 'Feminism and Pornography', *Feminist Review* 36, Autumn, 1990: 15–18.

Evans, Mari (ed.) *Black Women Writers*, Doubleday, New York, 1984.

Ewert, Jeanne C. 'Lost in the Hermeneutic Funhouse: Patrick Modiano's Postmodern Detective' in Walker, Ronald G. and Frazer, June M. *The Cunning Craft*, Western Illinois University Press, Macomb, 1990: 166–73.

Faludi, Susan *Backlash*, Chatto & Windus, London, 1992.

Felman, Shoshana (ed.) *Literature and Psychoanalysis*, Johns Hopkins University Press, Baltimore, 1977.

Fiske, John, O'Sullivan, Tim, Hartley, John and Saunders, Danny (eds) *Key Concepts in Communication*, Methuen, London, 1983.

Foucault, Michel *Discipline and Punish: The Birth of the Prison*, translated by Sheridan, A., Peregrine Books, Harmondsworth, 1977.

—— *Power/Knowledge: Selected Interviews and other Writing 1972–77*, ed. Gordon, Colin, Harvester Press, Brighton, 1980.

—— *The History of Sexuality Vol. 1: An Introduction*, Peregrine Books, Harmondsworth, 1984.

Fowler, Roger (ed.) *A Dictionary of Modern Critical Terms*, Routledge, London, 1987.

French, Marilyn *The War Against Women*, Hamish Hamilton, London, 1992.

Freud, Sigmund *Introductory Lectures on Psychoanalysis*, translated by Strachey, James, Pelican Freud Library vol. 1, Penguin Books, Harmondsworth, 1973.

Freud, Sigmund *The Interpretation of Dreams*, translated by Strachey, James, Pelican Freud Library vol. 4, Penguin Books, Harmondsworth, 1976.

—— *On Sexuality*, translated by Richards, Angela, Pelican Freud Library vol. 7, Penguin Books, Harmondsworth, 1977.

—— 'The History of the Psychoanalytic Movement', translated by Brill, A. A. (1917), in Strachey, James (ed.) *Historical and Expository Works on Psychoanalysis*, Pelican Freud Library vol. 15, Penguin Books, Harmondsworth, 1986.

Freud, Sigmund and Breuer, Josef *Studies on Hysteria*, translated by Strachey, James and Alice, Pelican Freud Library vol. 3, Penguin Books, Harmondsworth, 1974.

Freund, Elizabeth *The Return of the Reader: Reader Response Criticism*, Methuen, London, 1987.

Frosh, Stephen *The Politics of Psychoanalysis*, Macmillan, London, 1987.

Frye, Northrop *Anatomy of Criticism*, Princeton University Press, New Jersey, 1977.

Fuss, Diana *Essentially Speaking: Feminism, Nature and Difference*, Routledge, London, 1990.

—— (ed.) *Inside/Out: Lesbian Theories, Gay Theories*, Routledge, London and New York, 1991.

Gallop, Jane *The Daughter's Seduction: Feminism and Psychoanalysis*, Cornell University Press, Ithaca, 1982.

Gamman, Lorraine 'Watching the Detectives', in Gamman, Lorraine and Marshment, Margaret (eds) *The Female Gaze*, The Women's Press, London, 1988.

Garber, Marjorie 'Black and White TV: Cross-Dressing the Color Line', in *Vested Interests: Cross-Dressing and Cultural Anxiety*, Routledge, London and New York, 1992: 267–303.

Gatens, Moira *Feminism and Philosophy: Perspectives on Difference and Equality*, Polity Press, Cambridge, 1991.

Gates, Henry Louis Jnr *Black Literature and Literary Theory*, Methuen, London, 1984.

—— (ed.) *'Race', Writing, and Difference*, University of Chicago Press, 1986.

—— 'In Her Own Write', Introduction to *Six Women's Slave Narratives*, Oxford University Press, Oxford, 1988.

Gerrard, Nicci 'Sleuth Sayings', *Observer*, Sunday 27 June 1993: 62.

Gilman, Sander L. 'Black Bodies, White Bodies', in Gates, Henry Louis Jnr (ed.) *'Race', Writing, and Difference*, University of Chicago Press, Chicago and London, 1986: 223–61.

Gledhill, Christine *Home is Where the Heart Is*, BFI/Macmillan, London, 1989.

Grella, George 'The Hard-Boiled Detective Novel' in Winks, Robin W. (ed.) *Detective Fiction: A Collection of Critical Essays*, Spectrum Books, Prentice-Hall, New Jersey, 1980: 107–20.

Griffin, Christine 'Cultures of Femininity: Romance Revisited', CCCS Occasional Papers, University of Birmingham, 1982.

Griffiths, Sian 'Opportunity Knocks Again', *The Higher*, 8 November 1991: 8.

Gunn, Daniel *Psychoanalysis and Fiction*, Cambridge University Press, Cambridge (USA), 1988.

Halprin, Sara '*The Color Purple*: Community of Women', *Jump Cut: A Review of Contemporary Media* 31, 1986: 27–8.

Hamer, Diane 'I Am a Woman: Ann Bannon and the Writing of Lesbian Identity in the 1950s', in Lilly, Mark (ed.) *Lesbian and Gay Writing*, Macmillan, London, 1990: 47–75.

Harasym, Sarah (ed.) *The Post-Colonial Critic: Interviews, Strategies, Dialogues*, Routledge, New York and London, 1990.

Hartmann, Heidi 'The Unhappy Marriage of Marxism and Feminism', in Sargent, Lydia (ed.) *Women and Revolution: A Discussion of the Unhappy Marriage of Marxism and Feminism*, South End Press, Boston, 1981: 1–41.

Hebdige, Dick *Subculture: The Meaning of Style*, Methuen, London, 1979.

Heilbrun, Carolyn 'James, P.D.', in Reilly, John M. (ed.) *Crime and Mystery Writers*, St Martin's Press, New York, 1980: 857.

Hobby, Elaine and White, Chris (eds) *What Lesbians Do in Books*, The Women's Press, London, 1991.

Holland, Norman N. 'UNITY IDENTITY TEXT SELF', *Proceedings of the Modern Languages Association* 90, 1975: 813–22.

hooks, bell *Ain't I a Woman: Black Women and Feminism*, Pluto Press, London, 1982.

—— *Yearning: Race, Gender, and Cultural Politics*, Turnaround Press, London, 1991.

Hubly, Erlene 'The Formula Challenged: The Novels of P. D. James', *Modern Fiction Studies* 29 (3), 1983: 511–21.

Hughes, Robert *The Shock of the New*, BBC Publications, London, 1980.

Hull, Gloria T., Bell Scott, Patricia and Smith, Barbara (eds) *All the Women are White, All the Blacks are Men, But Some of Us are Brave: Black Women's Studies*, The Feminist Press, Old Westbury, New York, 1981.

Hutcheon, Linda *The Politics of Postmodernism*, Routledge, London, 1989.

Jaehne, Karen 'The Final Word', *Cineaste* 15 (1), New York, 1986: 60.

Jaggar, Alison M. *Feminist Politics and Human Nature*, Harvester Press, Brighton, 1983.

Jeffreys, Sheila 'Butch and Femme: Now and Then', in The Lesbian History Group (eds) *Not A Passing Phase*, The Women's Press, London, 1989: 158–87.

—— *Anticlimax*, The Women's Press, London, 1990.

Jones, Ann Rosalind 'Inscribing Femininity: French Theories of the Feminine' in Greene, Gayle and Kahn, Coppelia (eds) *Making a Difference: Feminist Literary Criticism*, Methuen, London, 1985: 80–112.

Kaplan, Cora 'An Unsuitable Genre for a Feminist?', *Feminist Review* 8, 1986: 18–19.

Kaplan, E. Ann 'Is the Gaze Male?' in Snitow, Ann Barr et al. (eds) *Desire: The Politics of Sexuality*, Virago Press, London, 1984: 321–38.

Keating, H. R. F. *Murder Must Appetize*, Lemon Tree Press, London, 1975.

Klein, Kathleen Gregory 'Patricia Highsmith', in Bakerman, Jane S. (ed.) *And Then There Were Nine . . . More Women of Mystery*, Bowling Green State University Popular Press, Ohio, 1985.

—— *The Woman Detective: Gender and Genre*, University of Illinois Press, Urbana and Chicago, 1988.

Knepper, Marty 'Agatha Christie – Feminist', *Armchair Detective* 16 (4), Winter, 1983: 398–406.

Knight, Stephen *Form and Ideology in Crime Fiction*, Macmillan, London, 1980.

Kolodny, Annette 'Dancing Throught the Minefield: Some Observations on the Theory, Practice and Politics of a Feminist Literary Criticism', *Feminist Studies* 6 (1), 1980: 1–25.

Krzowski, Sue and Land, Pat (eds) *In Our Own Hands*, The Women's Press, London, 1981.

—— (eds) *In Our Experience*, The Women's Press, London, 1988.

Leitch, T. M. 'The American Detective Hero', *Modern Fiction Studies* 29 (3), Autumn, 1983: 475–84.

Lesbian History Group (eds) *Not A Passing Phase*, The Women's Press, London,1989.

Lewis, Reina 'Only Women Should Go to Turkey: Henriette Browne and Women's Orientalism', *Third Text* 22, Spring, 1993: 53–64.

Light, Alison *Forever England: Femininity, Literature, and Conservatism Between the Wars*, Routledge, London, 1991.

Lovell, Terry *British Feminist Thought*, Basil Blackwell, Oxford, 1990.

Maddi, F. R. *Personality Thories: A Comparitive Analysis*, The Dorsey Press, Homewood, 1980.

Maio, Kathleen L. 'A Strange and Fierce Delight: The Early Days of Women's Mystery Fiction', *Chrysalis* 10, n.d.: 93–105.

Mayne, Judith *Revision: Essays in Feminist Film Criticism*, American Film Institute, Los Angeles, 1984.

McHale, Brian *Postmodernist Fiction*, Routledge, London, 1987.

Meissner, William W. *The Paranoid Process*, Jason Aronson, New York, 1978.

Meyer, Richard 'Rock Hudson's Body', in Fuss, Diana *Inside/Out: Lesbian Theories, Gay Theories*, Routledge, New York and London, 1991: 259–88.

Mitchell, Juliet *Psychoanalysis and Feminism*, Pelican/Penguin Books, Harmondsworth, 1974.

Modleski, Tania *Loving with a Vengeance: Mass Produced Fantasies for Women*, Methuen, London, 1984.

—— *The Women Who Knew Too Much*, Routledge, London, 1989.

—— *Feminism Without Women: Culture and Criticism in a 'Postfeminist' Age*, Routledge, London, 1991.

Moi, Toril *Sexual/Textual Politics: Feminist Literary Theory*, Methuen/Routledge, London, 1985.

Moraga, Cherrie and Anzaldua, Gloria (eds) *This Bridge Called My Back: Writings by Radical Women of Color*, Kitchen Table Press, New York, 1981.

Moretti, Franco *Signs Taken for Wonders*, Verso, London, 1988.

Morris, Virginia B. 'Arsenic and Blue Lace: Sayers' Criminal Women', *Modern Fiction Studies* 29 (3), 1983: 485–95.

Mort, Frank 'The Domain of the Sexual', *Screen Education* 36, Autumn, 1980: 69–84.

Muller, John P. and Richardson, William J. (eds) *The Purloined Poe: Lacan, Derrida and Psychoanalytic Reading*, Johns Hopkins University Press, Baltimore, 1988.

Mulvey, Laura *Visual and Other Pleasures*, Macmillan, London, 1989.

Munt, Sally R. 'The Inverstigators: Lesbian Crime Fiction', in Radstone, Susannah *Sweet Dreams: Sexuality, Gender, and Popular Fiction*, Lawrence & Wishart, London, 1988: 91–119.

—— *New Lesbian Criticism: Literary and Cultural Readings*, Harvester Wheatsheaf, Hemel Hempstead, and Columbia University Press, New York, 1992.

Neale, Stephen *Genre*, British Film Institute, London, 1980.

Nelson, W. and Avery, N. 'Detective Story to Detective Novel', *Modern Fiction Studies* 29 (3), 1983: 463–74.

Nestle, Joan *A Restricted Country*, Sheba Feminist Press, London, 1988.

Nichols, Margaret 'Lesbian Sexuality: Issues and Developing Theory', in The Boston Lesbian Psychologies Collective (eds) *Lesbian Psychologies*, University of Illinois Press, Boston, 1987: 97–125.

Nichols, Victoria and Thompson, Susan *Silk Stalkings: When Women Write of Murder*, Black Lizard Books, Berkeley, 1988.

Nicholson, Linda J. *Feminism/Postmodernism*, Routledge, London, 1990.

Norden, Barbara 'Campaign Against Pornography', *Feminist Review* 35, Summer, 1990: 1–8.

Nozick, Robert *Anarchy, State and Utopia*, Basic Books, New York, 1974.

Nye, Andrea *Feminist Theory and the Philosophies of Man*, Routledge, London and New York,1989.

Olivier, Christiane *Jocasta's Children: The Imprint of the Mother*, translated by Craig, George, Routledge, London, 1989.

O'Reilly, Emma-Louise 'Little Sister Hits the Trail', *Guardian*, 26 May 1987: 10.

Palmer, Jerry *Thrillers: Genesis and Structure of a Popular Genre*, Edward Arnold, London, 1978.

—— *Potboilers: Methods, Concepts and Case Studies in Popular Fiction*, Routledge, London, 1991.

Palmer, Paulina 'The Lesbian Feminist Thriller and Detective Novel', in Hobby, Elaine and White, Chris (eds) *What Lesbians Do in Books*, The Women's Press, London, 1991: 9–27.

Paulin, Tom 'Mortem Virumque Cano', *New Statesman*, 25 November 1977: 745.

Philips, Deborah 'Mystery Woman – Patricia Highsmith', *Women's Review* 6, 1986: 14–15.

Pick, Daniel *Faces of Degeneration*, Cambridge University Press, Cambridge, 1989.

Porter, Dennis 'Detection and Ethics: The Case of P. D. James', in Rader, Barbara A. and Zettler, Howard G. (eds) *The Sleuth and the Scholar: Origins, Evolution and Current Trends in Detective Fiction*, Greenwood Press, New York, 1988: 11–18.

Pratt, Mary Louise 'Scratches on the Face of the Country: Or What Mr Barrow Saw in the Land of the Bushmen', in Gates, Henry Lois Jnr (ed.) *'Race', Writing and Difference*, University of Chicago Press, Chicago and London, 1986: 138–62.

—— *Imperial Eyes: Travel Writing and Transculturation*, Routledge, London, 1992.

Pratt, Minnie Bruce 'Identity: Skin, Blood, Heart', in Bulkin, E., Pratt, M. B., and Smith, B. (eds) *Yours in Struggle: Perspectives on Anti-Semitism and Racism*, Long Haul Press, New York, 1984: 9–63.

Propp, Vladimir *Morphology of the Folktale*, University of Texas Press, Austin, 1968, 2nd edn.

Pykett, Lynn 'Seizing the Crime: Recent Women's Crime Fiction', *The New Welsh Review* 2, Summer, 1989: 24–7.

Rabinowitz, Peter J. 'Chandler Comes to Harlem: Racial Politics in the

Thrillers of Chester Himes', in Rader, Barbara A. and Zettler, Howard G. (eds) *The Sleuth and the Scholar: Origins, Evolution and Current Trends in Detective Fiction*, Greenwood Press, New York, 1988: 9–29.

Rader, Barbara A. and Zettler, Howard G. (eds) *The Sleuth and the Scholar: Origins, Evolution and Current Trends in Detective Fiction*, Greenwood Press, New York, 1988.

Radford, Jean (ed.) *The Progress of Romance: The Politics of Popular Fiction*, Routledge & Kegan Paul, London, 1986.

Radstone, Susannah (ed.) *Sweet Dreams: Sexuality, Gender, and Popular Fiction*, Lawrence & Wishart, London, 1988.

Reddy, Maureen T. *Sisters in Crime: Feminism and the Crime Novel*, Continuum Books, New York, 1988.

Register, Cheri 'American Feminist Criticism: A Bibliographic Introduction', in Donovan, Josephine (ed.) *Feminist Literary Criticism: Explorations in Theory*, University Press of Kentucky, Lexington, 1975.

Rich, Adrienne 'Compulsory Heterosexuality and Lesbian Existence', in Snitow, Ann Barr, Stansell, Christine and Thomson, Sharon (eds) *Desire: The Politics of Sexuality*, Virago Press, London, 1984: 212–41.

Rodgerson, Gillian and Semple, Linda 'Who Watches the Watchwomen?: Feminists Against Censorship', *Feminist Review* 36, Autumn, 1990: 19–24.

Ruehl, Sonja 'Inverts and Experts: Radclyffe Hall and the Lesbian Identity', in Brunt, Rosalind and Rowan, Caroline (eds) *Feminism, Culture and Politics*, Lawrence & Wishart, London, 1982: 15–36.

Rush, Florence 'The Great Freudian Cover-Up', *Trouble and Strife* 4, Winter, 1984.

—— 'Hysteria or Resistance – Dora the Great Freudian Cover-Up Part II', *Trouble and Strife* 15, Spring, 1989.

Russ, Joanna 'Somebody's Trying to Kill Me and I Think It's My Husband', *Journal of Popular Culture* 6, Spring, 1973: 666–91.

Said, Edward *Orientalism*, Routledge & Kegan Paul, London, 1978.

Sayers, Janet *Mothering Psychoanalysis*, Hamish Hamilton, London, 1991.

Semple, Linda and Coward, Rosalind 'Women at the Scene of Crime' ICA talk, London, 19 January 1988. Published as 'Tracking Down the Past: Women and Detective Fiction', in Carr, Helen (ed.) *From My Guy to Sci-Fi: Genre and Women's Writing in the Postmodern World*, Pandora Press, London, 1989: 39–57.

Shaw, Marion and Vanacker, Sabine *Reflecting on Miss Marple*, Routledge, London, 1991.

Showalter, Elaine (ed.) *The New Feminist Criticism*, Virago Press, London, 1986.

Siebenheller, Norma *P. D. James*, Frederick Ungar, New York, 1981.

Simmonds, Felly Nkweto 'SHE'S GOTTA HAVE IT: The Representation of Black Female Sexualty on Film', *Feminist Review* 29, 1988: 10–22.

Skinner, Robert E. *The Hard-Boiled Explicator: A Guide to the Study of Dashiell Hammett, Raymond Chandler, and Ross Macdonald*, The Scarecrow Press, London, 1985.

Slung, Michelle *Crime on her Mind*, Random House/Parthenon Books, New York, 1975.

Slotkin, Richard 'The Hard-Boiled Detective Story: From the Open Range to the Mean Streets', in Rader, B. A. and Zettler, H. G. (eds) *The Sleuth and the Scholar: Origins Evolution and Current Trends in Detective Fiction*, Greenwood Press, New York, 1988: 91–100.

Smith, Barbara 'Towards a Black Feminist Criticism', *Conditions Two*, 1970: 25–44.

Smyth, Cherry *Lesbians Talk Queer Notions*, Scarlet Press, London, 1992.

Snitow, Ann Barr, Stansell, Christine and Thomson, Sharon (eds) *Desire: The Politics of Sexuality*, Virago Press, London, 1984.

Spivak, Gayatri Chakravorty 'Three Women's Texts and a Critique of Imperialism', in Gates, Henry Louis Jnr (ed.) *'Race', Writing, and Difference*, University of Chicago Press, Chicago and London, 1985: 262–80.

Steele, T. 'Myth and Ritual', *Modern Fiction Studies* 29 (3), 1983: 435–50.

Steven, Peter (ed.) *Jump Cut: Hollywood, Politics, and Counter Culture*, Praeger Press, New York, 1985.

Stimpson, Catherine 'Zero Degree Deviancy: The Lesbian Novel in English', in Abel, Elizabeth (ed.) *Writing and Sexual Difference*, Harvester Press, Brighton, 1982: 243–59.

Stuart, Andrea '*The Color Purple*: In Defence of Happy Endings', in Gamman, L. and Marshment, M. (eds) *The Female Gaze*, The Women's Press, London, 1988: 60–75.

Symons, Julian *Bloody Murder*, Viking, London, [1972] 1985.

Taylor, Helen 'Romantic Readers', in Carr, Helen (ed.) *From My Guy to Sci-Fi: Genre and Women's Writing in the Postmodern World*, Pandora Press, London, 1989: 58–77.

Thomson, Liz 'Shooting From the Hip and the Lip', *Books* 6 (3), 1992: 4.

Thurston, Carol *The Romance Revolution: Erotic Novels for Women and the Quest for a New Sexual Identity*, University of Illinois Press, Champaign, 1987.

Todd, Janet *Feminist Literary History*, Polity Press, Oxford, 1988.

Tong, Rosemarie *Feminist Thought: An Introduction*, Unwin Hyman/ Routledge, London, 1989.

Turner, Jenny 'Right-ons', *London Review of Books* 13 (20), 24 October 1991: 22–3.

Tyler, Carole-Ann 'Boys Will Be Girls: The Politics of Gay Drag', in Fuss, Diana (ed.) *Inside/Out: Lesbian Theories, Gay Theories*, Routledge, London, 1991: 32–70.

Vance, Carole S. *Pleasure and Danger: Exploring Female Sexuality*, papers from the conference 'Towards a Politics of Female Sexuality', Barnard College, New York, 1982, Routledge & Kegan Paul, Boston, 1984.

Volosinov, V. *Marxism and the Philosophy of Language*, Seminar Press, New York, 1973.

Walker, Ronald G. and Frazer, June M. (eds) *The Cunning Craft*, Western llinois University Press, Macomb, 1990.

Wald, Gayle F. 'Strong Poison: Love and the Novelistic in Dorothy Sayers', in Walker, Ronald G. and Frazer, June M. (eds) *The Cunning Craft*, Western Illinois University Press, Macomb, 1990: 98–108.

Wall, Cheryl A. *Changing Our Own Words: Essays on Criticism, Theory and Writing by Black Women*, Routledge, London, 1990.

Wallace, Michele *Black Macho and the Myth of Superwoman*, Verso, London, [1978] 1990.

Weedon, Chris *Feminist Practice and Poststructuralist Theory*, Basil Blackwell, Oxford, 1987.

Weir, Angela and Wilson, Elizabeth 'The Greyhound Bus Station in the Evolution of Lesbian Popular Culture', in Munt, Sally (ed.) *New Lesbian Criticism*, Harvester Wheatsheaf, Hemel Hempstead, and Columbia University Press, New York, 1992: 95–114.

Williams, Gwen 'Fear's Keen Knife: Suspense and the Female Detective, 1890–1920' in Bloom, Clive (ed.) *Twentieth Century Suspense*, Macmillan Books, London, 1990: 37–50.

Williams, Raymond *The Country and the City*, The Hogarth Press, London, 1985.

Willis, Ellen 'The Conservatism of *Ms.*', in Redstockings (eds) *Feminist Revolution*, Random House, New York, 1975: 170–1.

Willis, Susan *Specifying: Black Women Writing the American Experience*, Routledge, London, 1990.

—— *A Primer for Everyday Life*, Routledge, London and New York, 1991.

Wilson, Elizabeth *Mirror Writing: An Autobiography*, Virago Press, London, 1982.

Winks, Robin W. 'The Sordid Truth: Four Cases', in Winks, Robin W. (ed.) *Detective Fiction: A Collection of Critical Essays*, Spectrum Books, Prentice-Hall, New Jersey, 1980: 215–18.

—— *Detective Fiction: A Collection of Critical Essays*, Spectrum Books, Prentice-Hall, New Jersey, 1980.

Wolff, Janet *Feminine Sentences: Essays on Women and Culture*, Polity Press, Cambridge, 1990.

Worpole, Ken *Dockers and Detectives*, Verso, London, 1983.

—— *Reading by Numbers*, Comedia, London and New York, 1984.

Young, Iris 'Socialist Feminism and the Limits of Dual Systems Theory', *Socialist Review* 10, 1980: 169–88.

Zimmerman, Bonnie 'What Has Never Been: An Overview of Lesbian Feminist Criticism', in Greene, Gayle and Kahn, Coppelia (eds) *Making A Difference: Feminist Literary Criticism*, Methuen, London, 1985.

Index